Ancient Encounters

— ✹ —

*Kennewick Man
and the First Americans*

James C. Chatters

— ✹ —

A TOUCHSTONE BOOK

PUBLISHED BY SIMON & SCHUSTER

New York   London   Toronto   Sydney   Singapore

TOUCHSTONE
Rockefeller Center
1230 Avenue of the Americas
New York, NY 10020

First Touchstone edition 2002

TOUCHSTONE and colophon are registered trademarks
of Simon & Schuster, Inc.

All photographs and illustrations are courtesy of the author unless otherwise stated.

For information regarding special discounts for bulk purchases,
please contact Simon & Schuster Special Saltes at 1-800-456-6798
or business@simonandschuster.com

Designed by Katy Riegel

Maps by Jeffrey L. Ward

Manufactured in the United States of America

1   3   5   7   9   10   8   6   4   2

The Library of Congress has catalogued the Simon & Schuster edition as follows:
Chatters, James C.
Ancient encounters : Kennewick Man and the first Americans / James C. Chatters.
p.   cm.
Includes bibliographical references.
1. Kennewick Man.   2. Human remains (Archaeology)—Washington (State)   3. Indians of
North America—Anthropometry—Washington (State)   4. Indians of North America—
Washington (State)—Antiquities.   5. Washington (State)—Antiquities.   I. Title.
E78.W3 C417 2001
979.7'01—dc21   00-054754

ISBN 0-684-85936-X
0-684-85937-8 (Pbk)

To Jenny Elf,
My love, my strength, my inspiration,
and
To future generations of Americans,
whose right to know the full story
of their homeland's past was
the motivation for this book

Acknowledgments

THIS BOOK COULD not have come into being without the help of many people who, wittingly and unwittingly, contributed to the story. The initial recovery and analysis were very much a community effort. Will Thomas and David Deacy responsibly reported their find to the authorities, who, led by Sergeant Craig Littrell, quickly responded. Floyd Johnson gave me the opportunity to investigate the Kennewick skeleton thoroughly. Ray Tracy and John Leier of the U.S. Army Corps of Engineers arranged for the ARPA permit, and Tom McClelland, Kenneth Reid, Scott Staples, and Scott Turner helped recover the bones from the beach. Kenneth Lagergren, DDS, x-rayed the teeth, and John Umbright and Carl Senekham of Kennewick General Hospital produced X rays and CT scans of the spear point in the pelvis. Without the assistance of Ron Gerton, I could not have produced a cast of the skull from which the facial reconstruction was produced through the skill of Tom McClelland. My daughter, Claire Chatters, produced detailed drawings of Kennewick Man and, later, Buhla.

I am grateful to those who provided me with the opportunity to study other ancient skeletal materials, including Amy Dansie, Nevada

State Museum; Steven Hackenberger, Central Washington University; John Harris and Christopher Shaw, Page Museum of Los Angeles; Thomas Hester, Texas Archaeological Research Laboratory; Barbara O'Connell and Susan Myster, Hamline University; Max Pavesic, Boise State University; James Woods, College of Southern Idaho; Robert Yohe, Idaho Historical Society; and especially Al Redder of Waco, Texas. The analysis of Stick Man was made possible through location fees paid to Central Washington University by WGBH, Boston.

The following individuals graciously shared their discoveries and knowledge about First American issues and offered thoughts on the interpretation of Kennewick Man's characteristics: C. Loring Brace, University of Michigan; George Gill, University of Wyoming; Richard Jantz, University of Tennessee, Knoxville; Grover Krantz, Washington State University (retired); Catherine MacMillan, Bone-Apart Agency (deceased); Walter Neves and Max Blum, University of São Paulo; Douglas Owsley, Smithsonian Institution; Joseph Powell, University of New Mexico; Christopher Ruff, Johns Hopkins University; and D. Gentry Steele, Texas A&M, offered their ideas about physical anthropology. Jane Buikstra, University of New Mexico; Christopher Kontogianis, M.D., Kennewick, Washington; David Mohler, M.D., Stanford University; and Philip Walker, University of California, Santa Barbara, helped me interpret Kennewick Man's injuries. Betty Pat Gatliff, John Gurche, and Sharon Long provided helpful comments on the facial reconstruction. Frederika Kaestle, Yale; Theodore Schurr, Southwest Foundation for Biomedical Research; and especially David Glenn Smith, University of California, Davis, consulted on mitochondrial DNA. John Southon, Lawrence Livermore National Laboratory; Thomas Stafford and Skye Sellars, Stafford Research Laboratories; and R. E. Taylor and Donna Kirner, University of California, Riverside, shared their knowledge of radiocarbon dating. And James Adovasio, Mercyhurst College; Robson Bonnichsen, Center for the Study of the First Americans; Bruce Bradley and Michael Collins, Texas Archaeological Research Laboratory; Michael Crawford, University of Kansas; Thomas Dillehay,

Acknowledgments

University of Kentucky; James Dixon, Denver Museum of Natural History; Theodore Goebel, University of Nevada, Las Vegas; C. Vance Haynes and Marta Lahr, Oxford University; David Meltzer, Southern Methodist University; W. Roger Powers, University of Alaska; Dennis Stanford, Smithsonian Institution; and Lawrence Straus, University of New Mexico, conferred with me on the timing and routes of early migrations. Many of these same individuals read and commented on portions of the manuscript. Peter Schoonmaker read and commented on the complete manuscript.

The effort to learn about America's remote past is threatened by political forces, so the assistance of attorneys and members of Congress is becoming increasingly important. I wish to thank Alan Schneider and Paula Barran for so ably pursuing the Kennewick Man case, Congressman Richard "Doc" Hastings and his staff for authoring an amendment to NAGPRA, and Senators Slade Gorton and Patty Murray and Congressman George Nethercutt for inquiring into the activities of the Corps of Engineers. Thanks especially to Mike Lee of the *Tri-City Herald* and Cleone Hawkinson of Friends of America's Past for keeping the public informed.

Finally, there are those whose encouragement and counsel have kept me going throughout the long Kennewick Man ordeal. My heartfelt thanks to Dick Daugherty, Tom McClelland, Doug Owsley, Doug Preston, Gentry Steele, and especially Kent and Carol Richert and Jake and Claire Chatters for their patience, loyalty, and kindness.

Contents

Prologue

THE OLD MAN stopped on the trail, suddenly in a cold sweat, and leaned against a welcome boulder. His hip was aching again. It had troubled him some during the winter—the cold always awakened unwelcome reminders of his active youth—but all through the early spring he had felt vital and strong. While the young men hunted the bison cows when they left the herd to give birth to their calves, he had remained in camp, telling stories to the young children and enjoying bawdy banter with the women as he helped them prepare hides for clothing and shelter. But now the pain had returned, and with it this time had come that greatest of terrors: fever.

One calm, warm afternoon, while the women were cutting meat into strips for drying, he had left the clamor of camp and walked alone out onto the plain, taken as he always was by the stark beauty of the new grass and the brilliant yellow, pink, and lavender of the spring flowers. Under their blanket of soft green, the rolling hills and canyon clefts had taken on a colorful sensuality that belied their aridity. As a breeze rippled over a rounded slope, he had thought again of his young wife of so many winters past. They, his bride and he, had been on just such a walk as this, escaping the prying eyes of their companions to share a private moment in the warmth of an April afternoon. The Others, springing from their canyon ambush, had fallen upon the couple without warning. He had struggled valiantly to save her from her captors. He had nearly lost his life trying. But he had never seen his mate again.

Lost in bittersweet reverie, he had passed into the shade of a gray cliff, where the ground was still moist from a rain that had fallen the morning before. Stepping on a wet, moss-covered stone, he had lost his footing and fallen hard on his right buttock, tearing the skin around an ancient wound that never seemed to heal completely.

Now, many days later, the hunt was over, and the People were again on the move. They carried the dried meat and newly tanned skins in great loads on their backs and were making their way slowly toward their fishing place on the Great River. The weather was unseasonably warm, and for the past three days heavy clouds had blanketed the faraway mountains.

"My load is too light, Uncle." The youth his sister had borne three hands of winters ago walked up to his side. "Will you trade bundles so that I might try to carry yours?"

Grateful for his nephew's discretion and proud of the boy's growing strength, the old man exchanged packs with him, and together they resumed their march. But soon this weight, too, became more than he could bear. His bones began to ache, his blood thundered in his ears, and his vision narrowed until he could see little more than the trail at his feet. His body felt as if it would burst into flame.

Just when he felt he could bear no more, he caught the screeching cries of white waterbirds on the breeze, and a moment later he smelled the snow in the water of the Great River. A painful few steps more, and the surging waters came into view.

Salvation! The cold river would quench his fire.

He threw down his burden and stumbled down the rocky bank toward the torrent, heedless of the danger of a river in freshet.

"Rest with me, Uncle, I'm tired," the boy had begun, but to the boy's dismay the old man threw off this respectful attempt with a grunt. He was now just a few steps from the water's edge.

"Uncle! The water's too high! Already the river is rising!" he cried, abandoning formality in his alarm. "Uncle, you do not swim!"

"I will only walk in the shallows to soothe my old bones. Insolent child," the old man replied.

He stepped into the water. "Hu-uh!" He gasped. Yes! This icy flow would take away the fever and the pain. He stepped deeper, water now reaching to his knees.

Others who had reached the river before them heard the boy's shouts and came running.

Another step, and his wounded hip would feel the soothing fluid. Another step and . . . the bottom was gone!

He felt the cold slam into his fever-racked body, taking his breath away. He tried a few feeble strokes, paddling with his stronger right arm, but the boy was right. It was to no avail. His body went numb.

The pounding in his head soon ceased as his family's cries died away in the distance. He could now hear only the crackling of stones on the river bottom and the music of sand in the water rushing past his ears. Only brown twilight reached his eyes.

Then came darkness, silence . . . and peace.

Part I

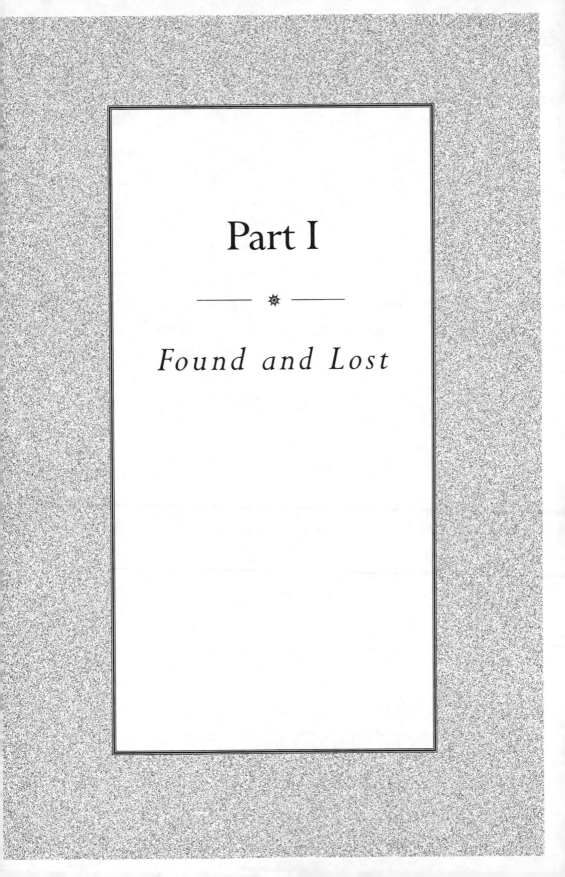

Found and Lost

1

The Stone Had Teeth

THE CALL CAME early Sunday evening, July 28, 1996. On the line was Floyd Johnson, coroner of Benton County, Washington, for whom I serve as a forensic anthropologist from time to time.

"Hey buddy," he said, "I've got some bones for you to look at. Some kids were wading in the river at the boat races and found a skull. Have you got time to look at it?"

"Sure," I answered. "We're just sitting around. Bring it on over."

It was not a long wait, but however short they are, these moments between hearing of a find and actually seeing it always fill me with anticipation. Old or recent, intact or deteriorated nearly beyond recognition, bones always have a story to tell. They chronicle early growth, life experience, death, and even what has happened to the body after death. Muscle ridges, wear and tear—arthritis, bone growth along ligaments and tendons, and fractures—record patterns of physical activity. Diseases and injury leave their mark in patterns of bone dissolution, atrophy, regrowth, and overgrowth. Cuts and bullet holes offer mute testimony to the manner of death. Then there are the all-important clues to identity—height, sex, age, and facial structure. All in all, it's a grand puzzle, and I love a good puzzle. But more than that, it's an introduction to someone new, someone whose story I will come to know well.

Floyd arrived carrying a five-gallon plastic bucket containing a drawstring plastic bag from a clothing store (police evidence containers are a constant source of wonder and amusement), and we sat down on the front porch. Opening the drawstring, I looked down at the first piece, the braincase, viewing it from the top. Removing it from the bag, I was immediately struck by its long, narrow shape and the marked constriction of the forehead behind a well-developed brow ridge. The bridge of the nose was very high and prominent. My first thought was that this skull belonged to someone of European descent. The bone was in excellent condition, having the tan, almost golden color of bone that has lain in the ground for some years but not long enough to deteriorate. All the breaks were fresh-looking, which told me that the skull had been complete until it was disturbed. A second fragment in the bottom of the bucket caught my eye, and I picked it up. It was the upper jaw. Thin walls of bone projected forward along the sides of the nasal opening, and an immense bony spine extended beneath it. Clearly, the nose had been huge. The tooth row also appeared to project slightly, and there were distinct deep depressions behind the ridges formed by prominent canine teeth. Called a canine fossa, this is an archaic characteristic common to many European skulls. So far, the characteristics were consistent with my initial sense that this was a white person, a Caucasian.

I turned the bone to inspect the underside, and what I saw seemed at first to be at odds with the rest of the picture. The teeth were worn flat, and worn severely. This is a characteristic of American Indian skeletons, especially in the interior Pacific Northwest, where the people ate stone-ground fish, roots, and berries and lived almost constantly with blowing sand. My mind jumped to something I'd seen when I was fourteen years old, working at an ancient site on the Snake River in Washington called Marmes Rockshelter. I saw the narrow-headed skull of a person who had died between 5,000 and 7,000 years ago being preserved in plaster for transport to the Washington State University laboratory. It stared at me from that long-ago memory through empty eye sockets. "Paleo-Indian?" came the involuntary thought. "Paleo-Indian" is the label given to the very earliest American immigrants, traditionally presumed to be early versions of today's Native Americans.

No, I thought, that can't be. The inhabitants of the Americas had had broad faces, round heads, and presumably brown skin and straight black hair. They had come over from Siberia no more than 13,000 years ago across the Bering Land Bridge and therefore resembled their modern-day Siberian relatives. This was no Paleo-Indian—was it?

"This looks like a white person," I told Floyd, "but it also could be very old." And I explained to him what I was noticing.

"How old?" he asked.

"It would have to be more than five thousand years, because everything I know of from after that time resembles modern Indians."

"I thought it looked old. But five thousand years! Amazing," he exclaimed.

I looked again at the braincase and, noting that the sutures—the seams between the independent growth centers of the skull—were all closed and nearly all obliterated, realized that this was an "aged" individual. Advanced age (beyond forty-five years when using suture closure as the measure) could account for the extreme tooth wear, so I put the thought of great age out of my mind. Prehistoric Northwest Indians had usually lost nearly all of their teeth by this age, but this man had a full set.

"So what do you think?" asked Floyd. "Is it an old Indian or what?"

"I don't think so, but I need more information to be sure. Is there any more out there?"

"They said there are other bones where these came from," he replied, "but I haven't even been out there myself yet. Do you want to go take a look?"

On the way to the site of the find, Floyd told the story of the discovery to me and my wife, Jenny, who had been watching the initial

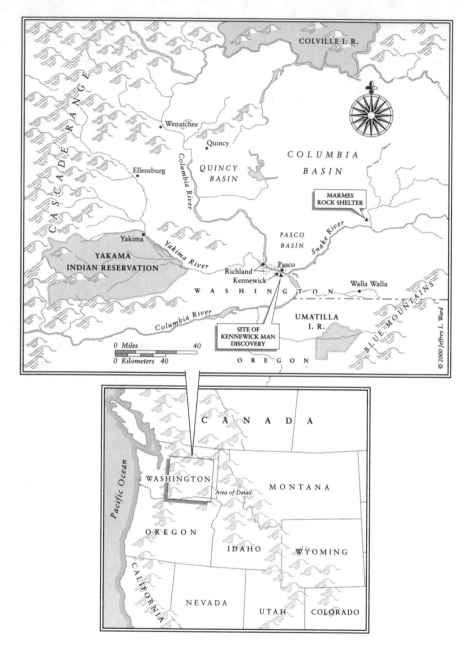

South Central Washington.

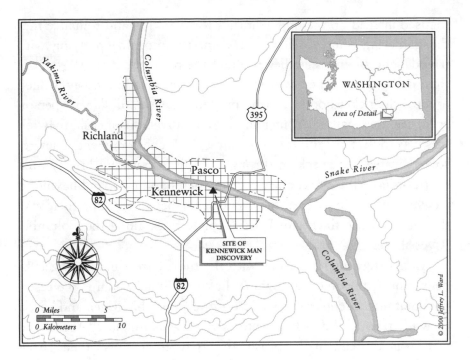

Kennewick and the Tri-Cities area.

exchange and came along to see how things turned out. I later learned the details from the discoverers themselves.

❈

Saturday and Sunday had been the days of the Columbia Cup, an unlimited hydroplane race on the Columbia River that culminated a summer-long Tri-Cities tradition of parades, sports, and music events called Sunfest. (The Tri-Cities are Richland, Kennewick, and Pasco in Washington State, about 140 miles southwest of Spokane.) The national-caliber race draws tens of thousands of tourists, who flock to Columbia Park in Kennewick to watch the finals. Much of the indigenous population of the Tri-Cities flees the crowd and deafening roar of the thunder boats, but among the largely youthful audience on this day were Will Thomas and Dave Deacy of nearby West Richland.

The two college students had little interest in the races but were focused instead on the opportunities for drinking and romance that the gathering offered. They had spent the morning partying with friends, and by the time they reached the park, the races were more than half over and they were more than a bit drunk. As they walked toward the ticket booth, which charged an eleven-dollar-per-person entry fee, they paused. Young and perennially short of cash, they felt this was too steep a toll for only half a day's entertainment. They resolved instead to sneak in through a 1,000-foot-long brushy area that bordered the entrance. A beer in each hand (to avoid having to pay high prices for beer at the event), they began working their way through a dense thicket of Russian olive trees along the Columbia River shore.

After struggling for a while with the thorny trees in dizzying 108-degree heat, they moved down to Lake Wallula, which is the reservoir that now occupies this stretch of the Columbia River, and began to wade through knee-deep water a few yards offshore. About 150 feet from the end of the brush, they paused to finish their beers, which were contraband in the race-viewing area. Will thought he saw something in the water a few yards ahead. Peering into the river, made murky by the wakes of the thunder boats, he could just make out a smooth round stone about the size of a cantaloupe. It looked like a skull. This was a great chance, he thought, to spook his gullible friend, Dave.

"Look over here, dude," he joked, pointing into the water. "We have a human head."

"Get out!" Dave retorted in disbelief. He was not taking the bait.

"No, really, man, it's a head. There's a dead body here! Somebody's been murdered!"

Reaching down as Dave moved closer, Will freed the object from the mud and lifted it from the water. Beginning to chuckle at his cleverness, he turned the object over in his hands. Then his laughter died.

The "stone" had teeth.

It really *was* a human skull. What should they do? Will, recovering from the initial shock and now considerably sobered, thought the bones were evidence of a crime or perhaps the remains of a drowning victim. He knew they should call the police, but Dave wanted no part of that. He had other priorities. They had, after all, come to the park with a purpose. There were parties to join, so they settled on a plan. They would watch the rest of the races, finish their partying, and then report their find to the authorities. In the meantime, to protect the skull from other spectators and two small boys who were playing on the nearby bank, they hid it in the bushes.

"It was *my* find," Will said later. "I didn't want anybody else to find it and get the credit!"

Once the races ended and the crowd dispersed, they returned with the police and retrieved their prize. The police then called Coroner Johnson.

❄

Floyd, Jenny, and I arrived at Columbia Park as the sun was setting. The cloudless sky was turning from azure to indigo, a rosy glow on the horizon framing Rattlesnake Mountain to the northwest and reflecting off the quieting waters of the Columbia River. Immense locust trees made gnarled black silhouettes against the darkening sky. We drove to the shore and stood with a pair of uniformed officers, taking in the scene and enjoying the cool breeze off the river. A jet boat cut a coral streak through the water off to the east, reflecting the sunset.

"Here they come," Floyd announced.

The police boat of the city of Kennewick, which manages the park, pulled in with a crew of officers and Columbia Basin search-and-rescue personnel. Floyd and I climbed aboard, and the boat pulled away. I expected a long trip and was puzzled as the boat nosed back to the bank only about a hundred yards upstream.

"What's up?" I shouted over the roar of the engines. Then, seeing an officer waving from the shore, "Did we forget someone?"

"No," someone called back. "This is where they found the skull."

I began to take in the setting, the first step in understanding what is known as the context of a discovery. The bank had been eroded by the river to a vertical cut about five feet high. Below it the land stair-stepped down to the water, indicating successive layers of increasingly fine sand and silt—finer sediment is more resistant to erosion. A dense thicket of orchard grass, milkweed, thistle, willow, and Russian olive crowded the land surface above the bank, with patches of cattails marking pockets of standing water. Irrigation seepage or a natural upwelling of groundwater makes this part of the park unsuitable for the manicured lawns that cover most of its four-mile length.

Sergeant Craig Littrell beckoned Floyd and me downstream. As we picked our way along the water's edge, we saw a scatter of debris, rusted and encrusted with sand—horseshoes, square and round nails, glass shards, bits of ceramic dinnerware, sawed bones, and the skulls of sheep and deer—the kind of trash typically found near homesteads of the late nineteenth and early twentieth centuries. Looking up, I saw more of the same protruding from the bank just beneath the jumble of vegetation.

When we reached the officer, he pointed into the water, saying, "That's where they found the skull, right next to that clump of grass that just shows above the water." A row of river cobbles lay at his feet, probably stacked by the boys Will and Dave had seen playing nearby.

The light was rapidly fading, but I could just see two vertebrae beneath the water, which by now had begun to clear. To the left were pieces of leg and arm bones and a scattering of rib fragments. The way the pieces lay disarticulated on the sand, they must have washed out from somewhere nearby. Turning, I searched the cut bank for the telltale outline of a pit caught in profile or bones poking from the soil. Finding none, I returned my attention to the water.

Darkness was closing in. We decided to gather up the exposed bones lest they be rediscovered in the morning by people less responsible than Will and Dave had been. I kicked off my sandals to feel any bones that might be invisible just beneath the mud, waded into the cool water, and began picking up fragments and handing them to Floyd: vertebrae, bits of rib, bones from both arms, part of a femur (thighbone), fragments of cheekbone, and part of a lower jaw. One of the search-and-rescue volunteers turned on his powerful spotlight as darkness overcame us. The beam played through the water, casting eerie shadows from the two halves of the pelvis that lay like complex abstract forms, all curves and hollows. Near them was a rusted knife with a bone handle and pewter inlay—a product of the late nineteenth century. We gathered these up and called it a night.

"What do you think now?" Floyd asked as he drove Jenny and me back home with the collection of bones. "Is it as old as you thought?"

"This is not an easy call," I told him. "It's going to take some time to figure out."

"What do you think so far, though, with what you have?" he asked.

"If I had to make a call right now, with the physical characteristics and the association with all that historic trash, I'd say this was a member of a pioneer family. Probably somebody who'd been buried in a family plot next to a homestead. But we're missing most of the lower jaw and some key parts of the face, and that leaves racial identification in doubt. I'll have to look at what I've got to see if the issue can be resolved. If not, we may have to come back and look some more."

"It's old, though, right? You know, not a recent death." By this he meant not within the last decade or so.

"Right. He's been there awhile."

❁

Back at home, I took the bones downstairs to my laboratory and laid them out on a worktable to dry gradually beneath a layer of plastic. *What is your story, old man?* I wondered as I went off to bed, unaware of the adventure that lay before me.

A Question of Time

SKULL FOUND ON SHORE OF COLUMBIA announced a headline on page 5 of the Monday-morning edition of the *Tri-City Herald*. A skull with apparently worn-down teeth had been found, it said. Police had no idea of its origin and would be sending it to the State Crime Lab for analysis. "State Crime Lab," I chuckled, amused at the new status conferred on my small consulting business. I have been an archaeologist in the Pacific Northwest for forty years and now own and operate Applied Paleoscience, which provides services in archaeology, paleoecology (the study of past environments), and forensic anthropology. I identify and analyze bones for the coroners of Benton and Franklin Counties, and it was in this capacity that I had been drawn into the Kennewick Man case. The "State Crime Lab" the paper was referring to was really the lower floor of my split-level home.

I had no sooner read the brief story when, at 7:30 A.M., I had a call from my colleague Ray Tracy, a great gentle bear of a man who is an archaeologist with the Walla Walla District, U.S. Army Corps of Engineers. Columbia Park is owned by the Corps, and anything found there is under its jurisdiction. Ray's coworker, District Lead

Archaeologist John Leier, had received a call from the Umatilla tribe demanding that the Corps take possession of the newly discovered skeleton and turn it over to them. Armand Minthorn, a tribal representative, was claiming that because the Umatillas had resided along the Columbia River and the skull had been found in the river, they should have the bones immediately. The worn teeth were proof enough for them that this was an Indian skull. Ray had been delegated to look into the matter and had called Floyd Johnson, who had directed him to me. Could I tell him anything about the skull? I had not yet started the investigation, I replied, but might have some answers by midafternoon.

A new intern from nearby Central Washington University was scheduled to begin working with me that day on a collection of 6,000-year-old animal bones from a cave in the nearby Cascade Mountain Range. That plan would change, but I doubted he would be disappointed. I phoned and told him that he would have to assist me with a new forensic case that had just come in.

There was plenty to be done in the meantime. Forensic analyses make up only about 2 percent of my work. At the time of the discovery I was conducting several studies for the U.S. Forest Service, seeking, through analysis of plant pollen sequences taken from lakes and bogs, to document the postglacial history of forest ecosystems and determine the natural cycle of forest burning and regrowth. Foresters would use the results to develop more ecologically sensitive policies for forest management. Not only was it fascinating work, but some reports were due. I had also been retained to analyze animal remains from a site on Washington's Puget Sound and needed to finalize plans for a site visit. Then there were some leads to be followed toward future contracts—more than enough for a week's work, even without the new distraction.

Although I had other work to do, I began to walk over every few minutes to clean and inspect the skeleton, which for record-keeping purposes I had designated merely "Columbia Park I." During one of those stolen moments I noticed something in the right ilium—the broad, thin blade of spongy bone that forms the upper part of the pelvis and serves as an attachment surface for the gluteus maximus and other major muscles of the legs and back. Beneath encrustations of cemented sand, I could just make out a gray object. I tapped it with a dental pick; it was hard, but because I could only see an area .25 inch (6.4 mm) in diameter, I could make out nothing more. One thing was certain: the object was embedded beneath the natural surface of the bone. The object peeked through an oval window in the outer, cortical layer of the ilium. A depressed, crescent-shaped area beside the window and smooth, hard bone on the window's rim showed that the bone had been infected but had later healed extensively before death. My heartbeat accelerated, and my hands began to shake. Something was embedded in this person's hip! I'd worked on several other skeletons with stone arrow points in their bones—ancient American Indian homicides. This could be another such case. But this victim seemed different from any Indian I had ever seen. Was this the first known northwestern example of an early trader who had met his fate at the hands of local tribesmen, or was the gut instinct I had suppressed the day before correct—was this a Paleo-Indian, one of the earliest inhabitants of the Americas? If the latter was true, the embedded object could be one of the first examples of conflict early in the history of the Western Hemisphere. I chided myself to reel in the wild speculation; there were plenty of other possible explanations.

Just then Scott Turner, my new intern, arrived, and we set about trying to learn some basic information about this individual. It was a large, robust male who, from the few bones we had in hand, appeared to be in late middle age. The right humerus (upper arm bone), which was the only complete limb bone we had, was from a person who had stood about 5 feet, 9 inches tall. The characteristics of the skull seemed to be those of a non-Indian and were more like those of a European, as I'd noticed earlier, but we clearly needed more fragments.

❈

We were interrupted by a call from a young reporter who had been assigned to follow up on the skull story for the *Tri-City Herald*.

"I understand from Sergeant Littrell that you're working on the skeleton the boys found at the boat races," he began. "He said that you identified it as the bones of an early European settler. Is that true?"

Man, news travels fast! The ink wasn't even dry in my notebook, and the press was already in on the details.

"That's not entirely accurate," I corrected him, trying to keep the story under control. "I don't know what to think yet; it's a little ambiguous. The skull does have a lot of European characteristics and was found associated with domestic trash from early this century or late last, so we might just have someone buried in the family plot behind a homestead. But I haven't finished my investigation yet, and I'm not ready to make an identification. We're missing some key pieces of the skull that we need for identification."

"But you do think it's an early settler?" he pressed.

"I'm not ready to say that," I cautioned. "This is very much a work in progress."

✳

At that point Ray Tracy called again, and I gave him much the same information I had given the reporter. We talked about the need for additional bone fragments and the possible ways of solving the identification question if the needed facial bones were not forthcoming, touching on the possible need for radiocarbon dating and even DNA analysis if I failed to find what I needed to resolve the identification issue.

✳

"This," I explained to Scott after the second call, holding up the ilium containing the mystery object, "is one reason I can't make a definitive statement."

"What is it?" he asked.

"I can't tell from what little is showing," I began. "It could be corroded metal. Lead, for example, can take on a hardness like that—it could be shrapnel from the Civil War . . . or the Spanish-

An example of a Cascade Point similar to the one found in Kennewick Man's pelvis. (Drawing by Sarah Moore)

American War. Could be he was a miner who had a piece of stone fired into his hip by an errant blast. Or it may be a stone arrow or spear point—a projectile point. From the gray material, which could be a fine-grained igneous rock like basalt or andesite, it could even be a Cascade Point."

He knew of Cascade Points from his classes on regional archaeology at Central Washington University. They dated from around 5,000 to 9,000 years ago and were definitive of the second earliest well-documented culture to occupy the interior Northwest, after the Clovis culture

"Cooool!" he exclaimed. "Way cool!"

From that moment on, for Scott, the skeleton was "Cascade Man." He talked of nothing else. The other possibilities had been eclipsed.

The object in the pelvis had become the burning issue for me as well. I called Kennewick General Hospital, which provides X-ray and computed tomography (CT) scans for the coroner's office, and arranged to take the pelvis in at 7:00 P.M. After physicians' hours, the hospital has only emergency cases and can more easily find time for the dead.

That was still hours away, so, after a call to Floyd Johnson for his approval, Scott and I went back to Columbia Park to look for more bone fragments. Arriving at the discovery site around 5:00 P.M., we found that the water level in the reservoir had been lowered nearly two feet since the night before, creating a broad, muddy beach. Wave action from boat wakes had exposed more bones, which lay like driftwood among soil concretions, dead fish, rubber tires, and an old bicycle frame. Nearly two hours of carefully searching the mud and scratching with our fingers through windrows of debris that lay high on the beach rewarded us with dozens more fragments, including vertebrae, ribs, arm and leg bones, and some of the small bones from hands and feet. Most important, we had found the right ramus, the vertical portion of the lower jaw that attaches it to the cranium. As the skull's other characteristics had led me to expect, it was narrow and angled strongly backward, a characteristic of Europeans and Africans. The jaw of an American Indian male would have been much broader, forming a right angle with the horizontal, tooth-containing portion of the jaw.

On our way to the hospital for the X rays, I cautioned Scott not to expect too much. The jaw showed more European-like character-istics, so we were probably not looking at a Cascade Point in the bone. But he was not dissuaded, certain that he was playing a part in a major discovery.

✾

At the hospital we met John Umbright, the head X-ray technician, who had helped me with cases before. After explaining what we hoped to learn, we laid the pelvis on the X-ray table and joined him on the other side of the radiation barrier. The first picture was nearly blank, showing little more than the outline of the bone. The machine had been set for an intact body, not dry bone.

He lowered the radiation intensity and tried again. The bone was visible this time, its structure illustrated in exquisite detail. We could see the healed bone as a densely white area beside the opening that had exposed the gray object. The edges of the window could clearly be seen, an elongated oval inside which was . . .

"Nothing," I said aloud in frustration. "Do you think an intermediate setting would show anything?"

"No," he replied, "it's invisible in both images. Nothing will show if it's stone."

Silica, which is a major component in most rocks, behaves just like glass, which is a form of silica; X rays pass right through it. Bone stops X rays because it contains potassium and calcium, both of which are metals. At least we knew now that the object was stone, but that told us little about what it was. We decided to do a CT scan, which might allow us to separate the bone from the less radioopaque stone inside it, but that would have to wait until the next evening, when the machine would again be free.

Scott left for home, still talking about the articles we would write about "Cascade Man" and leaving me to ponder what was becoming an increasingly puzzling case.

❋

After a light and troubled sleep, I rose early Tuesday, resolved to get a better look at the stone object. From the equipment shelf I chose a fine wooden probe and a dropper bottle containing a 10 percent solution of hydrochloric acid, which I used in the field to test soil for carbonates. I diluted the acid further to keep from damaging the bone and began placing tiny drops on the cemented soil around the healed window in the ilium. When the acid stopped fizzing, I scraped gently to remove the softened soil and then repeated the process.

Soon I could make out faint flake scars—the ridge-and-groove texture left by the chipping process that is used to shape raw stone into tools. Following the stone along the upper edge of the oval window, I exposed an edge and, to my surprise, broke through the cement to the other side of the bone. There was a second, smaller window in the back side of the ilium as well. In the space between the openings was about .5 inch (1.27 cm) of a very sharp, serrated edge. Around the lower lateral edge of the oval opening, I at first thought I was looking at the broken tip of the blade, but I soon realized that this end of the object did not have a sharp, broken edge. Instead, its surface curved gradually to a rounded base that appeared to have an intentionally dulled edge. This was definitely a projectile point, but there were no notches or shoulders for attaching it to a shaft. Scott was going to love this—an unnotched, convex base and serrated edges are hallmarks of the Cascade Point style.

I called my friend Dr. Kenneth Reid, who is a specialist in stone tools and owns a small archaeological consulting firm similar to mine. I told him what I was working with and asked if he could come look at the projectile point and perhaps help me recover more of the skeleton. We could also work on one or another of the contract reports on which we were collaborating. Glad for an excuse to escape from the office, he agreed to make the two-and-a-half-hour drive over from Pullman and would arrive in midafternoon.

Stopping for breakfast, I glanced through the morning's paper. This time, the story had moved up to page 3, under a headline that read SKULL LIKELY EARLY WHITE SETTLER. So much for the case being a work in progress. This was going to set off some fireworks.

As if on cue, the phone rang with another call from Ray Tracy. The Umatillas had read the paper and were already demanding a second opinion. "Find out what it is," Ray quoted Armand Minthorn as saying, "but don't do any study."

"That's going to be *real* easy," I said sarcastically.

He chuckled.

Of course I would need to study the bones in order to make an identification. So would anyone who was going to give us a second opinion.

I told him we had recovered more bone fragments the previous day and that I was more certain now of the skull's European characteristics. I still needed to recover some facial bones and teeth to firm up the identification. I told him that I wanted to sift the loose mud to recover the scattered remains.

He called back a few minutes later. He had discussed my plans to screen the mud with his superiors. They knew of the historic artifacts on the beach and were concerned that we might encounter some of them or even some prehistoric artifacts in the process of our work. Because of that concern and because they were under such close scrutiny by the Indian tribes, they wanted me to have an ARPA permit. ARPA is the Archaeological Resources Protection Act of 1979, which makes it a crime to collect artifacts and other archaeological materials (including ancient human remains) from federal land without a permit from the landholding agency. An ARPA permit would establish the proper paper trail within the agency, he said, and protect Corps officials from undue harassment.

I complied immediately in a letter to Richard Charlton, Corps of Engineers Real Estate Division, dated July 30:

> Under the authority of the Coroner of Benton County, Washington, I am conducting a forensic investigation of human remains found Sunday, July 28 at Columbia Park. . . . In order to solve issues of age and racial affiliation, it may be necessary to revisit the site of the find and obtain more skeletal material from eroded sediments and to inspect the cut bank from which the bones apparently weathered. Since the land is owned by the U.S. Army Corps of Engineers, I am requesting an ARPA permit for the period between July 28, when remains were turned over to me, and August 3, a period of one week.

The retroactive nature of the request was a precaution. I did not want myself, Scott Turner, Floyd Johnson, or any of the law enforcement personnel to be charged with an ARPA violation just for doing our jobs. I popped the letter in the fax and mulled over the second-opinion issue.

In order to gather full forensic measurements on this skeleton, I would need some very specialized measuring instruments and a set of templates for estimating age from the pubic symphysis (the area above the genitals where the left and right halves of the pelvis meet).

The nearest institution that owned these things was Central Washington University, located 110 miles north in the town of Ellensburg, where I had formerly taught archaeology and physical anthropology. Ellensburg was also the home of Catherine (Katie) MacMillan, a retired physical anthropologist. Katie was perfect for a second opinion.

Katie and I had been acquainted since our student days at Washington State University—I as a freshman, she as a returning graduate student. She was a tall, imperious woman with graying blond hair and a smoker's husky voice. With students and colleagues alike, she was fond of posing a question and fixing the victim with her intense gray eyes, brows raised, awaiting the answer. A miss earned a loud "Baaaaan—WRONG!" She was intimidating and entirely unswayed by others' opinions of her or her ideas.

In retirement, Katie had opened a forensic consulting business called the Bone-Apart Agency to supplement her income. A mutual friend had confided to me that a year previously, when Katie and I had both been on the same murder case—she working for the prosecution, I advising the defense—Katie had been annoyed to learn that I was working in forensic anthropology. The central Washington area was hardly big enough for one forensic anthropologist, let alone two. Who would be a better choice for a second opinion than a brutally honest competitor? I arranged for us to meet at the Anthropology Department at CWU, where Katie was analyzing some skeletons. I packed the Columbia Park bones into my ancient Toyota pickup and made the two-hour drive.

❀

At CWU, Katie, as usual, simply looked over the rims of her reading glasses and snapped, "What have you got?" I opened the box and placed the skull fragments, femur parts, and left half of the pelvis on the tabletop. Not wanting her assessment tainted by the apparent spear wound or my own opinion, I kept the right ilium hidden in a separate box and said simply, "See what you think. I need an opinion on race, but afterward I want to work with you on the aging."

While Katie worked, I talked to Steve Hackenberger, the CWU Anthropology Department chair, showing him the right ilium I had withheld from Katie.

"Look at this," I whispered, showing him the ilium with its gray prisoner. "Look like a Cascade Point to you?"

"Well, maybe. Kind of looks like it. But you know, those things aren't very limited in time. Jeffrey Flenniken [one of the country's best flintknappers—a world-class replicator of stone tools] is pretty skeptical about that point style. He says that these leaf-shaped points like Cascade pretty much run the gamut timewise. He's seen the same style in early photos of Indians in Western Oregon—historic pictures of people using the same leaf-shaped spear points.

"Why don't you just get a radiocarbon date?" he suggested.

※

"OK." Katie was finished. "Male Caucasian," she announced.

"You sure?" I asked.

"Easy call," was the firm response.

"The face?" I probed.

"White guy."

"Mandible?"

"White guy."

"Femur?"

"A white guy, *Jim!*" She was becoming annoyed.

"OK, OK," I placated her. "But what about this?" And I placed the right ilium with its gray enigma in front of her.

Her eyes widened. Out rolled a soft, gravelly chuckle. "What's that doing in there?"

"Does this change your thinking?" I asked.

She looked over the skull fragments again, turning each piece slowly in her hands and holding the facial bones together to inspect their orientation. Then she looked up with a shrug.

"If these bones were brought to me and the stone wasn't in there," she declared firmly, "I'd have to say Caucasian."

After we had taken measurements and worked out an estimate of the man's age (forty to fifty-five years), I thanked Katie and made her promise to send a letter summarizing her observations to Coroner Johnson. Then I sped back to Richland in time to greet Ken Reid.

A slender, soft-spoken Vietnam veteran, Ken, who is now state archaeologist for Idaho, specializes in the analysis of stone tools and the debris from their manufacture—a field known as "lithic technology." He and I had recently worked together on a Cascade Culture site in Hells Canyon of the Snake River, he studying the stone and I the animal remains. The report we were writing on that work was the primary business reason for his trip to see me. He had also been working for several years on a method for matching tools made from glassy volcanic rocks to their quarries of origin. He was particularly interested in andesite, an igneous rock that I suspected was the raw material of the Kennewick projectile point. I asked what he thought of the gray object in the pelvis. As I expected—Ken characterizes himself as "pathologically prudent"—he was noncommittal.

"I wouldn't be too eager to call that a Cascade Point," he said, squeezing out the words. "And it could be andesite, but it could also be dacite [another igneous rock] or even siltstone. We'd have to analyze it to find out."

Analyzing the stone would be difficult. The point was firmly locked into place and could not be removed for sampling without breaking the dense, healed bone from around it. That would be intentionally damaging the bone and was out of the question. If we couldn't identify the material, though, at least the CT scan might help us to identify the point itself.

Eager for a resolution, we reached the hospital at five, but the CT scanner turned out to be in use on live patients and we had to remain in the waiting room for nearly an hour. I took the unexpected opportunity to brief Ken on what we were there to accomplish.

X-ray and CT-scan machines both do their work with beams of X rays, but in very different ways. A standard X-ray machine shines a single, broad beam of radiation through the subject and creates a two-dimensional image of its radio-opaque contents, just as a beam of light exposes photographic film. The image is collapsed and is thus difficult to interpret; bones and foreign objects are shown overlaid on one another in what can be a confusing jumble. To locate a foreign object or interpret an injury, the radiologist usually needs to take X rays from multiple angles. A CT scanner solves this problem by shining narrow X-ray beams from multiple locations around the subject as the radiation source rotates. The detector, which also rotates, receives this series of images and transmits them to a computer, which combines the data into a narrow vertical "slice." Multiple slices taken at intervals through the object can be combined to create a three-dimensional image that physicians use to inspect injuries in bone and cartilage. In our case, because of the multiple views it offered, this machine might allow us to—in effect—see the projectile point by looking "around" the bone rather than through it. If so, we could use a lower beam strength that would not pass through the stone so readily and thus would keep it visible.

Finally the last patient left and we were introduced to the technician who was operating the CT scanner that evening. They had an unexpectedly full schedule, he said, so we immediately set to work.

I began by positioning the pelvis on the bed of the scanner. In moments, images began to appear on the screen. The first showed only bone, the walls of the healed window clearly visible. But the next frame displayed an irregular white form where the projectile point would be, and in the third the object took shape. It was more than two inches (5 cm) long and .8 inch (2 cm) wide—much larger than I had expected.

We could clearly see the rounded base and serrated edge that were visible to the naked eye, but in place of the expected sharp tip at the opposite end there was only a broad, wavy edge. By the fifth scan, this broad end began to disappear again, while the basal end remained on the screen. This was an indication that the end of the point opposite the base was much thinner. The point had originally been shaped like a willow leaf, almost bipointed, with a wide blade and a narrow, rounded base. Apparently it had struck something solid, probably the pelvis itself, which sheared away its tip in what is known as an impact fracture. The resulting thin, freshly broken, and therefore very sharp edge had then chiseled its way deeply into the bone.

The technician printed the images on X-ray film. For future reference, I asked what he had named the file on his computer tape, should we need additional copies or want to look at the point in three dimensions. He shrugged apologetically: he hadn't saved the file. There was no time to redo the scans; another patient was already being wheeled into the exam room. We took our film, grateful for at least the one copy, and departed.

❀

That evening, Ken and I reviewed the evidence. The skeleton had Caucasoid characteristics—both Katie and I had seen that independently. At the very least it was physically distinct from skeletons of American Indians of the last several thousand years. The skeleton was associated with what looked like a homestead of late-nineteenth- or early-twentieth-century date, yet the only artifact that was certainly associated in time with the skeleton was the large spear point in its pelvis. The point itself was no real help in solving the puzzle. Stylistically, it could, Ken agreed, be from almost any time—or any place, for that matter. Yes, it looked like the local Cascade type, but Australian Aborigines had been making nearly identical serrated-edged, leaf-shaped spear points, called Kimberlys, well into the twentieth century. The bone had been healed for at least many months, probably many years, before death, easily enough time for the man to have traveled around the world. Our man could have been a trader, or a sailor perhaps, who had gotten into trouble with Stone Age people somewhere during his wanderings, years before his death on the Mid-Columbia. If we could identify the source of the stone, we could narrow down the geography but still would not be able to place the skeleton in time.

"You could radiocarbon-date it," Ken said, echoing Steve Hackenberger's suggestion.

"Right," I responded ruefully. "And if it comes back something like five hundred years, the Indians will be all over me." The Sahaptin-speaking tribes of Washington and Oregon—Yakamas, Umatillas, and Nez Percés—had become increasingly opposed to any analysis that would destroy bone.

We let the issue drop.

The next morning, armed with our ARPA permit, which had arrived the previous afternoon, we set out with five-gallon buckets and a fine-meshed archaeological screen to recover as much of the skeleton as we could from the beach at Columbia Park. We supported the screen against a tussock of drying grass about 15 feet (4.5 meters) downstream from where Will and Dave had found the skull and began to sieve the mud. We would scoop up a bucket full of the saturated goo, slog through knee-deep water to the screen, pour the muck into the screen, and wash it through with bucket after bucket of water. This was exhausting and unproductive. Not only did the clay-rich mud stick together so well that it took tens of gallons to screen a single bucketload, but in the first four buckets, we found only one cervical (neck) vertebra and a few bone scraps. To make matters worse, the washing clouded the water and, with our vision obscured, we risked breaking with foot or bucket edge the small, delicate facial bones we were so keen to find.

We needed a better tactic and switched to mimicking the wave action that had exposed the bones in the first place. We tried standing offshore and using the buckets to splash water against the beach; ten splashes, then wait for the water to drain off, then ten more. On the first try, we exposed two vertebrae and a portion of the right lower jaw. Next came more vertebrae, a third molar, and a part of the left tibia. As we threw water at the muck, the lighter bone fragments floated free, wash onto the higher shore, and remained there as the water drained away.

※

That afternoon, I added forty more bone fragments and became aware of a pattern. Five rib fragments showed signs of having been severed and later healed. It appeared that if the person had been standing, the breaks would have been vertically aligned, as if they had been cut by some straight edge, such as that of a saber. Closer inspection would later show them to have been fractured rather than cut and aligned on both sides of the breastbone rather than one side, but at the time the pattern seemed to fit with the steel knife and physical characteristics as just one more piece of evidence dating the man to the historic period. Still, there was that problem of the spear point.

I began telephoning trusted colleagues for advice. Everyone offered the same solution: get a radiocarbon date. One was Dr. Tom Green, director of the Arkansas Archaeological Survey, who had had an experience similar to my own. Several years before, as the state archaeologist for Idaho, he had been involved in the discovery near Buhl of a partial female skeleton that was so well preserved he had thought she was less than 8,000 years old. He submitted bone to a commercial laboratory for a radiocarbon date and was stunned to learn she had died more than 12,700 years ago! That find had forced him to become familiar with literature on the earliest North American skeletons.

"Gentry Steele did several papers on an analysis of the Paleos," he recalled. "Seems to me the males were long-headed, with big faces."

"The skelton I have here is long-headed, but the face . . ." I thought out loud. "I suppose it's pretty big, long anyway, but not especially wide. Was there anything else about them?"

He didn't recall the details offhand but said he would send along copies of Steele's articles.

❋

My colleagues had told me what I had known all along to be the best scientific course of action, but still I was hesitant. The evidence was pointing almost equally in opposite directions. If I went by the physical features, supported by Katie MacMillan's assessment, the steel knife, and what looked in this context to have been saber-severed ribs, the skeleton would become Kennewick's earliest pioneer—a trapper or explorer of whom there had been no written record, or perhaps a sailor who had come inland to settle on the wide Columbia River. He would be honored, become a local hero of sorts. If I went on the spear point alone, plus Tom Green's brief description of Paleo-Indian males, this could be one of the earliest examples of interpersonal conflict yet found in the Americas, but the remains would immediately be claimed by local tribes without further study. By running the radiocarbon date, I would solve the age question, but if the bone dated to before European contact but was not truly ancient, I would be berated by tribal officials for having destroyed some of the bones. I did not relish the prospect.

As I sat pondering what to do, staring all the while at the skeleton laid out on my exam table in its protective plastic bags, Jenny walked into the lab.

"So how's 'Kennewick Man'?" she asked brightly, using that term for the first time.

"As well as can be expected, but I'm having an awful time," I complained. I described my dilemma in all its convoluted detail.

At length she put a hand on my shoulder, gave me an earnest look, and declared, "If it's an ancient Indian, that makes him my ancestor, and I want to know how old he is." Jenny's great-great-grandmother was a Haida Indian from southeastern Alaska; one of her great-grandfathers was a Chippewa from northern Minnesota. Her maternal grandmother described her heritage as "Heinz 57," although her Tennessee origin and high cheekbones bespoke a Cherokee ancestry.

Jenny's words brought the issue home: our family had a stake in this that went far beyond resolving a scientific dilemma. If I were incredibly lucky and this did turn out to be a very ancient American, and if he had contributed his genes to modern Indians, then he was an ancestor of Jenny's and of our daughter and all her descendants. I no longer saw a downside to radiocarbon-dating the skeleton, and resolved to see it done.

I wanted someone who would be able to do the job with the absolute minimum of bone. The smallest amounts of material are dated by a method called accelerator mass spectrometry, or AMS, and my connection to the AMS world was John Southon, a researcher at Lawrence Livermore National Laboratory, with whom I had been discussing a research collaboration. John told me that Ervin Taylor at the University of California, Riverside, had recently been dating a lot of very small samples of human bone and would be a good choice. John would do the mass spectrometry for free, as a research sample, as long as no court issue was involved (national laboratories don't like that sort of publicity). I assured him there was none, since the specimen was in any case not a recent murder victim.

Erv Taylor said he would be glad to help. Now in his early sixties, Erv had written a major text on radiocarbon dating and had been a colleague of my late father, who had operated a radiocarbon-dating laboratory at Washington State University until his retirement.

I explained my situation and that we did not want to use any more material than absolutely necessary out of respect for the skeleton and to avoid upsetting any potential relations whoever they might prove to be. Southon, I told him, was willing to do the AMS part for free.

"We can work with as little as ten milligrams of carbon," Erv said in short, clipped tones. This is a piece of bone about the size of a shelled sunflower seed. "The price, with Livermore eating the cost of the AMS, is four hundred dollars. We've been dating quite a few early skeletons lately. Why do you think it might be old?"

"Two main reasons," I replied. "There's a stone point that might be early healed into the pelvis . . ."

"That's a good start."

". . . and there are carbonate concretions on the bone."

"The carbonate doesn't mean anything," he said dismissively. "Formation rate is too locality-specific. If you decide to run the date and get it in right away," he continued, "we can do it in two weeks to a month. Call Donna Kirner—she runs the lab—to make arrangements."

❈

Thursday, after a series of calls to other clients and a serious attempt to put in some billable time, I reached Floyd Johnson and explained why I felt radiocarbon dating was our only option. He wondered if we couldn't just run DNA analysis to solve the identity question, but I explained that I thought it was still too expensive—about $1,000 to $2,000 per sample. The radiocarbon dating would be only $400.

"Oooh . . . I don't think I can do it, buddy," he said apologetically. "My whole budget for forensic work is only two thousand dollars this year."

This was a blow. Too much was at stake here to drop the testing now. I had to know if this was a pioneer or one of the earliest Americans. I offered to forgo my fee for this case and the last one as well, for which I had not yet sent Floyd a bill. The total would save the county more than $400, but for a self-employed consultant like me, taxes would take nearly half of that, so I was really giving up only a couple of hundred dollars to solve an exciting puzzle and get this man properly taken care of.

He thought a moment, then agreed, asking me to draft a letter for his signature requesting that the work be finished by the time he returned from vacation in about three weeks.

Now only one step remained: getting approval from the Corps of Engineers. The coroner's authority in forensic investigations is supposed to be total, a policy that prevents people in power from abusing the system. Nonetheless, I did not want to get into trouble with the Corps, which is a powerful federal agency in the Northwest and a sometime client.

Friday morning, I put in a call to Ray Tracy and explained the situation: we had an apparently European skeleton with a possibly ancient stone projectile point embedded in it. We needed a radiocarbon date to solve the conundrum and had made arrangements at a top-flight laboratory.

"Sounds like the best approach," he said simply. Then, after a moment: "This could be really exciting. If it really is only about a hundred years old, though, as you seem to think, the Corps will have to communicate directly with the coroner to determine ownership and disposition of the skeleton."

"How is it going with the tribes?" I asked.

"Oh, John [Leier, his superior] has been talking to them," he replied. "The Yakamas are OK, just said, 'Keep us informed'; the Umatillas are resigned to the process.

"Anyway," he closed, "it looks to me like the progression of analysis is going as it should, with care and sensitivity."

❈

Now all that remained was to choose the sample to be submitted. For this, I needed a piece of bone that was most likely to be free of contamination from more recent carbon. I also have a personal rule, derived nearly a decade before from a conversation with the late Sarah McCraggie, then a ninety-year-old elder of the Okanogan tribe of north-central Washington. She believed that people's body parts needed to remain together in the ground so that when the Creator called on them to live again, they would be whole. For this reason, I try to use a part that a person could function without in life—a toe or finger bone, a tooth, or a twelfth rib. This time I chose the fifth metacarpal of the left hand—the bone that connects the little finger to the wrist. It was suitable not only because many people function perfectly well after losing their little fingers but also because this bone was the best preserved in the entire body. I had found it while cleaning soil from inside the braincase, to which rodents had probably moved the bone long ago (skulls make great rodent homes; the walls rarely cave in). Housed there, the metacarpal had been protected from water flowing through the soil and had been spared the mineral encrustation found on and inside other bones (a fact that supported my suspician that the carbonate crust on the bones was a result of recent irrigation). It would thus have the least contamination of any bone. It was small, weighing only 2.6 grams; the laboratory would need only a small part of it for the date.

On Monday I packaged the metacarpal for shipment to the University of California, Riverside. Along with it went a submittal form, estimating the age at 150 to 250 radiocarbon years, but possibly 5,500 to 9,500 years, plus the coroner's signed letter of request.

We would soon know the age of Kennewick Man.

✻

A week later, Donna Kirner, specialist of the UC Riverside radiocarbon dating lab, phoned to inform me that the collagen, the principal protein in bone and the target of our dating efforts, was in excellent condition and would provide a reliable age estimate. She thought it likely that the bone contained intact DNA and wondered if we had considered trying to use DNA for identification of ethnicity. I expressed my belief that DNA work was too expensive, but she told me that a graduate student at the University of California, Davis, Frederika Kaestle, was extracting DNA from old bone and might be interested in assisting us in the Kennewick case. There should, she said, be enough bone left over from the radiocarbon dating for a series of DNA analyses.

I contacted Kaestle the same day and was told with assurance that by using mitochondrial DNA she would be able to tell the coroner whether or not the skeleton was that of an American Indian or a European. She would speak to her professor, David Glenn Smith, who she felt would approve of her assisting us at no cost. She would need only about a quarter of a gram per analysis and would need to do two analyses to achieve a reliable result.

Kaestle was talking about analyzing mitochondrial DNA, not the form of DNA that is used in criminal trials. DNA exists in two forms in our bodies, the long double-helix strands of fifty to one hundred thousand genes that are found in the cell nucleus and mitochondrial DNA, or mtDNA, which occurs in small bodies, called organelles, in the cytoplasm, the substance that surrounds the nucleus of the cell. Whereas nuclear DNA provides the blueprint for producing the proteins that make up our bodies and the enzymes that operate them, mtDNA is a separately self-replicating ring of just a couple of dozen genes that create and operate the mitochondria. Mitochondria are structures that convert sugars into the energy that fuels our bodies. There are only two sets of nuclear DNA in each cell, but there can be thousands of essentially identical mtDNA rings. During sexual reproduction, the mitochondria are present in the maternal egg cell but are absent in the sperm cell provided by the father. Thus, mtDNA is inherited only in the maternal lineage. Mutations in its circular molecule can be used to show genetic relationships between people, living or dead, but only along the maternal line.

DNA is a surprisingly stable molecule and under the right circumstances can last for as many as tens of thousands of years. Dry or permanently frozen environments seem to be the best for DNA preservation. In the relatively closed environment of bones and teeth, DNA can persist, at least in fragments, long after a person's death. By dissolving the mineral and protein portions of bone, DNA specialists like Kaestle can isolate the DNA fragments, multiply them, and use them to determine the maternal lineage to which a person belongs.

Genetic researchers at the University of California, Davis, and others at Arizona, Emory, Michigan, New Mexico, Utah, and Yale universities (to name a few) have been extracting mtDNA from modern peoples throughout the world. They have found that it occurs in only a couple of dozen general patterns, called haplogroups. Each haplogroup is believed to represent the descendants of a single female, and these groups tend to be strongly geographically distributed. Groups A, B, C, and D account for the majority of American Indians but also occur in eastern Asia, along with E, F, G, and Z. Types H, I, J, K, T, U, V, and X occur primarily among people in western Eurasia and North Africa. L predominates in Africa and all other haplogroups descend from it. This modern geographical distribution means that mtDNA can be extracted from bones and used to help establish the ethnicity of the dead. Hence our interest in having Kaestle extract the DNA from the bone fragment left over from the radiocarbon date on Kennewick Man. If the radiocarbon date came back at only 150 to 200 years, and there was still an argument over the man's ancestry, the DNA would tell us whether he was modern European or American Indian.

When Floyd Johnson returned from his vacation on August 19, I informed him of the possibility of using DNA in our attempts to identify Kennewick Man, and he immediately approved. I called Donna Kirner and asked her to send the bone she was not using for dating to Kaestle, who had received approval from her professor to conduct the studies for us.

✺

Things were now in motion: a radiocarbon date would tell us when the man died, and if that was ambiguous, we would soon have the DNA results as a backup. One additional project remained to be initiated.

Early in the case, Floyd had expressed an interest in having a facial reconstruction done on the skull. He had seen one produced for the coroner of Franklin County and thought it would be interesting to see what this early Kennewick pioneer had looked like. I too had been interested in producing such a reconstruction but was uncomfortable building up clay on the skull itself. We needed to produce a cast of the skull and work from that. If the skeleton proved to be recent, as I expected, we would get a look at the face of the pioneer. If it was ancient, we would have a copy of the skull for study in case the bones were reburied by local Indian tribes. For this, we needed a mold. I ordered materials and enlisted the aid of a skilled friend, and we scheduled the mold making for Friday, August 24, planning to work on the mold through the weekend.

The morning of August 24, I was standing at the top of the stairs, saying good-bye to my son, Jake, who was departing for his senior year in college, when the telephone rang. It was Donna Kirner.

"Hi, Jim. We have your date," she said teasingly.

"How'd it come out?" I asked.

"It's just preliminary. John [Southon] just got the results off the accelerator."

"OK. Give it to me."

"Are you sitting down?"

✺

Radiocarbon dating was developed in 1950 and soon revolutionized archaeology and its sister sciences of paleoecology and geomorphology. Before Willard Libby of the University of California, Los Angeles, developed the method, archaeologists either used historical records for dating or estimated ages of their finds using assumed rates for the deposition of geologic layers. Although it was initially greeted with skepticism, the method is now so widely accepted and readily available that it has become just another measuring tool, little different from a tape measure or a balance. Individual radiocarbon dates may be controversial, but the radiocarbon method itself is not.

The method is founded on several basic facts. Carbon, which is the primary building block of living things, occurs naturally in three alternative forms, called isotopes. Carbon 12 and 13 are stable, but carbon 14, which represents only one one-hundred-billionth of a percent of all carbon, is radioactive. One half of it is constantly decaying into stable nitrogen 14 every 5,560 years, a value known as the half-life of carbon 14. Dates are given as years B.P., or before present.

Although carbon 14 is continuously decaying, it is also constantly replenished by cosmic radiation striking nitrogen molecules in the atmosphere, thus maintaining a global balance. Carbon, including carbon 14, combines with oxygen to form carbon dioxide, which is taken in by plants during photosynthesis. Animals eat the plants, thus incorporating carbon 14 into their bones, skin, muscles, and other organs. When people eat the plants and animals, we too become slightly radioactive. As long as we remain alive, the carbon 14 in our bodies remains in equilibrium with the atmosphere. As much new carbon 14 is being taken in as decays into nitrogen. When we die, however, the equilibrium is broken. No new carbon 14 is taken in; now there is only decay of the carbon 14 that the tissues already contain. The clock is ticking.

Radiocarbon dating is the process of extracting carbon from preserved ancient tissues—in this case bone collagen—and measuring how much of the original carbon 14 has been lost through radioactive decay. Collagen is a fibrous protein that creates the soft matrix of our bones, on which mineral crystals are deposited to produce the hard skeleton. The process that extracts carbon from bone protein and measures carbon 14 by accelerator mass spectrometry (AMS), the method that was used for Kennewick Man, includes about 150 separate steps and is far too complicated to describe here. But in the end, the Kennewick Man sample had about 33 percent of the assumed original amount of carbon 14. Using a standard half-life of 5,560 years, that calculated to . . .

"Well," Donna repeated, "are you sitting down?"

"I'll take it standing," I answered. "What's the number?"

"Eighty-four hundred years!"

"All right!" I shouted, causing Jake, who was just walking out the door, to look up in alarm. "The skeleton," I told him. "It's eighty-four hundred years old."

"O-kaay . . ." Jake, an economics major, was not impressed. "I've got to go if I'm going to make Portland before dark." And he was gone.

"What's the exact number?" I asked Donna.

"I don't know. John just called me with the preliminary result. It's not official yet, but I thought you'd want to know right away."

"I appreciate it. Do you know what that eighty-four hundred calibrates to?" I would need this to translate the date into calendar years for Floyd and others.

"We don't usually calculate that. We just work in radiocarbon years, but I can include it for you if you want. It'll be around ninety-five hundred years."

❇

Radiocarbon years and real years are not the same thing, hence the calibration. When Libby developed the radiocarbon dating method, he assumed that the proportion of carbon 14 to other carbon isotopes in the atmosphere had been constant throughout the 50,000-year period that can be dated by his method. This assumption has since proven to be false. Radiocarbon experts such as Minze Stuiver, professor emeritus at the University of Washington, have used tree rings and carbon trapped in annual layers in lakes, oceans, and polar ice caps to demonstrate that the proportion of radiocarbon in the atmosphere has varied through time. Radiocarbon dates thus can differ from actual ages by more than 1,000 years. The reason for this discrepancy is primarily that the cosmic radiation striking the earth has not remained constant. During periods of high solar activity, the flow of matter outward from the sun—known as solar wind—increases and effectively blows the cosmic radiation away from the solar system. During these times, less carbon 14 is produced, so dates from these times are correspondingly older than they should be. Likewise, when solar activity is low, radiocarbon ages are too young. By dating hundreds of samples of known ages, Stuiver and his colleagues have produced a calibration curve for radiocarbon ages that now extends more than 14,000 years into the past. The curve is not smooth, however, so that some radiocarbon ages correspond to more than one calendric age. Thus the radiocarbon age of Kennewick Man—which turned out to be 8,410±60 B.P.—is actually between 9,330 and 9,580 calendar years, or from about 7330 to 7580 B.C. Throughout the rest of this book, I will give ages in calendar years, not radiocarbon years.

❁

Kennewick Man was 9,500 years old! *Now* I sat down, my mind flooded with all the ramifications of this outcome. The impact on my understanding of the prehistory of the western United States and the peopling of the Americas was immediate. On a local scale, I had always been taught to expect continuity between the most ancient inhabitants and modern Northwest Indians, yet this man bore no resemblance to the aboriginal peoples of the Columbia River basin. What was this Caucasoid-looking man doing here? Why had conflict—represented by the spear wound—appeared so early in the region's history? On the scale of the hemisphere, the impact was even greater.

Just a few days before, I had received a package from Tom Green containing copies of articles by D. Gentry Steele and Joseph Powell on the results of their analysis of Paleo-Indian skulls. They had confined their analysis to North American specimens older than 8,500 radiocarbon years, an age insignificantly different from the 8,400-year result on Kennewick Man. Because most early skeletons are so fragmentary, their first study, in 1992, had been limited to two males and two females. Here in my laboratory lay the remains of an almost perfectly preserved skeleton old enough to be included in their analysis—a 50 percent increase in the sample of measurable males!

But my excitement at the prospect of contributing so substantially to the body of knowledge about America's past was overshadowed by my realization that there would be precious little opportunity to study this exciting discovery. A 1990 federal law known as the Native American Graves Protection and Repatriation Act, or NAGPRA, was being used by the Indian tribes to reclaim all ancient human skeletons, regardless of their age and often with little or no opportunity allowed for scientific investigation. Because the age meant that Kennewick man was not a pioneer, by process of elimination he would be assumed to be Indian. How could I do justice to this important find with limited resources in what might be very little time?

3

An Opportunity Lost

NINETY-FIVE HUNDRED years ago, nearly all human beings lived by hunting, fishing, and gathering. The only exceptions were the incipient farmers in the mountainous regions of the Middle East and possibly some parts of highland New Guinea. Everyone, everywhere, still lived in the stone age.

At the time of Kennewick Man's discovery, there had been only two finds of human remains in the Pacific Northwest that were his age or older. One was a group of cremated skeletons from Marmes Rockshelter on Washington's Snake River dated approximately 11,700 years old; the other was the superbly preserved partial skeleton of a young woman from near Buhl, Idaho, who died approximately 12,800 years ago. Kennewick Man was nearly intact, making him the most complete ancient skeleton in the region and, I was to learn later, one of only two complete early skeletons from the entire continent. This was truly a find of major proportions.

The afternoon of August 24, after hearing from Donna Kirner, I contacted Floyd Johnson with the news. He was understandably awestruck. He would need to contact the mayor of Kennewick immediately, he said. Despite the fact that the corps of Engineers owned the land, the city managed the park and the mayor would want to call a news conference to announce the discovery.

I advised caution, however, because this was just a preliminary result. Numbers can sometimes change between preliminary and final results due to problems with an entire run of samples on the mass spectrometer. I never report preliminary dates, especially when working with local Indian tribes. It has been my experience over the last twenty years that they take the first statement on any issue to be true and regard any revision of that statement as a lie. We needed to be reporting only one number, and that should be the official one.

Fortunately, the mayor agreed to wait before making any public announcement. Things might have gone smoothly from there if not for another discovery the next day.

✵

Midafternoon on the next day, while taking a break from casting the Kennewick Man skull, I received another call from Floyd. More bones had been found at Columbia Park by a medical illustrator who had been walking the beach, on the lookout because of newspaper reports of the initial discovery.

"I think these are all animal bones," Floyd began, entering my lab with a large body bag in tow.

I unzipped the brown plastic bag, and there lay dozens of fragments in tones of white, brown, green, and almost black. Among them were jackrabbit and muskrat bones, but the majority were human. At least two adult humeri—bones of the upper arm—were immediately evident, one slender and long, the other short and robust. There were also bones of a child. All had been found about a mile and a half upriver from where Kennewick Man had lain.

There was not enough of any one skeleton for me to determine race or age, so again we drove to the park. After about an hour of searching the shore and feeling in the soft reservoir mud, we recovered enough material to identify the dead as American Indian. We stopped at that point and returned to the laboratory. Once I had them laid out, I was able to distinguish at least four and as many as five people: two adult males, an adult female, and one or two children. Their broken bones had been pounded by waves and stained black by rotting leaves.

✵

Monday morning, August 26, I received another early-morning call from Ray Tracy of the Corps. He had heard a rumor of the new discovery and wanted details. I wondered how he had heard, since Floyd had tried repeatedly over the weekend to contact John Leier, but without success.

I told him that yes, the remains of at least four or five people had been found, but not from the same location. Their skeletal characteristics resembled those of American Indians from the last 2,000 to 3,000 years of local prehistory, but no artifacts that might have allowed us to narrow down the age had been associated with them. He asked me to write a letter to the Corps about this new discovery, which I agreed to do immediately.

"What's the status of the radiocarbon date on the first skeleton?" he then asked. "Weren't you expecting it about now?"

Preliminary date or no, there was no avoiding a direct question, so I gave him the news, hoping that Donna Kirner would be sending the official date that day and that there would be no change in the final numbers. I told him of my concern about holding off on the news conference, and we agreed that tribal authorities should be notified before any public disclosure so that they might take part in the announcement. I was not in charge, however, I cautioned him, and might not be able to determine the timing of the event.

"I'd better tell John Leier," he said, and hung up.

I'd barely put the phone down before it rang again.

"Hello, *Jimmy,*" growled Jeff Vanpelt, head of the Cultural Resources Office of the Confederated Tribes of the Umatilla Indian Reservation. The Umatillas are a group of about 2,000 American Indians descended from the Walla Walla, Cayuse, and Umatilla tribes, who reside in northeastern Oregon about sixty miles from the Tri-Cities. I had known Jeff for seven or eight years. Our relationship had begun well but had become increasingly difficult as the tribe's political power had grown during the 1990s.

"Why were five *tribal members* collected on Saturday and nobody was informed?" he shouted. "Haven't you heard of ARPA? Haven't you heard of NAGPRA?"

"I was called in by the coroner, Jeff." I tried to be patient, but "Jimmy" is not what I prefer to be called, and Jeff knows that. "They were eroded out, just like the first one a month ago. We just picked them up from the surface and secondary mud. The coroner tried to call John Leier . . ."

"And you collected the bones of an eighty-four-hundred-year-old *tribal member!*" Obviously he'd already heard from the Corps.

"I had a permit," I replied. I wanted to question his use of "tribal member" but thought better of it. There was no need to inflame the situation.

"You had a permit to collect the remains of one tribal member? Why weren't we consulted? I'll see to it that you're charged for violating ARPA and NAGPRA, *Jimmy*. And I'll have the coroner and the guys that found it arrested too!"

"Whoa, Jeff." I tried to defuse the situation. "Take a step back."

"Take a step back? *Take a step back?*" he shouted. "You collect the remains of six tribal members, and you want me to take a step back? You grave-robbing motherfucker!" He slammed down the telephone.

This was bad. With just one ancient skeleton, there might have been a chance to work out time for analysis, but now that five others had entered the picture and Vanpelt had thrown down the gauntlet, there would be no room for negotiation.

❁

The official radiocarbon date arrived from Donna Kirner later that day. Fortunately it had not changed: eighty-four hundred years B.P. A news conference was called for 11:00 Tuesday. The word was leaking out, and the city wanted to make an official announcement before everyone heard the news. I called Ray Tracy to see if the other tribes had been contacted. Nobody likes to be blindsided with important news if they feel they have a stake in it. The Yakamas and Nez Percés had been informed, he said, as well as the Umatillas. Vanpelt, he said, had given John Leier the same treatment he had given me.

"What about the Colvilles?" I wanted to know. The Colville Confederated Tribes occupy a large reservation in north-central Washington. Their ancestors include the Columbia or Sinkaiuse people, who formerly occupied the Columbia River not far north of the Tri-Cities, and some of the Palus, who lived just to the east of us. Their historian, Adeline Fredin, had maintained an interest in the cultural affairs of the Tri-Cities area. I had been working with the Colvilles for more than a dozen years, most recently having been asked by them to relocate, recover, and analyze more than forty skeletons that had been excavated from several recent cemeteries of the Colville Confederation's member tribes. It had been a good relationship. They liked my work and had usually requested state-of-the-art analyses on the skeletons. An announcement made without their advance knowledge would not only ignore a legitimately interested party but would jeopardize that working relationship.

"John isn't going to contact them," Ray answered. "He considers this to be outside their area of interest."

"But something this early is in everybody's interest. Please suggest it," I urged.

"OK, but it's John's call."

I tried to reach Adeline Fredin with the news, but she was not in, and I could do no more than leave a message.

The situation was becoming increasingly tense. With the Umatillas' assertion that Kennewick Man was a tribal member, it was clear that they would be demanding repatriation of the remains in short order, citing NAGPRA as authority for their claims.

NAGPRA was enacted by Congress to right a historical wrong. Tens of thousands of American Indian graves had been excavated by archaeologists in the past 150 years, too often without any sort of consultation or cooperation with the direct descendants of the dead or the tribes whose cemeteries were being disturbed. Looters had desecrated untold thousands more. NAGPRA established a procedure whereby skeletons and associated grave goods and "sacred objects" in federally funded institutions were to be inventoried and, where possible, returned to direct descendants or affiliated tribes. Skeletons found during new archaeological excavations or discovered inadvertently, as Kennewick Man had been, were also covered under the law.

Over a career that by 1996 spanned thirty-six years, I had never recovered recent human remains, meaning remains a few hundred to a couple of thousand years old, without some cooperative arrangement with tribal entities. In my experience the tribes had been little interested in very ancient remains, such as those from Marmes Rockshelter, about which they had no oral history. After NAGPRA was enacted, however, activists among the local tribes had begun to claim all precolonial human remains as ancestors, no matter how ancient. This had created tensions in what had formerly been a positive working relationship.

Given my past experience with government agencies, which have little stamina for controversy, I fully expected the Umatillas' demand for Kennewick Man to be complied with in short order. I would, I estimated, have little more than two weeks to continue studying the skeleton before it was lost to science—and the public—forever. I was not in a position, through either expertise or equipment, to do full justice to such an important discovery on my own. I needed help. I needed advice.

My first contact was with Gentry Steele of Texas A&M. He was the senior author of the articles Tom Green had sent me on Paleo-Indians, and I wanted at the very least to complete the measurements he needed to further his research. When I spoke with him that afternoon, I introduced myself and explained the details of my dilemma. I told him I had an ancient skeleton that was sure to be "repatriated" in short order and I needed help.

"Well," he began calmly, soothingly, in a soft central Texas drawl, "you can't be sure it will be repatriated; its antiquity raises issues of biological affinity. These early people definitely look different from the later ones, and we can't be sure from skull characteristics who's related to whom."

That was surely true here, I told him, but I had no confidence whatever that the Corps of Engineers would attempt to analyze the situation that carefully. What, I asked would he do in my place, given what I saw as very little time to work?

"If you do nothing else, get a cast," he said, and was pleased to learn that I was in the last stages of producing a mold.

"You also need to get a second opinion on the original skeleton," he went on. "Somebody else needs to get in there and validate your measurements for the discovery to have scientific reality. I'd like to do it, but I couldn't get there anytime soon. Ask Bobby Hall. She's a colleague of mine up there at Oregon State University and is well versed in all the measurements I take. And if you can't get her, I'd try Doug Owsley. Do you know Doug? At the the Smithsonian? He's been doing a lot of measurements of ancient skeletons around the country. He has a whole team that comes in to do it."

"We met once long ago," I said. But the mention of the Smithsonian made me raise my guard. As the major national institution, it has an air of great power and insensitivity to local investigators. I have a fear of the Pros-from-the-Big-City coming in to take over. "I'll try Bobby," I told him, "we're already acquainted, and she's close by."

"Talk to Amy Dansie, too. She's dealing with a similar problem there at the Nevada State Museum and might have some useful advice."

I reached Amy Dansie early Tuesday morning. Yes, she said in a firm, husky voice, she had a similar problem: very ancient skeletons from federal land. She had developed a long-term research program to conduct extensive studies and had two early skeletons dated so far that were more than 10,000 years old. A male mummy from Spirit Cave had been dated at Erv Taylor's U.C. Riverside laboratory to about 10,700 calendar years, and another she called Wizards Beach Willie was only slightly younger. I asked her to describe them physically.

"Doug Owsley, Richard Jantz, and Gentry Steele were here to study them earlier this year," she answered, "and they all see major differences between the early skeletons and later Indian people. The heads are long and narrow, the faces are small compared to Native American faces."

"You're going to lose them?" I asked.

"Well, we could"—her voice took on a tone of determination—"but thus far we are calling them unaffiliated. We have the Paiutes down here, who by their own oral traditions came recently into Nevada. They talk about taking the land from the Zaideka—Tule Eaters—who they call the 'redheaded giants.' But the skeletons are at risk because federal agencies are giving in to new claims by the Paiutes that they were created in their present territories and have 'always been here.'

"We're doing OK so far because the evidence of Paiute immigration is so extensive. We even have the backing of our legislature and the governor, who just gave us money for research for this year and an annual study budget. If you need money for your work, we may be able to help."

"I have nothing here. I'm doing this alone and have no political connections or institutional backing. But I don't want to see this incredible discovery lost forever. But if I fight, the tribes will turn on me. I have a good working relationship with most of them now . . ."

"Jim," she tried to interrupt in a sisterly tone.

". . . and can't afford to lose it. I don't want to turn against the tribes, but they're asking too much this time. I feel like I'm failing an important responsibility if I don't stand up to them, but . . ."

"Jim." She finally got my attention. "Don't be ashamed of standing up for science."

❖

At Kennewick city hall, the press and city officials were assembled in the small yellow-walled City Council Chambers. Mayor Jim Beaver, Coroner Floyd Johnson, and I sat at a front table. To our right, facing us, were people I took to be city staffers interested in the discovery. The array of media people was much smaller than I had expected. I recognized the *Tri-City Herald* reporter. Only two of the local TV stations were represented.

The mayor introduced us, telling the assembly that we had made a startling discovery in the course of investigating the skeleton found at the Columbia Cup Races in July. I looked at Floyd. His hands were shaking, and he was fingering a packet of photographs he had taken of the skeleton a few weeks earlier. When he spoke, his voice quavered. He told of the discovery during the boat races and the conundrum we had faced between the seemingly European physical characteristics and the spear point in the pelvis. Then he gave them the punch line: "Yesterday we got the results, and the bone dates between ninety-two hundred and ninety-six hundred years old. Dr. Chatters can tell you what he learned about the skeleton."

I then summarized what I knew up to that point: "What we have is the most complete early skeleton ever found in the Pacific Northwest. This one is about ninety percent complete, missing only a few bones of the hands and feet. The remains are from a male who stood about five feet, nine inches tall. He had a long, narrow skull with a narrow face and receding cheekbones, unlike the short, round skulls with broad, flat faces that we see among the recent American Indians of this area. It also lacks the flattening at the back of the skull that results from a child's being reared on a cradle board, which also differs sharply from modern Indians. His bones are strong and well developed, indicating a healthy childhood. He lived to be around forty to fifty-five years old but still had all of his teeth at the time of his death. He had been repeatedly injured, with a blow to his chest that broke several ribs, injuries to his left arm, and of course the healed wound from a stone spear point in his right hip.

"What makes this find so significant is that we don't have much evidence about what was going on in this area more than nine thousand years ago, so it's quite exciting to turn up someone who lived then and whose body tells us so many stories. From him we'll be able to gain a much better understanding of the physical characteristics and lives of Paleo-Indians of that time.

"I'd like to compliment Will Thomas and Dave Deacy for being so responsible. Many people wouldn't have reported this find. I think these two deserve a medal for how they handled their discovery."

When I had finished, the floor was opened to questions, which came in a flurry from all directions, reporters and onlookers alike. The issues people asked about have become familiar in the years since the discovery. The first came from one of the TV reporters.

"What's a European doing here nine thousand years ago?" she asked. This was not an unexpected question, given the history of the discovery to date. Floyd had, after all, just explained that we had conducted the dating because of the apparently European features and seemingly contradictory projectile wound.

Floyd looked to me for the answer.

"We're not saying this *is* a European," I corrected, trying not to sound too much the college professor. "His skull and leg bones share some characteristics that are also found in Europeans today, but what they probably represent are archaic characteristics that were common to early modern humans and are simply retained in Europeans, south Asians, and some others."

"Where do you think he came from?" asked another reporter. "Was he a lone wanderer just passing through?"

"No, he was probably from this region. I suspect he was probably even born within one to two hundred miles of where he died."

"Why was his skeleton so well preserved?"

"The soil in the nearby riverbank, which I think he washed out from, is fine-textured and has a high calcium carbonate content, both of which are perfect for bone preservation."

"If he's been there nine thousand years, why wasn't he found before?"

"We had that severe flooding last February, and I think it was that event that washed his remains out of the riverbank. The area where he was found is brushy and probably doesn't get the kind of visitor traffic that the developed parts of the park do."

"Is he the oldest human skeleton ever found in the Northwest?"

"No," I responded, and told them of the Buhl and Marmes discoveries.

"What did he die from?" asked John Stang, the reporter from the *Tri-City Herald*. "Was it the spear point?"

"Possibly, but the spear wound had healed for a long time before his death. He could have died from a reeruption of the infection from the wound. There is an indication of an active infection in the bone of his skull, which I suppose could be related to the spear wound."

"What happened to his people?" asked someone from the gallery. "Did they die out?"

"We don't know. Possibly. But given the thousands of years ago that he lived, and assuming he had any children of his own, he probably could be considered ancestral to all modern American Indians." Then, to drive the point home, I asked, "How many of you have Indian ancestors—that you know of?"

About one third of those present raised their hands, including, to my surprise, Floyd Johnson and Jim Beaver. Floyd, I later learned, had an Indian grandmother; the mayor is one quarter Cherokee.

"Well," I continued, addressing the raised hands, "he's probably an ancestor of all of you. In fact, given the four hundred fifty or so generations since he died, he is probably an ancestor of everyone."

"Will the skeleton be on display in a museum anytime soon?"

"No."

"Do you have any pictures we could use?" one of the TV reporters asked.

"Yes, we have a few . . ." Floyd reached for the envelope containing the photos of the skeleton and began to open it. I laid my hand gently on his arm and said softly in his ear, "We don't want to show those."

"Why not?" He was truly perplexed but showed no irritation.

"Some of the tribal folks get very offended when we show pictures of skeletons in public." In particular, one of my Umatilla friends had a thing about photos being taken, let alone shown. He wouldn't let anyone videotape him out of what he described as the personal desire to have no image of himself left behind walking and talking after he was dead. "It would just inflame the situation."

Floyd understood immediately. "No," he answered the reporter, "we have photographs but prefer not to display them out of sensitivity for the beliefs of some Native Americans."

This did not go over at all well with the press, particularly the young reporter who had made the request, but Floyd stuck to his position.

"We'll have drawings that you can use in the near future," I offered in consolation. "Check with us in a few weeks."

"OK, folks," Jim Beaver cut in, aware that the situation was getting uncomfortable for Floyd and me. "We have time for just one last question." The *Herald* reporter raised his hand. "Yes, John."

"Coroner Johnson, what was your reaction when you found out how old the skeleton was?"

"I could see from the teeth that it was fairly old," Floyd responded softly. "That's why I took it to Dr. Chatters. But I was astounded when I found out how old."

Another reporter asked, "What about you, Dr. Chatters?"

I thought a moment. "Well," I mused, "it's like I've been following this man's tracks for my whole life, studying the things he left behind: campsites, dwellings, trash piles. I thought I knew who I was following—what he looked like. But then I finally caught up with him, and he turned around . . . and he wasn't who I expected to see."

✹

After returning to my lab from the press conference, I took several calls from media people before managing to reach Roberta Hall at Oregon State University. She would have loved to come, she said, but she was leaving for Australia the next day. She could, however, lend me some measuring equipment, and she suggested that I contact Doug Owsley in her place.

It was midafternoon. With the three-hour time difference, the Smithsonian would already be closed. In any case, my thoughts of a collaborator were derailed by another call from Ray Tracy, who was arranging a meeting between the Corps, the coroner's office, and the Indians the next day at Columbia Park. Could I be there, he asked, to talk about the most recent skeleton find? I was reluctant, as such meetings had become increasingly uncomfortable over the years. This one promised to be even less amicable than most, but I hoped that by being accommodating I could buy some time, so I agreed.

✹

When we assembled next morning en route to the park, Ray was accompanied by John Leier and a man who was introduced to me as Lee Turner, the colonel's executive assistant. Each Corps of Engineers office has a largely civilian staff directed by a military officer, usually a colonel. Lieutenant Colonel Donald S. Curtis, Jr., was the current commander of the Walla Walla District office. At the park we found five Indian men standing in the shade by their car. All but one were short and stocky with broad faces, black hair, and bronze complexions. Most wore braids. I recognized three of them and walked up to shake hands all around. Among them was Louie Dick, an intelligent, understanding, good-humored man from the Umatilla tribe who had once been a guest in my home. Rex Buck, leader of the tiny Wanapum band and an important regional religious leader, stood with him. I had worked with Louie Dick and Rex Buck on a number of occasions, most often in my former role as lead archaeologist for the Hanford Nuclear Reservation, just outside the Tri-Cities. The relationship had generally been a good one. On one occasion, a white paper I drafted led to reclamation of a sacred mountain; on another I helped relocate rubbings of rock art that now lies beneath a reservoir near the Wanapums' village and was invited to join them in a group photograph during an occasion that commemorated the event. We also had worked together on the repatriation and reburial of several skeletons. I knew both men had strong feelings about human remains, so after an exchange of pleasantries, I spoke gravely.

"I know we have different ideas of what respect is, but I want to assure you that to the best of my ability, within my understanding of the word, these remains are being treated with respect."

Some nodded, but others gave no response.

John Leier came over to introduce us all, directing me last to the one man who differed in appeareance from the others.

He was Armand Minthorn, a small, very thin man with a broad, acne-scarred face, who took my hand in the gentle handshake— really more of a hand clasp—that I have come to know as typical of Indian traditionalists. I recognized him then and smiled. He looked just like his brother Phil, who had worked for me for two years when I was a manager of the archaeology program at the Pacific Northwest National Laboratory. After we exchanged pleasantries and news of Phil, the Corps people got down to business.

"Now, exactly where were those five skeletons found?" Leier asked, and I directed the assembled group to the river's edge, where erosion had cut a crescent-shaped block from the bank and now threatened to take away part of the park road.

Just then another car arrived and two more Indian men came toward us. An average-sized, plump man was introduced as Paul Minthorn [no relation to Armand], and we shook hands. The other was a tall, long-faced, balding man with wavy, shoulder-length brown hair and deep-set eyes: Jeff Vanpelt. When I extended my hand, he simply glared and refused to take it. This was a breach of etiquette I had never seen before among Indians, even in tense situations. Courtesy is displayed at all times. Personal feelings are saved for speech making and even then are usually expressed indirectly.

Turning to the riverbank, I explained how the bones had been found among the rocks at the shore and that no sign of a grave pit or any remaining bones could be found in the bank. Vanpelt, who had climbed down the five-foot-high vertical bank and was searching the shore, raised his hand holding a small chip of stone and angrily yelled, "There are artifacts down here. You should have known immediately that these were tribal members!"

"There are one or two," I replied impatiently. "There are artifacts scattered thinly all along this shoreline for miles. That doesn't mean they are associated with the skeletons."

He made another angry protest and returned to his searching.

Lee Turner, a tall, thin, stooped-shouldered man with a bland face and unctuous manner, turned to the men who stood assembled beside the road. He explained that he spoke for Colonel Curtis, who was out of the area and was regrettably unable to be present in person. Then he asked in a placating tone, "What is it you want done here?"

Armand Minthorn took a step forward, straightened his slender frame, and looked sternly up at Turner.

"These remains and the other ones [meaning Kennewick Man] should not have been disturbed. They have to go back in the ground immediately," he insisted.

"Of course," Turner responded in the same tone, as if he were responding to a command from a superior. "The colonel has made this his top priority."

The words brought my heart into my throat—there might be less time than I had thought for me to learn about the discovery of a lifetime.

After we returned to the shade by the parked cars and the talk turned to Kennewick Man, Vanpelt angrily accused me of saying the skeleton looked like a European just to get around NAGPRA and find a way to study it.

"I know you, *Jimmy*," he said. "You're a scientist. You're always trying to push the envelope of knowledge!"

It was meant as an accusation, but was to me one of the nicest compliments I have received. The exchange clearly made some of the traditionalists uncomfortable. Louie Dick admonished us that it was not right to speak in angry tones and accuse each other. I knew the reason. Such actions are generally unacceptable in any context, but especially so when remains of the dead are exposed. Followers of some of the Christian-influenced cultural revivalist religions that sprang up in Washington and Oregon in the 1880s believe that as long as the dead are out of the ground, they can hear whatever is said. When they reach the spirit world, they report what they have heard to the Creator. Then, when other people die, the Creator, like Saint Peter at the gates of Heaven, holds them accountable for their actions in life, including behavior reported by the spirits of those who preceded them in death.

Unchastened, Vanpelt continued to glower.

Armand Minthorn, who stood beside him, spoke. "It's too bad that a bone was destroyed for a radiocarbon date, but what's done is done." Then, addressing Turner, he continued sternly, "We don't want no more analysis."

"Of course," Turner replied, his eyes on his shoes. "The Colonel has made this his top priority."

Turning toward me, Armand repeated, "I want you to promise there won't be no more analysis."

This took me aback. The last thing I wanted to do was stop studying Kennewick Man. But I thought that Armand Minthorn's chief concern was the destruction of bones. "The bone that was sent to the Riverside lab is all that will be destroyed," I told him.

That wasn't good enough. Minthorn and Vanpelt tilted their heads together and moved perceptibly closer to me, as cops do in an interrogation when they want to intimidate a suspect.

"We want you to promise there won't be no more analysis," Minthorn repeated, menacingly.

Just then it occurred to me: there were seven tribal representatives, four Corps staffers, and me. It *was* intimidating, but, more significant, there was no coroner present. He was the man with jurisdiction over the bones. Evidently, in their minds, I was there as the coroner's representative. But I could not represent him. Although I have since been deputized, I was then only an occasional contractor. I had to be careful in what I said so that I would not compromise him. And I could only hope that Rika Kaestle had finished with the DNA.

"No analyses are planned that have not already been done."

They weren't satisfied but seemed to recognize that it was the best they were going to get. Armand moved on, addressing Turner again: "There's been too much publicity about this old skeleton already. We don't want no more publicity."

"Of course," Turner responded emphatically. "There won't be any more publicity."

Incredulous, I moved to face him. The Corps of Engineers was going to stifle the news media? He had no business making such a
promise. "Haven't you heard of the First Amendment to the Consti-
tution?" I asked angrily.

Turner acted as if I weren't there. One of the Corps staffers sput-
tered, "The First Amendment doesn't apply in NAGPRA cases."

I glared at him and snapped, "The First Amendment *always* applies!"

✹

Back at my lab that afternoon, I was convinced the situation was
truly desperate. Despite the skeleton's age, physical differences, and
probably widespread pool of descendants, the Corps was going to
cave in and immediately turn it over to the Umatilla tribe. Kennewick Man would be lost to science and the public store of knowledge. I put my professional ego aside, swallowed my fear of being
steamrollered, and put in a call to the Smithsonian. By a stroke of
good fortune, Owsley was in.

"Remains that important deserve the full battery of analysis," he
began after I had explained the situation, "and from what you say,
it's going to have to be done in a hurry." He had a grant that could
conceivably fund him and his study team, including a photographer,
measurement specialist, and one or more assistants to fly to the Tri-
Cities, but that would be expensive and he would not be able to
come for more than a week. Why didn't I just bring the skeleton to
him the week of September 8? It could be done with Smithsonian
funds, which he would request from Dennis Stanford, the chairman
of the Anthropology Department at the National Museum of Natural History and an expert in the early stone tool technologies of the
Americas. He would be interested in the spear point in the pelvis. All
I needed to do was send the Smithsonian a formal request for assistance. "We can have you in and out of here in two days," he concluded.

"I hope we'll still have the skeleton by then." September 8 was ten
days off.

"There's no reason for them to give it to the local Indians," he reassured. "I think a case can be made that the disposition of these early specimens has not been resolved. NAGPRA leaves opportunity for study of remains that are of national scientific significance, and this certainly meets that criterion." As a staffer of the National Museum, he was in a good position to make such a statement.

"But the way the Corps people are acting," I said, "I suspect that they're going to ignore that clause. I know these guys."

"Look, why don't you contact Rob Bonnichsen's lawyer? I don't know his name. I'm told he's an expert in NAGPRA law and can explain the process you could follow. Hang in there. We'll get it studied."

※

Floyd and I got together for tea late that afternoon outside a local bakery to review our options in the case. I briefed him on the meeting with the Corps and the conversation with Owsley. He approved of the move and promised to deputize me so I could transport human remains without legal liability.

The time frame was still worrying me. September 8 was a long way off.

"By state law," Floyd reassured me confidently, "I'm in charge of human remains until I've finished my investigation, and it isn't finished yet."

※

Thursday morning, I received a chilling call from Ray Tracy. His voice sounded tired.

"I've been directed to ask you this question," he began apologetically. "Just so you know it isn't coming from me, I'm going to read it verbatim: 'If you choose in the course of exercising your First Amendment rights to inform any of your colleagues of the Kennewick discovery, the Corps would appreciate knowing whom you contact.'"

It was right out of Orwell's *1984*. Big Brother had heard my comment about the First Amendment but wanted to contain me nonetheless.

"Well, thanks, Ray," I said flatly. "You can tell them I heard it." I had no intention of complying.

"What's happening? Do you think there's a chance I'll have time to study the skeleton adequately?" I asked with little hope.

"I can't tell you much," he answered wearily, "but let me just say that the Corps will not be the one to fight for science."

�֍

Convinced now that the Corps would buckle to tribal pressure, I called Rob Bonnichsen of the Center for the Study of the First Americans in Corvallis, Oregon. Though we had known each other for thirty-eight years, I didn't have time to chat. Briefly explaining the problem I faced, I asked for and received the phone number of Alan Schneider of Portland, the attorney who not only represented the center but also served on its board and was very knowledgeable about archaeological issues.

Alan was in when I called and freely shared his expertise, which proved to be considerable. Among other things, I learned that he taught NAGPRA law all over the western United States under contract with the U.S. Forest Service. As he spoke to me in his rapid-fire style, I was alternately encouraged and disheartened.

"Well, it's good if you have the coroner behind you on this one and he's willing to fight for the analysis," he said, "but it isn't going to hold the government for long. Federal law has supremacy on federal land, and NAGPRA overrides all other statutes.

"But don't give up hope," he went on. "Because this skeleton is so ancient it's arguable that these remains aren't Native American and that NAGPRA doesn't apply. The statute specifically states that 'Native American' refers to a 'tribe, people, or culture that is indigenous to the United States.' The operative word is *is*. It's present tense. The tribe, people, or culture still has to exist for the law to apply. If the Corps wants to, they can take the position that they don't know if it's Native American."

"I think they've already decided that it is, based solely on the radiocarbon date," I said.

"That's just the point," he went on forcefully. "It's old enough that if there's a genetic relationship with any later people, they could live anywhere in North or South America. The NAGPRA Review Committee has agreed that the law may not cover very ancient remains and recommended no action on them until Congress has modified the law. That should also apply to this case." The NAGPRA Review Committee includes three Native American religious leaders, three museum people appointed by the Secretary of the Interior, and one at-large member selected by the other members. They are charged with hearing disputed claims between tribes and with making recommendations for the disposition of human remains that cannot be affiliated with any modern tribe.

"And if the Corps still decides to turn them over to the Umatilla tribe?"

"Then the county's lawyer could demand retention of the skeleton on the grounds that the government was arbitrary and capricious in their decision—that it was a bad decision—and file an injunction in federal court to prohibit transfer until the case is resolved."

✹

On Friday, Doug Owsley confirmed that the Smithsonian had bought me a plane ticket for a September 8 flight to Washington, D.C. I tried to work on the remains but was stressed to the point that I felt like a donkey standing in a circle of haystacks, starving but unable to decide which was most important to get to first. Still unsure I would have the bones on September 8, I decided to make one more try at getting a colleague to come look at them, as insurance against their imminent seizure by the Corps. The man I persuaded to come was my former osteology professor, Grover Krantz of Washington State University, 140 miles away in Pullman.

Grover was an excellent osteologist and had been a fascinating teacher. He had worked with many collections of skeletons from Washington, California, the Great Plains, and elsewhere, and his observations would add to my own.

He arrived about midafternoon Friday, a tall, slightly stooped, big-boned man with a huge head covered by shaggy gray hair and beard. He sat down beside the skeleton, which I had laid out on the table for his inspection, then worked in silence, emitting only an occasional "Hmm" or "Mm-hmm!"

Finally breaking the silence as he looked at a photograph I had taken of the assembled skull, he said, "If you hold this in the Frankfort horizontal [a standard position for comparing skulls that puts the upper rim of the ear openings in the same horizontal plane as the lower rim of the left orbit or eye socket], you get into a little bit of trouble."

"Trouble?" I asked.

"The lower rim of his orbit is almost behind the upper, as in Caucasians," he replied. "That wouldn't be consistent with being an Indian."

"That's just the point!" I exclaimed. "There are a lot of differences!"

"Yes, that upper rim of the orbit is unusually sharp for a male," he continued. "That's a trait that's only common in Negroids. And that nose! That's the most projecting nose I've ever seen. Most people would first think of European origin from that trait alone." He was sure it would not be possible to fit this skeleton into any of the Indian tribes from western North America.

With that, he abruptly rose to leave. I was shocked. He had driven for three hours to get here and had stayed less than an hour. I had hoped he would remain awhile—help me take additional measurements and review my observations of the man's age and injuries. But now there might be no second analysis. Disappointed and disheartened, but feeling that asking him to stay would be presumptuous, I thanked him for coming and began to assemble equipment for photographing the individual bones of the skeleton. I would at least make a photographic record for others to see.

※

I had just set up when, shortly after five o'clock, the phone rang.

"Hey, buddy," Floyd Johnson began, "I've got some bad news for you. The attorneys are in it now. Andy Miller [the county attorney] has been talking to the Corps lawyer, and he forbids me to transport the bones anywhere."

"There goes the trip to the Smithsonian," I sighed.

"It's worse than that, buddy," he said sadly. "I've been ordered to stop all studies, take custody of the bones, and transport them to a secure place pending a meeting next week. I've got to come get the bones."

"I thought you were autonomous! That nobody could interfere until you finished your investigation!" I was hyperventilating. I felt dizzy. This couldn't be happening, not already!

"So did I," he said.

"How soon?" I hoped for the weekend.

"Now," he replied.

"But, Floyd, I haven't finished taking pictures yet. I have the skull but none of the injuries, none of the postcranial material!"

"I can delay for a couple of hours, but that's all. I'm under orders now."

❈

In panic, my hands shaking, I began to take black-and-white pictures of the fractured ribs, the spear-point wound, and anything else I could think of that needed to be documented. How could I photograph all of the bones with so little time? I grabbed my color camera and stood on the table above the assembled skeleton, my daughter, Claire, steadying me, but I could get only half of the bones in each frame. The film ran out after only two shots, and I hurriedly reloaded the camera.

Just then, my friend and sculpture instructor, Tom McClelland, arrived and, seeing my state of mind, asked if he could do anything to help. Jenny came in behind him.

"The video camera!" I suddenly realized. "We can get pictures of the skeleton with the video camera!"

"Jim, calm down," Jenny warned. She was clearly concerned. "You're going to have a heart attack. I'll get it for you."

She set the camera up on the tripod, then showed Tom how to operate it.

"Just pan back and forth over the skeleton and zoom in and out on the different bones," I instructed, while I began to take color photographs of the injuries to the bones.

The doorbell rang, and Jenny ushered Floyd into the lab, followed by a sheriff's deputy.

"Oh, God, Floyd, is it time already?" I exclaimed. "I'm not finished."

"It's OK," he said soothingly. "Take your time. Finish what you're doing. We can wait awhile." He and the deputy sat down, and I continued to snap pictures. Tom panned the camera scross the skeleton.

The phone rang. It was Alan Schneider. I told him that my worst fears were coming to pass. He asked to speak to Floyd and began to tell him what options remained. Floyd seemed encouraged. But I was only dimly aware of the conversation, lost in feelings of desolation as I busily clicked the shutter.

I finished my color photos and described the pathologies on the videotape. Then it was time. I had a large plywood box beside the exam table, waiting for the trip to Washington, D.C. Thinking it would be a sturdy resting place for Kennewick Man, I padded the bottom with bubble wrap and began to fill it with the bones.

Tom handed me plastic bags, and I placed bones in them a few at a time. We didn't label the bags; there seemed little reason for that. The bones would soon be back in the ground, where a new chemical environment would lead to their rapid destruction.

I began to pack the box. The large pieces of the femur were the first to go in, because they were the heaviest and might destroy smaller bones if I put any beneath them. In went the braincase beside the femur parts, still wrapped in its large protective plastic bag. Then, one by one, I gently added the smaller long bones, the vertebrae, pieces of the pelvis, the ribs, the small bones of hands and feet. The bones of the mandible and face went atop the skull. Finished, I screwed the wooden lid into place and reluctantly handed the box to Floyd.

"I guess that's it," I sighed, still shaking.

Floyd said something consoling and began to leave with the box. "Wait!" I cried. We had missed the rib fragments that lay in a separate tray opposite the exam table. Tom and I packed them in a smaller cardboard box and added them to Floyd's burden, and he walked slowly up the stairs and out to the patrol car.

Kennewick Man was gone.

✻

I felt a profound sense of loss. I had been given a gift from the past, an opportunity to learn from an ancient ancestor and to convey what he could tell us to future generations. I had not managed to learn from him all that he could tell me. I had not gotten the scientific corroboration needed to establish his validity as an early American. I had failed him. I had failed posterity.

To the Brink
of Oblivion

KENNEWICK MAN HAD come to us from long ago, with many stories to tell of his life, his times, and his people. I had begun to learn some of those stories, but with only one set of eyes, one set of skills, one set of knowledge, I could not hope to learn all that he had to say. This was especially true because my own study had been abruptly and prematurely halted. If Americans were to learn from this messenger from the past, other scientists would need to study him to contribute what they could from their disparate perspectives. In scientific terms, without at least one corroborating study, Kennewick Man would not truly have existed. The rapid reburial had to be forestalled. But how?

I sought advice, getting on the phone with old friends—men and women older, wiser, and more politically connected than I. Foremost among them was Dr. Richard Daugherty, a retired archaeology professor with whom I had first worked in 1962 at the age of thirteen. Doc, as we used to call him, had been well acquainted with Washington's congressional delegation from the 1960s to the early 1980s and had used these connections successfully in his work at the Marmes Rockshelter site and later to construct a museum on the Makah Indian Reservation. He was also, in the absence of my late father, the elder I looked to first for counsel. He greeted me warmly and offered sound advice.

"The first thing that I'd do," he began, "is get the congressional delegation involved. Call Slade Gorton and Patty Murray [Washington State's senators]. And don't worry about party loyalties. When it comes to archaeology, there are no sides to the aisle; you take your support where you can get it. Get your local congressmen on it too.

"Second thing I'd do is get the newspapers involved. Call *The Seattle Times, The Spokesman-Review* [Spokane's paper], and the Vancouver *Columbian*. Generate some public outrage. Finds like this are once-in-a-lifetime things. And see if you can get another tribe interested in filing a claim to keep the skeleton from going into the ground without study."

I immediately began following his advice. The afternoon of September 2 and all of Labor Day, I called and e-mailed colleagues across the country, including past and current presidents of the Society for American Archaeology, the United States' premier archaeological association, and old friends who had connections with Indian communities, the federal system, or the wealthy and powerful. Among them were David Hurst Thomas of the American Museum of Natural History, Rob Bonnichsen of the Center for the Study of the First Americans, and Doug Owsley of the Smithsonian. They expressed incredulity that NAGPRA could apply to such ancient remains, suggested additional contacts, including the Department of the Interior's chief NAGPRA officer, and promised to pass the word along to others. Each had a suggestion. Owsley offered to call Lieutenant Colonel Curtis of the Corps of Engineers. Bonnichsen had a contact in the Justice Department. Katie MacMillan and Grover Krantz, who had given second opinions on the skeleton, agreed to send letters to the coroner's office immediately, describing their observations of the skeleton.

Tuesday morning, I placed calls to Senators Gorton and Murray and Representative George Nethercutt, the congressman whose district included the Walla Walla Corps of Engineers offices. Floyd

Johnson knew our local congressman, Richard "Doc" Hastings, from school days and would seek his support. All wanted letters requesting assistance, so they could use them in pursuing their inquiries, letters I gladly supplied.

❋

Soon after, I spoke with Ray Tracy for the first time since the bones had been taken away. He tried to be encouraging.

"Even if the Corps establishes legal custody of the bones," he said hopefully, "it doesn't mean they will be given back to the Umatillas right away. There are two things that still have to be done. First, they have to determine who has possession of the bones, the Corps or the county. Second, they need to use the current information—the data you've collected—to make a decision. And that information says that the bones warrant further analysis."

❋

Ardis Dumat, staffer for Senator Murray, reported back to me on her office's efforts. It had placed an inquiry with the Corps, she said, "making a strong case for scientific research and making it clear that no cave-in by the Corps [to the conservative Indian position] was desired." Colonel Curtis, she said, "says he feels he's only obliged to follow the law. He has thirty days to reach an agreement on what to do with the bones." According to her, he had no interest in permitting scientific studies, asserting that the Umatillas would probably file an injunction against the Corps if the bones were allowed to go to the Smithsonian for even a few days. Ray's optimism began to appear unwarranted.

❋

Soon after, Linda Kirts, the Corps attorney who had ordered Floyd to put the bones into lockup, called to inform me that a meeting was being held at one that afternoon between the Corps, county attorney Andy Miller, Floyd Johnson, and me at the district attorney's office to discuss the next steps to be followed with the skeleton.

Floyd and I arrived first at the appointed place, followed soon after by the Corps contingent, which included Ray Tracy, John Leier, Lieutenant Colonel Curtis, and attorney Kirts. Kirts, a stocky woman in early middle age, swaggered in, her chin jutting forward. The other three, in marked contrast, shuffled in with downcast eyes—the uniformed colonel included. Even when we shook hands in introduction, they did not raise their eyes to ours. Then, to our surprise, there came a young Indian woman, who was introduced as a representative of the Yakama tribe. This, we had been led to understand, was to be a meeting between the Corps and the county. Why was she here?

As we filed into the meeting room, Kirts continued with the surprises. Requesting speakerphones, she proceeded to call attorneys and representatives from the Yakama, Colville, and Umatilla tribes. As those in the room were introduced, we heard from Marla Bigboy and Adeline Fredin for the Colvilles, Rory Flintknife for the Yakamas, and the attorney for the Umatillas, with a tribal member standing by. Andy Miller began to show signs of agitation; this was not the meeting he had agreed to.

Kirts then took charge of the meeting by asking the Indian representatives what they wanted done with the skeleton. The Yakama representative gave the standard reply that she wanted the remains reburied immediately with no more study. This sentiment was echoed by all other tribal representatives except the Colvilles, who expressed an interest in learning from the remains for the benefit of their members.

Discussion then turned to where the bones should be kept pending the outcome of the negotiations about their custody. All the tribal representatives concurred that the skeleton should be held by a neutral party, so their attention shifted to where the skeleton should be moved to. Kirts suggested the federal artifact respository at Pacific Northwest National Laboratory, which is located about four miles from where I live in Richland. Fredin said she would rather see the bones in "Chatters's lab" than with the coroner. At that time I was working with the remains of more than forty people affiliated with her tribe, so it was an expression of trust that I appreciated. Others disagreed with her, though, and the PNNL repository was agreed upon between Kirts and the tribes. After a brief conference we also agreed.

With the housing issue resolved to her satisfaction, Kirts moved on to the ownership of the skeleton, dropping a bomb with evident pleasure. The Corps, she proclaimed, was taking possession of the skeleton under the stipulations of my ARPA permit, copies of which she passed around the room. Indeed, Section 7 of the permit stated that the government could take possession of all collected materials at any time. The permit that I had requested at the Corps's suggestion, because of the possibility of finding artifacts while I recovered the skeleton, was now being used to circumvent the coroner's jurisdiction! The whole meeting had been a setup. At no time had our input been requested. We were livid.

Andy Miller, furious at having been deceived, turned bright red and left the room. Floyd and I followed him and reconvened in Andy's office to discuss the situation, for which we had clearly been unprepared. Unhappily, I acknowledged that the permit did give the Corps the right to commandeer anything collected under it. Andy Miller was not so willing to concede the issue, however, and told Kirts angrily, "We are not going to agree to your taking custody based only on your recitation of statutes that we are not familiar with." His staff, he said, would have to review the law before he was willing to proceed, and the meeting was over.

Floyd and I left together, angry at having been shoved aside so summarily. We discussed our options, which seemed to be few except to keep working the political angles. What about the cast and the DNA analysis that had been done at UC Davis? Should we tell the Corps? No, we decided. After the bullying treatment we'd just received, we would be cooperative, but only to the extent we were asked. As if we were being cross-examined in court, we would answer any direct question honestly but would volunteer nothing.

We went to prepare the remains for the transfer to PNNL, which entailed consolidating them into a single box. After being checked in by the evidence clerk, and accompanied by a sheriff's lieutenant, we entered the small square building behind the courthouse that serves as the county's evidence locker. Floyd climbed a ladder, unlocked his cabinet, and lifted down two boxes wrapped in evidence tape. I removed the tape from the large wooden box and, opening the lid, transferred the bags of rib fragments from the smaller container to the larger. Saying a silent "Good-bye, old man," I replaced the lid. Floyd retaped the box and, two days later, made the transfer to PNNL. By that time, Andy Miller had conceded the issue of custody.

❋

In an interview with a *Tri-City Herald* reporter later that Thursday, Corps public information officer Dutch Meier gave strong clues about the Corps's intent. He reported that the bones were being handled as American Indian remains. "The most immediate requirement is satisfying the tribes' desires to honor their ancestors and see those remains interred," he said.

When pressed about the scientific value of the bones, Meier acknowledged, "The Corps is trying to be sensitive to the tribes but is also cognizant that there may be other interests out there that may need to be considered, to include the scientific community among others. Before any decision is made, there is a lot of work to do."

❋

That Friday, September 6, following a business trip, I continued my telephone campaign, beginning with Timothy McKeown, the Department of the Interior official in charge of NAGPRA enforcement. Surely, I said, there must be some allowance in the law for truly ancient, unique fossils.

He expressed sympathy with my argument but said, "The section of the law that applies to your find is the section on inadvertent discoveries. The sections on museum collections and intentional archaeological investigations have stipulations for study. In the case of museums, if the remains are needed for completion of a study that is of major importance to the United States, then study can proceed for a limited time. But that's only for existing museum collections. Inadvertent finds don't have that stipulation.

"For inadvertent discoveries," he continued, "you go through a series of questions. Is there a lineal descendant?"

"That would be impossible to demonstrate," I said.

"Was it on Indian land?"

"No."

"Is it culturally affiliated with anybody?" he continued. "That is, is there shared group identity between the ancient and modern people?"

"That too would be impossible to demonstrate over such a time span."

"Remember," he cautioned, "the relationship doesn't have to be established with scientific certainty; it's based on the preponderance of evidence from archaeology, biology, geography, history, oral history, and folklore."

"Still impossible. There's no archaeology in this case, and the biology is completely different from the local Indians'. Oral history doesn't last that long."

"Then," he said, "the remains go to the tribe whose aboriginal territory it was, as established by the U.S. Court of Claims." That seemed to mean the Umatillas, since they claimed the Kennewick area as ceded land under the Treaty of 1855.

"So the law is set up so that all remains go to *some* tribe regardless of relationship?" I was incredulous. I hadn't understood this when the law was first enacted. It had seemed relatively benign on the surface. As I understood NAGPRA, it had been designed to return remains to their kin or to tribes that could demonstrate a close cultural relationship, but unaffiliated remains were not to be repatriated. Clearly, I thought, the law's intent was being perverted.

"There may be some good news," he said. "There are three angles that might work. The first would be to go outside the law, that is, to show they are not Native American. As defined by the law, a Native American is someone who is of or related to a people that is indigenous to the United States. The skeleton would have to fail to fit that definition. The second would be that the aboriginal territories may not have been resolved. Sometimes multiple tribes claimed an area, so there is no Court of Claims settlement due to the overlapping and conflicting claims. The final angle would be to insist that the Corps has a fiduciary responsibility to know what they have. That involves documentation."

❄

The Corps of Engineers began to receive tribal claims for Kennewick Man almost immediately. First, the Colville tribe made an informal request for nondestructive study of the bones the day they were moved from the coroner's locker. Then, on Monday, September 9, the Confederated Tribes of the Umatilla Indian Reservation (CTUIR) made their formal demand, claiming support from the Yakama, Nez Percé, Wanapum, and even the Colville tribes. The letter, written by Donald Sampson, the young tribal chairman, bore a remarkable resemblance to my conversation with McKeown the previous Friday:

> As you are aware, carbon testing on a portion of the human remains has determined that the remains are approximately 8,000 to 9,000 years old. Because of the age of the human remains, *a final determination on the cultural affiliation . . . cannot be reasonably ascertained.* Accordingly the CTUIR . . . provides notice to the Corps of Engineers of its claim to the human remains . . . based on the following: "a) the reasonable assumption that the human remains are Native American . . . ; b) that because of [their age] the cultural affiliation of the remains cannot reasonably be ascertained; c) on the fact that the human remains were excavated from federal lands within the aboriginal territory of the CTUIR as determined by the Indian Claims Commission in Docket No. 264" [emphasis added].

He included copies of Docket 264, which, interestingly enough, belies his claim. The land on which the skeleton was found had not been designated as the aboriginal territory of *any* tribe.

Publicly, the Umatilla tribe justified its claim on the basis of policy and religion, asserting that in its belief system it was considered disrepectful to conduct any studies of skeletons. Armand Minthorn, who was to become the Indian spokesman for much of the case, repeatedly asserted, "The fact that this man is nine thousand years old only strengthens our claim that he is an ancestor. Our oral history goes back 10,000 years. We know how time began and how Indian people were created. These lands have been used by our tribe since time began."

❀

There are indications that the Umatillas' claim was immediately accepted by the Corps of Engineers. I spoke with Ray Tracy on September 10, and he described having inspected the remains of Kennewick Man during a meeting with tribal representatives earlier in the day. It had been the first time any Corps representative had actually seen the bones.

"Things are moving really fast," he said. "I'm not sure what level of information I should give you." After a cautious pause, he confided, "The commander [Curtis] has made a decision, although I can't tell you what it is. In part, it's a desire to see the method played out. All I can say beyond that is, keep your eyes open in the media."

❀

On Wednesday, September 11, I received a request for information from Linda Kirts, dated the previous Friday. She wrote: "Please provide copies of all field notes, records, photographs and other data as required by Section 8(g) of the [ARPA] permit. We'd appreciate receipt of these on or before Tuesday [September 10], for use in meetings occurring September 10 and 11, 1996. . . . Please submit the final . . . report no later than September 18, 1996."

I immediately began to supply the requested materials, except the report, which I was not about to give them at this early stage and for which the permit contained no deadline. Although Ray Tracy indicated that the colonel's decision had already been made, I failed to see how the colonel could not take my observations into account. That day and the next, I faxed measurements, a listing of the bones, and my field notes. The notes were handwritten in my less-than-perfect scrawl, and the measurements were on student-prepared sheets rife with misspellings. If they wanted the information immediately, they would have to take it in its current condition. Over the next several weeks, Ray Tracy visited me to borrow photographs, X rays and CT scans. None of the photos or X rays that left my office was an original, however. The earlier telephone call requesting the names of any colleagues I had spoken to about the find had made me suspect the Corps's motives. I did not trust the Corps to return borrowed records and feared that it might attempt to confiscate everything I had assembled on Kennewick Man. With this in mind, I made multiple copies of important photographs and sent sets to colleagues for safekeeping.

The notes contained an accounting of all of the analyses Floyd and I had initiated, including the DNA work at UC Davis. That the Corps did not attempt to read those notes or give any weight to my observations during its decision-making process was evident from the fact that it remained unaware of the DNA work until *Science* magazine prematurely reported it in mid-October.

I needn't have bothered sending the records quickly. Curtis's decision had already been made. I was later to learn from the government's internal correspondence that on Monday, September 9, the first business day after he and I had spoken, Tim McKeown of Interior had had another communication about Kennewick Man, this time with Colonel Curtis. Curtis is reported to have said that he was comfortable with his decision and to have been assured by McKeown that he "could not have made a better decision." Four days previously, Dutch Meier had said that the Corps had a lot of work to do. That work must have been completed with remarkable speed— and entirely without information: Corps personnel not only had not had my records before making the decision, they had not even looked at the bones they were agreeing to hand over. They didn't do that until the following day.

On September 13, the Corps released to the press its intent to "repatriate" the skeleton to the five tribes. On September 17, Colonel Curtis published in the *Tri-City Herald* the first of two official announcements proclaiming this intent. The second would be published a week later, on September 24. Beginning on that date, the Corps was required to accept alternative claims and comments for thirty days, after which it could release the bones to the Umatillas, who publicly proclaimed their intent to bury the remains in a secret place once they were in tribal hands. If we were to save Kennewick Man from destruction, we had until only October 24 to do it.

❋

The need for political support had become urgent. Congressional staffs had responded with alacrity following my first request for aid, but additional inquiries had received the same response: the Corps was only following the law. The reply received by Congressman "Doc" Hastings on September 18, following the first legal announcement, summed up the Corps's position on the issue. Curtis wrote, ". . . applicable NAGPRA guidelines and definitions as currently drafted clearly indicate we must proceed with repatriation of the remains without additional study, unless desired by the involved claimant(s)." Then, following citation of the law and a definition of "Native American" right out of my conversation with McKeown, he continued:

> Examination/study of the remains did occur by a number of individuals, including the coroner's consultant, a forensic anthropologist. While we recognize the extent of study may not be to the level desired by the scientific community, the remains were examined and data collected. Concerned Indian tribes have requested that no further study of the remains be done. Again, we are trying to balance matters of great concern to both sides of this issue.

Following this brush-off, Hastings and Senators Gorton and Murray moved up the chain of command, writing to General Joe Ballard, commander of the Corps of Engineers, in Washington, D.C. In his October 4 letter to Ballard, Hastings again appealed for scientific study and urged the general to postpone action "until the [skeleton's] origins are determined conclusively or until Congress has the opportunity to review this important issue." Although these inquiries seem to have rattled down the chain of command, they were met with essentially the same "our hands are tied" response.

✻

With the Corps's announcement of its intent to "repatriate" Kennewick Man, I redoubled my efforts to involve colleagues in the fight. Another call to David Thomas would take me down the second of Doc Daugherty's suggested routes.

The problem, I complained to Thomas, was that NAGPRA was being applied beyond the original intent of Congress. I went on to relate some of the horror stories I had been hearing from around the country. He countered with horror stories of his own and related how the American Museum of Natural History had its hands full with demands for repatriation of not only skeletons but a broad array of objects that were being claimed as sacred.

I suggested that he challenge NAGPRA, since he was in a better political position than I and the law hit the museums harder than anyone. This he could not do, however, because to do so would be counter to both his museum's interests and the needs of his own research program.

During the 1990s, tribes had increasingly gained power over access to archaeological sites, even sites that were off reservations and (in some states) on private land. If an archaeologist these days wants to continue working, he has to stay in the tribes' good graces. It's a difficult task. I faced the same problem.

The way to make a change, he suggested, was to generate public interest through the news media. We had had local coverage, but he felt we should seek national exposure in a paper like *The New York Times*, and gave me the phone number of John Noble Wilford, the *Times*'s top science reporter covering anthropology and archaeology.

He was right, of course. The media's interest had already been piqued, but past experience had shown me that interest quickly wanes after the early reports of a discovery. Within two weeks, only a select few remember a new find and even fewer care. I called Wilford, but he was busy with another story, and it was not until September 24 that I heard from another *Times* reporter—Seattle Bureau Chief Timothy Egan.

Egan's story came out on September 30—front page news: TRIBE STOPS STUDY OF BONES THAT CHALLENGES ITS HISTORY. As Thomas had predicted, it unleashed a media feeding frenzy that would sweep across the United States and Europe, ultimately drawing attention in Japan, Korea, Brazil, Australia, New Zealand, and even Indonesia. Before the thirty-day comment period was up on October 23, the story had been picked up by *Time, Newsweek, The Economist, Archaeology* magazine, *Science*, ABC, PBS, and the Discovery Channel, to name but a few.

The media attention was welcome, but some of the directions the reporters chose to take their stories in were not. Instead of focusing on the fact that overzealous government application of an untested law was about to lead to the loss of a priceless storehouse of information, some reporters took a more sensationalistic tack. The battle they chose to highlight was between Western science and Native American religious beliefs. As had their local counterparts before them, they emphasized the "European" or "Caucasoid" characteristics of the skeleton. Some asserted that this one discovery had fanned theories that the first Americans had been European, a misinterpretation that would only become more exaggerated as time went on.

One negative side effect of the media interest brought the last of our analyses to a halt. Although Floyd and I had thought the DNA work had been completed at about the same time as we received the radiocarbon results, that was not the case. Rika Kaestle had not actually gotten the sample of bone until after the radiocarbon dating was completed. She had then left the country and had been incommunicado for several weeks. By early October, when I finally reached her, she had completed only the initial separation, just enough to know that the DNA was intact. Shortly after that, Ann Gibbons, a stringer for *Science* magazine, had learned from a source that the DNA work was under way. Wanting to break a new twist to the story and despite Rika's and my efforts to dissuade her from disclosing this information until the study was finished, she ran a news story about the work. The Corps, apparently never having read my notes and thus being unaware of the DNA analysis up to that point, acted swiftly to halt the analysis. In their zeal to report "news," the editors of *Science*, a publication of the American Association for the Advancement of Science, had inadvertently been instrumental in stifling research.

Another negative consequence of press interest struck even closer to home. On September 18, I received a chilling call from one of my chief business clients, with whom I had worked for more than a dozen years. It had received an unsigned letter from Harvey Moses, a member of the Colville tribe's Business Council. Recently, he alleged, I had "shown disdain for communicating with Indian people. Dr. Chatters identified human remains in Columbia Park near Kennewick as being very ancient and apparently felt that their importance to 'science' transcended Indian concerns." The letter went on to accuse me of deliberately withholding this discovery from "the Indian people" while I communicated with my colleagues, including the Smithsonian Institution. I had kept this secret, he alleged, for two months, despite the fact that my ARPA permit had required consultation with Indian tribes. He said that charges were being considered against me for violating the conditions of my permit.

I thought I detected Jeff Vanpelt's influence in the letter and later learned that he had been meeting with the other tribes, spreading the same vitriol he had directed at me in late August. Reports by the Associated Press that had "quoted" me as asserting that the skeleton was not an ancestor of modern Indians had also played a part. Another trigger, Adeline Fredin later told me, was that the Colvilles had learned of the find later than the other tribes, thus putting them at a disadvantage in pressing their own claim. Whatever the reason for his action, the councilman went on to assert that I had destroyed any credibility I had once held with the Colville tribes. He demanded that the client terminate my contract immediately.

True or not, this blatant attempt to interfere with a separate business relationship of mine posed a genuine threat to my livelihood and temporarily sidelined me from the battle to save Kennewick Man while I attempted to salvage my company. Fortunately, there were other soldiers in this fight, and their efforts would ultimately prove more effective than my own.

⁂

The Corps's publication of its intent to turn Kennewick Man over to the tribes invited comments and alternative claims to the skeleton, and the Corps received plenty. Letters, calls, and e-mail communications flowed in from all over the country from individuals and groups laying claim to the skeleton as a relative, and from scientists decrying the irreparable loss to knowledge and requesting the opportunity for study.

Claims came mostly from the Pacific Northwest—from people who were outraged by the Corps's precipitous actions and the tribes' claims to something that could not possibly be proven to be their kin. Most, like Patricia Lettau of Richland, Washington, Ken Gauntt of Pasco, and Dan Donaldson of nearby Prosser, seized on the idea of European appearance. Some of these comments were tongue in cheek, but Stephen McNallen of the Asatru Folk Assembly was quite serious. He represented "a religious organization dedicated to the native, tribal beliefs of Europe. Like Native American spirituality," he went on, "our religion places great emphasis on honoring our ancestors. . . . We claim these bones of our ancient kinsman on the grounds that we are more closely related to him than are the Native American tribes in the area." Several individuals, including Rosemary Thomas, mother of the young man who had found the skeleton in the first place, asserted both European and Native American ancestry.

Organization or individual, all received the same form letter from Colonel Curtis, the principal message of which was:

If you are claiming the remains as a lineal descendant, we need evidence that you can trace your ancestry directly back to the individual in question. If you claim the remains on the basis of cultural affiliation, i.e. as an Indian, you need to establish that you are the authorized representative of an established Indian tribe for purposes of asserting NAGPRA claims.

Curtis's response highlights one of the greatest flaws of NAGPRA. Unless you can prove lineal descent, you have no say whatever over what happens to ancient human remains in America, even if you are of Indian heritage. Only federally recognized tribes may make such claims. This effectively disenfranchises the millions of American citizens, like my own wife and daughter, who have Native American ancestry but who have no tribal membership.

An organization representing some one thousand such families, the Ethnic Minority Council of America, sent a strong message favoring scientific study of ancient remains. Believing that medical and scientific research on old skeletons is of utmost importance to descendants of those ancient dead, it called activist groups' wholesale reburial of unstudied remains "passive genocide."

The scientific community weighed in heavily on its own behalf. Anthropologists, geologists, and medical researchers from throughout the United States and even Great Britain made numerous calls and sent more than thirty-five letters of protest. Some correspondents represented professional and lay organizations boasting hundreds and even thousands of members. Most proclaimed the international significance of the discovery and decried the loss to global knowledge if a rare, ancient skeleton such as Kennewick Man were to be discarded so arbitrarily. J. David Mahan of Anchorage, Alaska, called it "a theft from our storehouse of global knowledge." To John Verano of Tulane University, it was "a tragic mistake." And Richard Jantz of the University of Tennessee wrote, "We are, after all, one species whose history should not be controlled by specific ethnic groups."

As their lay counterparts had, some of the scientists, including

Rob Bonnichsen, focused on the skeleton's dissimilarity from modern American Indians. Bonnichsen observed that many of the earliest North Americans had tended to have Caucasian-like characteristics, leading him to suspect that multiple physically distinct peoples had colonized the Americas. To Martin Kessel of Florida Atlantic University, this meant that "it cannot be automatically assumed that early American skeletons are ancestral to modern Native Americans."

Many asserted that NAGPRA had not been drafted to apply to such rare, ancient fossils and questioned the Corps's ability to link an individual of such antiquity to any living people. Michael Moratto, author of a comprehensive text on California archaeology, observed:

> As a specialist in the prehistory of western North America, I can assure you that *no* living society, native American or other, can credibly claim biologic or cultural affiliation with archaeological remains 93 centuries old. This time span represents nearly 500 generations. During this time, peoples entered the New World, moved extensively within it, evolved culturally, intermarried, and sometimes died out. The true descendant of people represented by [Kennewick Man] might be living in Central or South America, or might be extinct. To link them with historic or modern Indians near Richland is without substantive or legal merit.

Moratto and others declared that turning over the skeleton to the first group to claim it would be counter to the intent of NAGPRA, which, they noted, requires that an effort be made to locate affiliated peoples. "Repatriation" now, without the necessary studies to determine affiliation, would be premature, they argued. In taking such an action, the Corps might be giving Kennewick Man to the wrong people, possibly even to the descendants of his enemies.

A key element in many of the letters was the observation that NAGPRA did not prohibit study and in fact seemed to require it in order for "cultural" affiliation to be determined. Owsley, Jantz,

C. Loring Brace of the University of Michigan, and George Gill of the University of Wyoming expressed interest in working on this particular skeleton.

Eloquent as they were, the scientists' pleas met with even less success than the claims by laymen. Their letters went unanswered, every one.

✼

Doug Owsley was becoming particularly alarmed. In recent years, he had seen one ancient skeleton after another reburied without adequate, duplicated scientific study. In 1991, the 12,800-year-old Buhl skeleton had been turned over to the Shoshone-Bannocks of Fort Hall after only one incomplete study by a graduate student; in 1993, a 9,000-year-old partial male skeleton found in Hourglass Cave, Colorado, had been similarly treated. Alarmed at the disappearance of this priceless record after so little investigation and not one to be easily deterred, Owsley went all out for Kennewick Man. First, shortly after the Corps announced its intent to repatriate the skeleton, he set up a conference call with Colonel Curtis and Corps archaeologist John Leier.

"I mostly emphasized how very rare the find was," he later told me, "and how little we know about these early people. I told [them] how these early ones are very different and that we don't know how they tie to peoples later on. I pointed out that this find was of national significance and that the law did not prohibit study, especially of such important material. I tried different explanations and different angles, but I got nothing. It was like talking to a stone wall. It became *abundantly* clear that the colonel wasn't going to budge."

He shared his complaint with Rob Bonnichsen, who directed him to Alan Schneider, the attorney I'd already spoken with. Doug and Alan resolved to seek help from higher up in the Corps's system, calling Paul Rubenstein, chief archaeologist at the Corps in Washington, D.C., and Sonny Trimble, the Corps's lead curator. Rob Bonnichsen, communicating closely with them, moved up the chain of command and wrote an appeal to Major General Ernest Harrell, commander of the Pacific Northwest Division, and General Ballard in Washington, D.C., whom Representative Hastings and Senators Gorton and Murray had already unsuccessfully petitioned.

What Rubenstein told Schneider and Owsley suddenly explained the colonel's unwillingness even to discuss the possibility of scientific research. It seems that Curtis had given the tribes his word that there would be no more study until the repatriation process was complete. "Rubenstein told me," Schneider related, "that Colonel Curtis had a whole suite of other problems with the Indians and he wasn't about to let 'a bunch of old bones' get in the way."

At that point, *The New York Times* article appeared and identified the Umatillas as the lead tribe in the dispute. With the aid of Armand Minthorn's brother Phil, who was then on the Smithsonian's repatriation staff, Doug drafted a letter to Donald Sampson, the Umatilla tribe's chairman.

"The letter was from Dennis Stanford (the chairman of the Smithsonian's Anthropology Department) and me," Doug noted. "It asked for their approval to conduct nondestructive studies and described what we would do in some detail. We offered to work closely with them and include them in any announcements that were to be made. We sent the letter off in October and got no response whatsoever. Nothing."

※

The same *Times* article impelled Rob Bonnichsen to an inevitable decision.

"I had a contract with the Umatillas to work on a 12,000- to 18,000-year-old mammoth on their reservation," he told me. "It was interesting because a longbone fragment had a green bone break that could have indicated human involvement in the animal's death. We'd about finished the fieldwork when the first article broke in *The New York Times,* with me quoted as saying the Kennewick case was a 'battle over who owns the past.' That was pivotal.

"Jeff Vanpelt called me and said, 'We're not going to give you money on this contract if you're involved in Kennewick.' I said, 'Hey, they're not at all related!' Then my name appeared a second time, and I was fired.

"We were getting stonewalled by the Corps of Engineers' brass on study requests, and now this. It began to look like we were going to have to stand our ground in the Kennewick Man case and duke it out."

✵

Alan Schneider, Doug Owsley, and Dick Jantz, Doug's mentor and research collaborator, had reached the same conclusion.

"When I called Curtis and pressed him about the requests for study," Alan explained, "he acknowledged that he'd received letters from all over. He said they weren't denying requests for study, they simply weren't going to rule on them until after the thirty-day comment period had ended. This meant we had to wait until the decision was made, but by then there'd be no time to pull together any legal action to stop it."

"It was getting down to the wire," Doug told me. "It was already the eighth of October, and we were getting no response from the Corps or the Indians. It began to look like we would have to sue to block the transfer of the bones to the Umatillas."

Alan expressed his reservations and tried to dissuade the others from court action.

"I had already told them I really didn't want to do a lawsuit," Alan explained to me. "I told them what it would entail—it took a long time and a lot of work, and still you might lose. I said it was like a marriage. It would draw their attention away from their classes and research. It would take an emotional toll and might not be a popular choice among their peers."

"But we really had no choice," said Owsley. "I'm a pretty persuasive guy, so if I can't talk my way into something like this, with my research background and Smithsonian connections, some assistant professor or doctoral student doesn't have a chance. The future of our entire field was in jeopardy.

"We had been talking to colleagues about this eventuality and had some tentative commitments," he continued. "I had persuaded Dennis [Stanford] to come in with us and called George Gill, who was my professor at Wyoming. Dennis brought Rob Bonnichsen on board and Vance Haynes [of the University of Arizona]." Stanford, an expert on North America's earliest stone technologies, was curious about the spear point in Kennewick Man's hip. George Gill was interested in the evolution of what some anthropologists refer to as the Mongoloid trait complex, features shared by Chinese, Japanese, Koreans, Siberians, and many American Indian peoples. Kennewick Man, who seemingly lacked those features, was an important link in understanding when and how that human form had developed. Haynes, one of the country's foremost archaeological geologists, felt it important that the geologic context of the discovery be documented.

Bonnichsen contacted Gentry Steele. They had worked together on First American issues for many years, and Steele sat on the Scientific Committee at the Center for the Study of the First Americans. He was an obvious choice, since it was he who had revitalized the study of Paleo-Indian skeletons with his papers in the early 1990s. The final member of the team was C. Loring Brace, who had seen a photograph of me holding a slide of the Kennewick skull and felt it resembled the skulls of the Ainu, an aboriginal Japanese people in whom he had a keen interest.

For my part, I had mixed feelings about joining in legal action. I was particularly concerned about the impact it would have on my relationships with local tribes. Nonetheless, after the Colvilles' attempt to damage me financially, I was resolved to take the plunge. Alan saved me from making the difficult choice, however, by pointing out that one of the plaintiffs' claims would be that they had been denied an opportunity to study. Because I *had* conducted some studies, however incomplete, my involvement might cloud the issues in the eyes of a judge.

So there were eight plaintiffs. Together they were some of the most eminent scholars in their fields, a partial Who's Who of American physical anthropology and First American studies.

One issue remained to be resolved: Alan was unwilling to take on the suit unless he had a major firm to help carry the load. An independent attorney, he lacked the resources and time to wage what proved to be a protracted battle. He asked a colleague, Paula Barran, of the Portland firm of Lane Powell Spears Lubersky, if her firm would be willing to take on the case pro bono, and to his delight, they agreed. It was now October 11, and Alan had to be out of town for a few days for a conference. Before leaving, he provided Paula with some thoughts on NAGPRA law and an outline of a possible strategy for the lawsuit.

Over the weekend, nearly a dozen volunteers, led by Paula Barran, assembled what Alan Schneider calls a masterpiece. On Monday, October 14, they handed him a full set of legal papers for the suit. What made this feat all the more amazing was that not one of them had had any prior knowledge of, let alone experience with, NAGPRA.

The suit alleged in part that the Corps's decision to repatriate the remains was arbitrary and capricious, that it violated the plaintiffs' First Amendment rights of access to knowledge and of freedom from establishment of religion, their right to equal protection regardless of race, religion, or ethnicity, and the very law it purported to enforce. In the last claim, the complaint further alleged that the Corps had violated NAGPRA by determining that Kennewick Man was a Native American without sufficient scientific evidence, refusing to consider evidence to the contrary, deciding on repatriation without first determining the ethnicity and cultural affiliation of the skeleton, and denying scientific study that could have major benefit to the United States.

By Wednesday, the sixteenth, Schneider had the signatures of all eight plaintiffs to the complaint and by that afternoon had filed the suit with the U.S. District Court in Portland. The hearing on the scientists' motion for a temporary restraining order under this complaint was set for October 23, one day before the end of the comment period. The tribes had scheduled the reburial for as early as the twenty-fifth.

The hearing was held before John Jelderks, an experienced federal magistrate, who, after careful consideration, denied the scientists' motion. He did so because the issue was moot.

The Corps had informed the court that it had received conflicting claims for the skeleton and was required by law to address these counterclaims before it could proceed. At last, the Corps had halted its automatic acceptance of the tribes' position. Jelderks, recognizing that the scientific team might want to reopen its lawsuit when the government did make a decision, if that decision was against additional study, ordered the government to give the plaintiffs ten days' notice before taking any action.

Why had the Corps backed down? Besides the lawsuit, at least four other factors may have influenced its decision. First, the government had received many claims for Kennewick Man's bones. Although most of the claims were not from Indians and thus had no standing under the law, the Colville tribe and the Wanapum band of Priest Rapids had filed separate claims, and neither had mentioned deferring to the Umatillas. In fact, Adeline Fredin had told Rob Bonnichsen and me during an October 16 meeting in Seattle that the Colvilles wanted the repatriation stopped and a proper NAGPRA process initiated. They had requested that, pending completion of that process, the remains should be kept in their tribal repository, where they could be studied for the benefit of tribal members.

Second, the congressional pressure had stepped up as the comment period ticked away. On October 11, Senator Gorton and Republican Congressmen Hastings, Nethercutt, and Metcalf had sent a joint letter to Major General Ernest Harrell, urging him to allow scientists to examine the bones before deciding to release them to the tribes.

Third, on October 15, one day before the scientific team filed suit, the chief legal counsel of the Smithsonian Institution made an official request for the bones. The 1846 act creating the Smithsonian Institution, he argued, required that materials recovered from federal land be turned over to the museum. According to the attorney, this law said that "all collections of rocks, minerals, soils, *fossils,* and objects of natural history, *archaeology* and ethnology [made by or for the government], when no longer needed for investigations in progress shall be deposited in the National Museum" (emphasis added). These provisions of law, he contended, are mandatory and are neither superseded by nor contradictory to NAGPRA. The remains, he contended, should be turned over to the Smithsonian for analysis, to be conducted in collaboration with any tribe that was interested in the remains.

Finally, a memorandum written on September 3, 1996, and sent to Corps headquarters on October 16, the same day as the scientists' suit was filed, showed that the Corps's hierarchy was uncertain about the provisions of NAGPRA even while asserting to the public that the law was perfectly clear and that scientific study was prohibited. It read in part:

> A real serious issue regards the accidental finding of very ancient remains as has just recently occurred in [the Walla Walla District]. The proposed rules [for NAGPRA compliance] are silent and there is serious scientific disagreement about the disposition of such remains. . . . The fact is that we do not really know how very ancient human remains might be related to contemporary Indian peoples. This fact alone would seem to merit some intermediate screening process that would provide for some kinds of study by qualified professionals and organizations prior to reburial by remote ancestors [*sic*].

Ultimately, all of my old friend Doc Daugherty's suggestions had been followed, with or without my action, and individually or collectively they and the Corps's own uncertainty had tipped the scales. Whatever the reason for the Corps's change of heart, Kennewick Man had received a reprieve from oblivion.

5

The Battle for
Kennewick Man

IN THE FALL of 1996, the government and collaborating Indian tribes tried to force the plaintiff scientists to back down. First, the Justice Department tried to put pressure on the Smithsonian Institution, claiming that it was illegal for the institution's employees Doug Owsley and Dennis Stanford to sue another branch of the federal government. Despite concern for his job, Owsley stood his ground, asserting his right to sue as a private citizen. Stanford stood with him, and they ultimately won their point. Today the Smithsonian is strongly behind their quest to save and study Kennewick Man.

The tribes made an effort as well, using much the same tactic. As they had done with me, the Colville tribe wrote to the employer of each plaintiff, asking if the employer was aware that its staff members were engaged in the suit and wondering whether the institution wanted the reputation of trying to "hurt" Indian people. This campaign, too, was unsuccessful, but not without some cost to Rob Bonnichsen, whose department chairman at Oregon State University charged him with ethics violations because of his involvement in the lawsuit.

In February 1997, indirect means having failed, the Justice Department, which was handling the suit for the Corps of Engineers, attempted to have the scientists' suit (and a related suit brought by the Asatru Folk Assembly dismissed on the ground (in part) that the Corps had made no final decision that needed to be challenged. Magistrate Jelderks denied this motion. The Corps, he maintained, had indeed made a number of decisions—in asserting jurisdiction over the remains and deciding they had been Native American and that NAGPRA applied, that the remains had been found on aboriginal land of an Indian tribe, that there was a cultural relationship between the remains and a modern tribe, and that the remains should be turned over to a tribe for reburial. Had the plaintiffs not filed suit, he observed, all evidence indicated that Kennewick Man would already have been given to one or another Indian tribe.

In late March, the scientists submitted a detailed study plan and asked the court to grant them access to the skeleton. This plan outlined thirteen kinds of studies to be carried out by the plaintiff scientists and their associates, myself included. The bones would be examined and measured by Owsley, Jantz, Gill, Steele, and Brace, each of whom had his own distinct methods of gathering data. Owsley, Bonnichsen, and others would evaluate what is called the taphonomy of the bones—evidence that would indicate what had happened to the skeleton between death and discovery. Joseph Powell, who had coauthored several papers with Gentry Steele about Paleo-Indians, and Christy Turner of Arizona State University would study the teeth, take X rays, and make casts that could be inspected by scanning electron microscope for evidence of diet. The skeleton would be photographed thoroughly and molds, X rays, and CT scans made of the skull and other bones. In addition, we would remove small amounts of dental calculus (which is what the dental hygienist does when you have your teeth cleaned) and study it for fossils of the plant foods the man had eaten, take a thin section of bone from an arm or leg to aid in determining his age, and remove four grams of well-preserved bone for DNA analysis and additional radiocarbon dates. The same bone we used for dating would provide tiny samples for isotope analysis, a further aid to reconstructing Kennewick Man's diet. Direct work on the skeleton would take only about two weeks.

In response to this request, the government made another attempt to have the case thrown out. On March 23, the Corps of Engineers had finally recognized that the Umatillas' claim to the skeleton strictly on the basis of aboriginal landholdings was in fact false. The Corps published a recision of its intent to repatriate the skeleton and asserted to Magistrate Jelderks that the scientists' lawsuit should be dismissed, contending again that a final decision had not been made and that Owsley and his associates had no legal standing to challenge a NAGPRA decision because they were not Indians. They further argued against the proposed studies, asserting, in part, that NAGPRA did not allow studies of skeletons found inadvertently and that, besides, study was an unnecessary duplication of my work and that the handling and sampling of the bones would be too destructive.

Jelderks ordered a May hearing and heard arguments from the contending parties. He then took the matter under advisement and, on June 27, 1997, issued a blistering fifty-two-page opinion. He denied the government motion. He also denied the scientists' study request but without prejudice, meaning they could pursue their request again once the government had reached an official decision. Then he pointed out that the government's affidavits to the court clearly showed that its decision to hand over the bones to Indian tribes had not changed, and he ordered it to start its process of reviewing the case over again. The government was to answer seventeen detailed questions, including: Are the remains subject to NAGPRA? What does the statute mean by "Native American" and "indigenous"? If there was more than one wave of ancient migration to the Americas, or if there were subpopulations of early Americans, does NAGPRA apply to skeletons from a people who died out and were not directly related to modern Indians? What happens to the remains if NAGPRA does not apply or if no existing tribe is culturally affiliated with them? Are scientific study and reburial mutually exclusive? Do the scientists have a First Amendment right to study the remains? Is

NAGPRA silent on important issues of this case (such as what to do with culturally unidentifiable remains) that should be addressed by Congress? And so forth. In the meantime, Jelderks ordered the Corps to store Kennewick Man in a manner that would ensure his physical security and protect his scientific value.

By the end of summer 1997, it had become apparent that the last order was not being followed. First came the revelation that the Corps had on five occasions permitted groups of Indians to visit the bones, twice adding new, wet pieces they had collected from the beach at Columbia Park and at other times conducting religious ceremonies. The Asatru plaintiffs, being a religious organization, demanded equal opportunity and were granted a visit to the bones on August 27. What they reported after their visit shocked the scientific contingent. The bones were still being kept in unpadded, unmarked plastic bags in the original wooden box in which I had placed them. In the box with them now were ashes and boughs of cedar that had been placed there by the Indians during religious observances. Some of the plastic bags were not sealed, which meant that foreign material might have become mixed with the skeleton. This could contaminate the bones with new carbon, allow bacteria to enter them, and affect both radiocarbon dating and any potential DNA analyses. In addition, we learned two months after the court's order that the Corps had not yet assessed the condition and preservation needs of the skeleton and was keeping no access records for the room in which it was stored. In October, both plaintiff groups filed complaints, and the Corps made belated attempts to remedy the deficiencies.

A museum conservator was hired to assess the condition and curatorial needs of the bones, and on November 4, 1997, fourteen months after taking control, the Corps sent a team from its Mandatory Centers of Expertise to inventory and properly package (curate) the skeleton. Up until that time, the government had had no record, other than my notes, of what it had in its possession. The Corps's inventory seemed to reveal the presence in the collection of three pubis bones (parts of the pelvis). A human being has only two pubis bones. Corps spokesman Dutch Meier alleged that the extra bone had been in my original collection, which would indicate that a second person might have been mixed in with Kennewick Man. This revelation sparked speculation by the media and some of my less sympathetic colleagues that my research had been shoddy. Some even saw it as evidence that the entire discovery was merely a modern-day Pilt-down hoax—a reference to a fabricated missing link "found" in Great Britain in the early twentieth century. When pressed, a second Corps public relations officer admitted that this "extra" bone had been added to the collection by the Umatillas.

I found more bone, this time a fragment of rib, during a Corps-supervised geologic survey of the Kennewick Man site in early December 1997. Inspecting the site one last time in March 1998, just before the Corps buried it under tons of rock and sand, I noticed additional fragments—pieces of ribs and vertebrae. Rather than pick them up myself and risk accusations that I had violated federal law, I wrote to Lieutenant Colonel Curtis, and Corps archaeologists were sent to do the job.

Shortly after this, evidence surfaced that parts of the skeleton were beginning to disappear. The first report came in late March 1998. Paul Nickens, who had directed the archaeological program at Pacific Northwest National Laboratory at the time Kennewick Man had been placed in government custody, was hired by the Justice Department to compare my records with the inventory compiled by the Corps's curatorial staff. Trying to match my notes, drawings, and photos with the Corps's bone lists, he found an alarming discrepancy: pieces of both femur bones were missing.

When I had recovered Kennewick Man from the beach, his femurs had been complete, although each was in three pieces of about equal length. Each bone had been more than 18 inches long (45.7 cm). But by March 1998, four of the six pieces—the upper two thirds of the right femur and the lower two thirds of the left—were missing. Nickens further compared the new list with three pages of notes purportedly made by an archaeologist for the Umatilla tribe on September 10, 1996, when Ray Tracy and various tribal members had first inspected the skeleton. That list did not include the missing pieces either. In late March 1998, the government confessed this discrepancy to the court and issued statements to the press to the effect that the Justice Department was asking Floyd Johnson and me to account for the missing fragments. To many reporters, the clear implication was that one of us had stolen the bones.

Having had five witnesses to my transfer of the bones to Floyd Johnson, plus a videotape of the skeleton that I had packed in the box, I was able, through my attorney, to dispel these rumors. Floyd, a former major in the Sheriff's Department and a man with no motive for taking parts of the skeleton, was above reproach. Nevertheless, as late as the summer of 1999, Floyd and I were still being investigated by the FBI, which considered us its only suspects in the disappearance of the bones. None of the many others who had had access to the skeleton after September 5, 1996, was even being considered.

The tribes' anger was again openly directed toward me. The Nez Percé Tribal Council issued a policy statement declaring that no agency or business working in its ceded territories (off the reservation) that wanted the tribes' cooperation should engage in a contract with me. The Umatillas have proudly admitted doing the same. Although individuals could be sued if they committed acts such as these, known as "tortuous interference with a contractual business relationship," I had no legal recourse against the tribes because they are officially sovereign nations. Fortunately, the clients to whom such instructions were directed refused to be intimidated, and my business was unaffected.

More bones disappeared in late April, but this time nobody pointed a finger in my direction. Corps archaeologist John Leier had been taking part in a repatriation and reburial that included the five partial skeletons found in Columbia Park shortly after Kennewick Man. According to his court affidavit on the incident, he entered a set of shelves at the PNNL repository and removed the labeled box containing the Columbia Park bones. He then walked to the end of the corridor and handed the box to a tribal member. A second tribal member standing outside the shelving unit got his attention and began demanding the wooden box in which I had originally delivered the Kennewick Man remains, which Leier would not give him. While Leier was thus engaged, a third tribal member apparently walked into the shelving unit and removed a second box containing a human femur that was not scheduled for repatriation, some animal bones, and the rib fragment of Kennewick Man found in December 1997, which, for some inexplicable reason, had not been secured with the rest of the skeleton. Leier noticed that the additional remains had been taken only as the femur from the second box was being placed into a grave. He was subsequently removed from the Kennewick Man case and reassigned.

The scientists immediately filed a request for a hearing with the court, alleging continued lax security at the PNNL facility. They reiterated that the repeated, poorly documented visits by tribal personnel, the frequent addition of undocumented bones, the mixture of animal and human bones, the contamination with ashes and leaves, and now the repeated disappearance of parts of the skeleton was evidence that PNNL was not a suitable facility for a national treasure. To make the situation worse, several members of the tribes who claimed the Kennewick bones were employed by PNNL, and the laboratory's new archaeology director, who oversaw the repository where the bones were held, was the husband of the same Umatilla staff member who had written the September 10, 1996, inventory list that had surfaced in the spring of 1998. PNNL's ability to remain impartial thus came into question. The scientists requested that the bones be moved to a new, neutral repository with better security.

Magistrate Jelderks took immediate action, calling a hearing on May 28, 1998, to discuss these allegations and to attempt to remedy the deficient care being given to Kennewick Man. There were, he said, "serious questions about the physical security and scientific integrity of the remains."

The government, in a familiar pattern, entered the hearing asserting that no court action was necessary because it had already decided to relocate the skeleton to a larger facility. The Corps of Engineers had found that it was ill equipped to answer the many questions posed by Jelderks the previous June, perhaps in part because of Curtis's promise to the tribes that he would allow no further study. In March, the Corps had delegated the task of determining Kennewick Man's ultimate fate to the Department of the Interior. Interior consulting archaeologist Francis McManamon, a career government employee with little practical archaeological experience, told the court that he intended to commission studies of the skeleton to resolve the questions Jelderks had set forth the previous June and that the PNNL facility lacked an appropriate space in which to do the work. Therefore, he proposed to move Kennewick Man to the Burke Museum, which is affiliated with the University of Washington in Seattle.

At the close of the hearing, Jelderks directed all parties to work together to decide on a neutral repository or he would make the decision for them. He ordered the Corps to allow two representatives from the scientists to inspect the PNNL facility and determine if the bones were being properly cared for, and to participate in an inventory of Kennewick Man's bones before they were moved to a new facility. He also had some choice words for the government. The case was proceeding too slowly, he admonished, and he directed the government to develop a clear timeline for resolving the disposition of Kennewick Man.

"A year," he said, "should have been ample time to get the issues resolved or at least have a timeline. Hard questions don't get easier to answer with the passing of time. It's time for a resolution at your end."

Lieutenant Colonel Curtis, standing before the court in full uniform, snapped to attention and replied, "I understand my mission."

✡

The Interior Department devised a study plan that summer and began to implement it in October. The first step was to move the bones to the Burke Museum. The plaintiffs objected to this proposal because of antagonistic statements made toward some of the plaintiff scientists by a museum archaeologist. Jelderks was satisfied, however, that the Burke was reasonably neutral and ordered the transfer. The move

was a complex undertaking, entailing inventories and religious observances before the bones were taken from PNNL and after they arrived at the Burke. Despite Jelderks's order that two representatives
from the scientists could take part in an inventory of the bones, the
government balked at their inclusion, then wanted veto power over
individual participants. Specifically, they sought to exclude me, stating that my presence would be offensive to the tribes. They argued
that the PNNL room was too small to hold the five-member government team, a PNNL staffer, and one observer each from the tribes
and the Asatru Folk Assembly plus two scientists. The plaintiffs insisted that I be one of the two scientific observers, asserting that my
prior experience with the skeleton would save time and increase the
accuracy of the resulting inventory. Besides, I was the only one who
could assess how much the skeleton's condition had changed since the
government had taken control of it. The government also wanted to
prohibit any recording devices, such as the computer Owsley wanted
to use to enter his observations or even a tape recorder. Ultimately the
judge was forced to intervene again, dictating that I could not be ex-
cluded from the two-person team representing the Bonnichsen plaintiffs and that Owsley could use a tape recorder.

My role was to compare the skeleton as it appeared in fall 1998
with its condition when it had last been in my possession two years
previously. I was not happy with what I saw. Most of both femur
bones were indeed missing, and cracks in the cranium that had been
only hairlines in August 1996 had widened and lengthened, threaten-
ing to alter the skull's shape if they progressed further. New cracks had
developed in the skull base. The bone had been kept too long in too
dry an environment, unprotected, before the Corps had finally repack-
aged the collection. Doug Owsley and I, who were doing the scientific
inventory with minimal government assistance, worked all evening
and into the next morning attempting to document each of the more
than 350 bone fragments. That would be the last time he or I would
see Kennewick Man, unless the scientists ultimately won their case.

The next step in the government's study plan was to choose a
team to conduct initial studies of the skeleton, studies designed to de-

termine whether the skeleton was Native American under the terms of NAGPRA. McManamon and the Interior Department interpreted NAGPRA to mean that a Native American was anyone who had lived in America before European colonization. That meant the *only* criterion under the law would be age. If the results of this investigation were positive under their definition—as they surely would be—they would then devise methods to determine which tribe, if any, the bones were culturally affiliated with.

The study McManamon proposed had two parts. Consultants would first study the skeleton, the projectile point in it, and the soil adhering to it. If the results of this analyis were inconclusive, they would remove bone from the skeleton for an additional radiocarbon date. When asked by reporters why they did not simply rely on the original radiocarbon date to determine cultural affiliation, an Interior Department spokesperson said that they could not rely on it because the "wrong bone" had been used.

In February 1999, the study team was convened amid great media fanfare. Chosen to take part were physical anthropologists Joseph Powell of the University of New Mexico and Jerome Rose of the University of Arkansas, stone tool specialist John Fagan of Portland, Oregon, and archaeological geologists Gary Huckleberry of Washington State University and Julie Stein of the Burke Museum. Despite their eminent qualifications, none of the plaintiffs had been asked to take part. Powell, however, had been on the plaintiffs' proposed study team, and Huckleberry was a student of plaintiff Vance Haynes's.

The studies Rose and Powell conducted encompassed parts of the analyses in the plaintiff scientists' study plan but did not include all the measurements the scientists had recommended. They did not, for example, conduct a taphonomic study, and they failed to do casting, DNA analysis, dental calculus removal, and thin sectioning to determine age. The geologists sought to match soil from Kennewick Man's bones with soil the government had taken from the discovery site. Fagan's assignment was to identify the Cascade Point in the pelvis.

Their findings, which underwent intense scrutiny by the tribes and the executive branch of the U.S. government, were kept secret for nearly nine months, meted out slowly by the government in a series of leaks and statements to the press. The results proved to be inconclusive, although they generally corroborated my own observations. Based on the consultants' observations, Kennewick Man could not biologically be classified as an American Indian, and the spear point was of a style that had been too widely used for Fagan to assign it to a specific time. As McManamon stated it in what I found to be a gratifying echo of my own statements of nearly three years previous, "Although the [spear] point appears similar to ones used thousands of years ago, such points were still in use after the arrival of Europeans, so the point is not a strong indicator of chronological age." Only the geologists could provide an approximate estimate of the skeleton's age; it appeared to have come from strata older than 7,700 years, but even this conclusion was tentative.

By July 1999, McManamon had decided, over the objections of the Indian tribes, that he had no alternative but to run additional radiocarbon dates because his first round of studies had not given him the firm age estimate he sought. His plan was unusual. Ordinarily, results from two laboratories are considered scientifically defensible, but he elected to send four bone samples to different laboratories: two university facilities, UC Riverside and the University of Arizona, and two commercial labs, Beta Analytic, Inc., of Florida and Stafford Research Laboratories of Colorado. As soon as the government had its results, McManamon told the court, he would determine whether or not Kennewick Man was Native American and, if he was, begin a process to determine his cultural affiliation. This process would take one to two years. That was too much for the scientists. The government was dragging out its decision-making process so long that by the time it was resolved, the scientists' careers might be over. Their research was being impeded by a lack of access to this important fossil. In August 1999, they accused the government of stalling and asked the court to order the government to immediately make a final decision on whether their request to study the skeleton would be approved or denied. If the government failed to make a decision, the judge should construe this failure to be a de facto denial. Once the government, by decision or inaction, had denied the study request, they could proceed to trial. They hoped, Schneider and Barran said, that the case could be completed within the lifetimes of the plaintiffs.

Just before the hearing on the plaintiffs' motion was held, Mc-Manamon again took a large team to Seattle, this time to cut bone from Kennewick Man for dating. He had elicited recommendations for how the sample should be taken and how much material was needed. Three of the labs asked for no more than 1 to 2 grams of bone, but the fourth wanted 5 grams. Two of America's leading radiocarbon-dating specialists, Erv Taylor at Riverside and Tom Stafford, owner of Stafford Labs, emphasized that the preservation of bone protein varies widely within a single ancient skeleton. Mc-Manamon, they said, should take minute samples from several bones to determine which were best preserved and use parts of the most intact for dating. Their advice was not heeded. McManamon announced that his team would take 20 grams of bone, 5 for each lab. Working from someone's suggestion that the tibia was a good bone to use, they took a small rotary saw and sawed a chunk out of Kennewick Man's shin. They also sawed in half the first metatarsal—a large bone of the foot. Cleone Hawkinson of Portland, Oregon, the plaintiffs' witness to this event, found it distressing: "There was bone dust flying everywhere, and the cutting just seemed to go on and on for about twenty minutes. They had to keep stopping to wipe off their goggles so they could see to work. More than a gram of bone was removed just as sawdust"—enough, in other words, for one radiocarbon date, if the bone was in good condition.

Not counting dust, McManamon took more than 30 grams of bone, rationalizing his blunder by saying, "We wanted to make sure the labs had enough." My original sample had weighed only 2.6 grams, and that had been enough for dating *and* DNA work.

The plaintiffs—especially Owsley—and I were incensed. Doug and I had both observed that the tibia was the worst-preserved major bone in the skeleton and we would never have used it for a date. Besides, the government cut the tibia right at one of the key measurement points, reducing the skeleton's research value should we ever get another look at it.

It was disheartening to see the skeleton I had worked so hard to recover, and that had been one of the most complete early human fossils ever found in America, becoming smaller and smaller. First missing femur parts, then missing pieces of rib, and now this destruction. Kennewick Man had been a human being after all, and it seemed wanton desecration to hack pieces from him in a great politically motivated show of how the government can protect ancient skeletons from scientists.

Tom Stafford pulled out of the group that was to date the bones. He objected to the sampling methods, and to the contract the government wanted him to sign. He drafted a contract of his own, but McManamon wanted to cut out several key stipulations, including one that prohibited the Park Service from distorting his results. Tom's piece of Kennewick Man, which he wanted so desperately to study, went to Riverside.

※

The scientists' petition for an immediate answer to their request for study was heard before the court in September 1999. During that hearing, Magistrate Jelderks asked McManamon about his definition of Native American (any remains from before A.D. 1492). "Are you telling me," he probed, "that a skeleton 507 years old, or a thousand years, or ten thousand years, or even half a million years old, would be considered to be Native American under this statute?" McManamon conceded that it would be.

On September 24, Jelderks issued another directive: the government must tell the scientists on or before March 24, 2000, whether or not they would be allowed to study the bones. He also ordered the government to begin its cultural affiliation studies immediately, since it was highly unlikely that even if the 1996 radiocarbon date was off by a factor of ten, the bones would not fall within its definition of "Native American."

McManamon finally released part of the results of the February 1999 studies in November, but not until January 2000 did he make his determination that Kennewick Man was Native American. The radiocarbon dates had begun to come in by November, but the labs were reporting that the protein in the bones was poorly preserved. Arizona and Riverside refused to provide anything more than apparent ages on any of the samples. The remaining lab, in contrast, said the protein of its sample was well preserved. Government lawyers contacted me for information about how I had collected my sample. Why had the protein been so much better preserved in my sample than in the bones the government had selected? The samples they had chosen, the Interior Department's spokesperson later reported, were already turning to stone.

The single date they received, from Beta Analytic, was identical to the one I had obtained in 1996. McManamon, noting the match, declared that Kennewick Man was officially Native American. McManamon had already, under Jelderks's order, hired a group of four Northwest anthropologists to compile information on linguistics, folklore, archaeology, and human biology and burial practices for use in affiliating the skeleton, despite the fact that it is widely recognized, even by the Umatilla tribe, that it is impossible to affiliate *any* skeleton from 9,000 years ago with a modern culture.

At this point, unable to continue for lack of funds, the Asatru Folk Assembly dropped its lawsuit. Shortly thereafter, the government decided to conduct the one analysis the Asatru Folk Assembly had been requesting all along.

In early February 2000, Bruce Babbitt, Secretary of the Interior, decided to conduct DNA tests for the purpose of determining "cultural affiliation." Indian tribes objected that DNA testing violated their religion and that this was "reducing their identity to a genetic code." The scientists also had concerns with the government's belated decision to undertake DNA testing. Although they supported the concept of such testing and had included it in their study plans, they observed that DNA has no relevance to "cultural affiliation"— culture is learned and therefore independent of biology. But what

they objected to most was the fact that the government then requested and received yet another six-month delay.

This time, having been burned by its radiocarbon sampling error,
the government went directly to Owsley for his advice on how to
take DNA samples. He again told them to first test minute samples
to determine bone condition and offered to bring in his team to do
the work. Instead, the government elected to hire three other physical anthropologists and bring in David Glenn Smith (Frederika Kaestle's professor at UC Davis), Erv Taylor from Riverside, and the
Corps's curatorial team to take minute samples. After those were
tested, the government would extract new material for DNA testing.
Smith would be allowed to complete Kaestle's analysis, which had
been halted in 1996, and two other specialists, Kaestle—now at
Yale—and Andrew Merriweather of the University of Michigan,
would test other materials. It seemed the case would never end. (Ultimately, no DNA could be extracted from the bone samples selected
by the government team.)

✹

After four years (in fall 2000), the U.S government had spent an estimated $2 million fighting eight scientists who merely wished to study
for themselves an ancient American fossil that even the government's
own experts admit needs to be studied. In the process the government has denigrated and obstructed efforts by the scientists to learn
about its actions. After first declaring that the studies the scientists
proposed were unnecessarily duplicative, it hired other scientists to
conduct the same investigations the plaintiffs had requested, declaring that the plaintiffs, who are the leading experts in their fields, are
"biased" and, by implication, untrustworthy. While Kennewick Man
has been in its care, the government has lost some bones, damaged or
destroyed others, and, after claiming that the plaintiff scientists
could not study the skeleton because handling it would damage the
bones, has handled the skeleton or permitted bones to be handled on
at least nine occasions. The plaintiffs—Owsley, Jantz, Steele, Stanford, Bonnichsen, Haynes, Gill, and Brace—had proposed to con-

duct their studies in less than a month of actual time with the skeleton, at their own expense. If the results of their studies had led to Kennewick Man's reburial, he would have been back in the ground long ago.

On the positive side, when Kennewick Man was seized from my laboratory on August 30, 1996, I had despaired over my failure to give him his due. For this I had needed verification of my findings, including a positive result of the DNA analysis. The government's studies, however constrained by politics, have provided a measure of that verification, albeit tainted by lingering doubts about the reliability of research that is constrained by edicts from federal attorneys.

Part II

*

Death and Life

6

A Lifetime of Pain

KENNEWICK MAN WAS an enigma. He was approximately 9,500 years old, and he did not resemble modern American Indians. Who was he? Why was he here? Was he a unique individual or a member of a now-extinct population of early Americans? If such a people had existed, where had they come from, how had they gotten here, and when? While the legal battle dragged on, I made it my quest to find answers to these questions, poring over the results of my own incomplete studies of the skeleton, devouring the literature on the archaeology and biology of the earliest Americans, interviewing colleagues, and traveling thousands of miles to analyze for myself many of the oldest skeletons of this hemisphere. What I found was surprising, fascinating, and often poignant.

✵

Although the skeleton was no longer in my care, I still had my notes, extensive measurements of the skeleton and some from the skull, X rays of the jaws, femur, and pelvis, CT scans of the pelvis, humerus, and femur, photographs of the skull and of most of the pathological conditions of the skeleton, a videotape of the whole skeleton, and a cast of the skull—not an insignificant assemblage of data.

Over the next three years, I studied these records and shared them with colleagues from throughout the United States, seeking second opinions from physical anthropologists, paleopathologists, and orthopedic surgeons. I pored over anthropological journals and medical texts to learn more about the health impacts and prognosis of the injuries evident on Kennewick Man's bones. In the process, I learned a great deal about the life and death of a man who had lived and died ninety-five centuries ago.

Forensic anthropology, known as bioanthropology when remains are ancient and not related to a modern crime, bases its interpretations on extensive studies of modern human populations. More accurately, it uses samples of the dead from the populations that are to be found in autopsy rooms and medical collections. The largest and most used collections are the Terry at the Smithsonian Institution and the Hamman-Todd at Case Western Reserve University in Cleveland, Ohio, which together contain the bones of nearly three thousand people. The skeletons in these collections are largely from named individuals whose medical histories are known and are mostly European Americans and African Americans. Hispanics, Asian Americans, and American Indians are few. The bodies were either donated to science or were unclaimed by relatives after death. Working with these and other collections, researchers can study hundreds of individuals, examining physical characteristics of the bones for the most reliable indicators of sex, age, stature, weight, illness, injury, and race.

The easiest place to determine an individual's sex is the same dead or alive, in the pelvic area. The pelvis is made of two three-part bones, called os coxae, and a set of fused vertebrae called the sacrum. Each of the os coxae is made up of the ilium, the broad blade that forms the rim of the hip; the pubis, at the front center; and the ischium, on which we sit. These three elements meet in the hip socket, and the two os coxae join in front at a cartilage pad known as the pubic symphysis. Males have higher, narrower pelvises and females lower, broader ones. The difference reflects the need for the female pelvis to be able to support a developing fetus and to allow its head to pass through at birth. Males also generally have larger, more elongated heads, with more sloping foreheads, more prominent brow ridges and neck muscle attachments, thicker upper rims to their eye sockets, and wider, squarer chins than females. They are generally more robust and have more prominent ridges and projections on their bones for muscle attachment. Kennewick Man was, as the name implies, distinctly male in the characteristics of his pelvis and skull, and in his overall robustness.

Age proved to be a more difficult issue to resolve. Numerous aging methods are in current use, and new ones are being developed every few years. They include patterns of tooth eruption, fusion of the joint ends of bones with their shafts, changes at the junctions between bone and cartilage in the pelvis and ribs, closure of the sutures in the skull, and remodeling of the spongy bone in the joint ends and of the solid bone in long-bone shafts. Each method has its limitations and degree of accuracy. Most are subjective, leading to frequent disagreements among researchers about the ages of important skeletons. They also vary according to people's health and level of physical activity. I was able to use most of these methods of determining Kennewick Man's age, but there were some that I was not able to use in the time I had access to the remains. I could not, for example, look at the bone remodeling in the long-bone shafts, called osteon counting, because it requires cutting a thin section from the shaft of a long bone, which I could not do with the remains in the custody of others. Tooth eruption and the fusion of long-bone ends with their shafts were not relevant, either. Both processes, which are completed in the early twenties, are only useful for pinpointing the ages of children and adolescents. Kennewick Man, in whom these processes were completed, was fully adult.

Methods of examining changes in the contacts between cartilage and bone are applied to the pubic symphysis, the sacroiliac joint, and the junction between the fourth rib and the sternum. When a person is young, these surfaces have well-organized series of ridges and grooves and exhibit rounded edges. As we age, they first become smoother and distinctly rimmed, then begin to degenerate into irregular, pitted surfaces with jagged rims.

Closure of sutures in the skull is widely used for aging skeletons, but it is considered one of the least accurate methods. The human skull is made up of twenty-one bones that grow independently until we reach adulthood. This allows the brain to grow and makes it possible for different portions of the head and face to change shape more or less independently as we mature. It is in part this differential growth process that gives infants and children a smoother, rounder look than adults. Once skull growth is complete, in the mid- to late twenties, the jagged interbone contacts begin to knit together, first with narrow bridges of bone, then across broad fronts. By middle age, the bones are typically fused together, making the skull less resilient. By late middle age and early old age, the sutures are so thoroughly interconnected that they can no longer be seen clearly, a state known as obliteration.

Aging from the remodeling of trabecular, or spongy, bone in the joint ends is a relatively new method that relies on X-ray images of the clavicle (collarbone) and upper end of the femur. As aging progresses and the small bars of bone inside our joints, called trabeculae, are repeatedly removed and replaced, they become fewer and larger, a process called densification. As densification proceeds, the trabeculae, seen in X-ray view, form a series of distinct patterns. With advanced age, the trabeculae have become very few, reducing the weight-bearing capacity of the femur and contributing to that common malady of old age, hip fractures. To estimate age by this method, the forensic anthropologist compares the X rays of the femur or clavicle from his or her current case with photographic templates.

In working with Kennewick Man, I arrived at two age estimates. I determined the first in collaboration with Katie MacMillan when I took the skeleton to her for a second opinion two days after its discovery. It was this estimate that I reported to the press in late August 1996. Using photographic templates of pubic symphysis aging and observing the fully obliterated sutures in the skull, we arrived at an estimated age of forty to fifty-five years. Since then, I have rechecked the evidence, largely following a suggestion made by Doug Owsley during our inventory of the skeleton in fall 1998. He felt that the skelton was giving mixed signals about its age but that the bones didn't have the overall appearance of someone in late middle age.

With his concerns in mind, I rechecked the pubic symphysis during that inventory, reviewed my photographs of the right sacroiliac joint and the end of the fourth rib, and compared an X-ray scan of the femur, taken as part of the CT scan process, with published templates. The results corroborated Doug's suspicions, although they were ambiguous and overlapped my original estimate.

The closure of Kennewick Man's cranial sutures placed him between thirty-nine and sixty-five years. The pubic symphysis exhibited changes consistent with a man between twenty-four and forty-seven years of age. The sacroiliac joint showed an age of thirty-five to thirty-nine years; and the fourth rib indicated thirty-four to forty-six years. The trabecular changes in the femur, which were the least reliable in this case because the X ray was not taken specifically for this purpose, gave an estimate of forty to forty-four years. The results from every method overlapped in the thirty-five to forty-five-year range, but I see forty to forty-five years as the best estimate of Kennewick Man's age. Interestingly, Joe Powell and Jerome Rose, in their three-day, government-funded examination of the skeleton, concluded forty-five to fifty-five years from just the characteristics of the pelvis, although Joe confided to me that he felt the man was closer to forty-five. So let's just say he was probably in his forties.

❋

Estimating living stature from dry bones is an exercise that depends on the fact that the skeleton is the body's superstructure and as the bones grow, height increases. The mathematical relationship between height and the lengths of the bones that contribute to height—especially the long bones of the legs—is, therefore, a linear one. That is, as a long bone—let's say the femur, although any long bone will do—lengthens, stature increases proportionately. Thus, knowing the length of the femur alone, one can estimate the height of the living person.

The stature formulas most used by physical anthropologists were developed in the 1950s by Washington University anatomist Dr. Mildred Trotter. Trotter worked with the remains of World War II and Korean War casualties at the U.S. Armed Forces Human Identification Lab in Tokyo, measuring the limb bones from exhumed bodies and comparing them with the men's living heights taken from their military records. Because of the racial diversity of the military, particularly during the Korean War, she was able to devise separate formulas for whites, African Americans, Mongoloids (which included Asians and American Indians), and Mexican Americans. I tried to apply Trotter's formulas but immediately faced a problem. Kennewick Man lived before Trotter's racial groups diverged. Which equation should I use? The question was solved one day when I was talking with Christopher Ruff, a paleoanthropologist with the medical school at Johns Hopkins University. Why didn't I, he suggested, use the crural index, a ratio of tibia length to femur length, to decide which equation was the most appropriate? The crural index varies with latitude. People living in Arctic and north temperate zones tend to have relatively short tibiae (in fact, short limbs in general relative to their trunks) to help them retain body heat, whereas tropical people, who need to expel heat, have evolved relatively long tibiae (and long limbs relative to their trunks).

Kennewick Man had a crural index of 86, which is a tropical value closest to those of African Americans, Melanesians, Egyptians, Pygmies, and Arizona Native Americans among the peoples for whom crural indices are available. Because of geographical proximity and the great genetic distances between Africans and all other world populations, the best available equation was for Central American Indians. Using a femur length of 18.5 inches (470 mm), I averaged Trotter's equation and that of another stature researcher, S. C. Genoves, and came up with a height range between 5 feet, 7 inches and 5 feet, 10 inches (170 to 178 cm). For an early hunter-gatherer, he was tall.

To estimate body weight, I used equations worked out by Chris Ruff and his coworkers, who sought to devise formulas that were universal enough that they could be applied to earlier members of the genus *Homo* and even its Australopithecene forebears. The method I was able to use on Kennewick Man calculates weight from the diameter of the head of the femur (the ball joint of the hip). Using a femoral head diameter of 1.9 inches (49 mm), I obtained an average estimated weight of about 159 pounds (72.2 kg).

So Kennewick Man was approximately 5 feet 8 inches and 159 pounds (173 cm and 72.2 kg). I wondered what sort of a body build this would represent, so I asked my neighbor Kent Richert, a mathematician, if he would help me calculate a statistical relationship between height and body mass. Dividing height by the cube root of the weight (volume and therefore weight varies with the cube of linear measurement), he obtained an index of 0.0240. To get a sense of what this meant in terms of body build, I had him compute my own index. I stand five feet, 6 inches tall (168 cm) and weigh 145 pounds (65.8 kg), which gives exactly the same index. Kennewick Man was a man of medium build.

✸

In general, Kennewick Man's bones and teeth testify to good health, at least during his formative years. Two indications of this were his relatively great height (for his time) and strong bones, even for a man who was probably in his early to mid-forties. The matrix of his bones and teeth bore further testimony to a generally healthy, well-fed youth. As bones and teeth grow, their development can be temporarily interrupted or slowed by ill health and poor diet, both of which retard the flow of nutrients to growing hard tissues. In the teeth these interruptions show up as narrow horizontal grooves across the enamel called hypoplasias. Because tooth development is closely correlated with a child's age, it is possible to measure a hypoplasia's position on the tooth crown and use this to estimate the age at which a nutritional insult occurred. In the limb bones, these interruptions show up on X rays as zones of increased bone density, called Harris lines, that run perpendicular to the bone's long axis. They mark times when growth of the bone shaft (diaphysis), developing independent of the joint end (epiphysis), was temporarily slowed or halted. In a way, they resemble the rings of a tree. Periods of fast growth appear dark, those of slow growth appear light.

I could see no Harris lines in the X rays I had of Kennewick Man's femurs, but there were two small hypoplasias visible in the thin remnants of enamel on his teeth. One occurred in the lower canine and the other in the upper left second molar. Both were in positions that indicated growth interruption at about five to five and a half years of age. He may have gone hungry for a few weeks at this time in his life or suffered some minor infection. It is possible, too, that this interruption was caused by late weaning. Children go "off their food" briefly at weaning time, while their digestive system and tastes adapt to a fully adult diet and the absence of the rich milk from their mothers. Late weaning is a common characteristic of hunter-gatherers, who move their residences every few weeks or months. Because a mother cannot easily carry more than one young child, hunter-gatherers keep their birth spacing low by nursing children for prolonged periods.

❈

One clue as to why Kennewick Man was so well fed came from the carbon isotope composition of his bones, which Donna Kirner at the University of California, Riverside, had determined for us as part of the original carbon dating process. The ratio of carbon 12 to carbon 13 varies according to a person's diet, and is expressed as a difference from average carbon isotope ratios found in seawater. People whose dietary protein comes almost exclusively from marine sources—fish, shellfish, sea mammals—such as the prehistoric occupants of the Pacific Coast or the Mesolithic hunter-gatherers of Denmark, have carbon 13 values around −12 per mil (parts per thousand). Those with fully terrestrial diets, such as Plains bison hunters, for example, have values around –22 or –23. In Kennewick Man's case, the ratio was –14.9, which meant that marine foods accounted for about 66 percent of his protein intake. Since the Pacific Ocean lies more than 200 miles (320 km) away, he most probably obtained this marine protein from anadromous fish—fish that feed in the ocean and migrate up rivers to spawn—like salmon or steelhead trout.

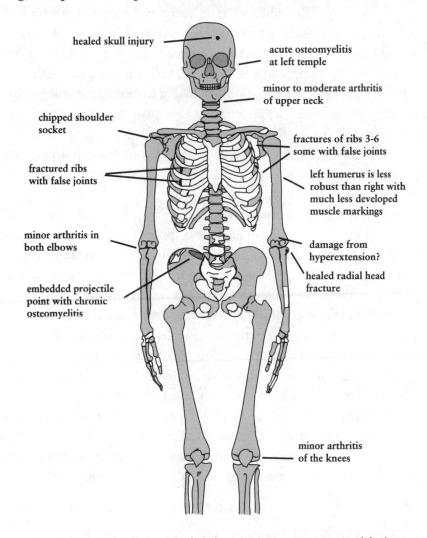

healed skull injury

acute osteomyelitis
at left temple

minor to moderate arthritis
of upper neck

chipped shoulder
socket

fractures of ribs 3-6
some with false joints

fractured ribs
with false joints

left humerus is less
robust than right with
much less developed
muscle markings

minor arthritis in
both elbows

damage from
hyperextension?

healed radial head
fracture

embedded projectile
point with chronic
osteomyelitis

minor arthritis
of the knees

Kennewick Man's bones (shaded) bear testimony to an active life that often led to injury and, eventually, to arthritis.

Although he may have been healthy early in life, Kennewick Man seems to have had a tough time in adolescence and adulthood. I have seen only one man with more injuries. That unfortunate, a modern forensic case, had been in a helicopter crash during the Vietnam War, a head-on collision between a motorcycle and semitruck after he recovered from the war injuries, and at least one later accident. Then he had been beaten to death by a neighbor.

As I looked over Kennewick Man's remains, I saw a man who had been damaged almost as badly. Starting from his head and working down, the defects were a small depression in the left forehead, damaged and healing bone in the left temple, arthritis in the upper neck, a chip off the socket of the shoulder blade, at least six broken ribs, injuries to the left elbow, and finally the most unusual injury, the spear point in his hip. What manner of accidents had befallen this man in antiquity? To interpret these injuries, one must journey into the most esoteric branch of physical anthropology, the discipline known as paleopathology.

A paleopathologist must interpret past injuries and diseases with fewer tools than doctors have at their disposal. Whereas a physician can use soft-tissue conditions and a wide range of biomedical tests—not to mention a patient's own testimony—to make a diagnosis, a paleopathologist works solely from modifications to bones and teeth. These modifications generally take two forms: bone loss and abnormal bone addition. A paleopathologist looks at the shapes, locations, number, and distributions of these bone changes, called lesions, taking into account the age and sex of the individual. The shape and pattern of defects in a skeleton are then compared with a catalogue of possibile medical conditions for the closest match or, more often, a set of possible alternative diagnoses. The process is highly subjective, leading to frequent differences of diagnosis and adding a strong personal component to the paleopathologist's pronouncements.

❖

The dent in Kennewick Man's forehead was a .24-inch (6-mm) diameter pit located .87 inch (22 mm) left of the midline and 1.6 inches

(40 mm) from the upper rim of the eye socket, near what was probably his hairline. The floor of the shallow depression was hard cortical bone, and it was surrounded on the skull surface by a narrow, irregular band. This irregular surface is evidence that there was a minor secondary infection in the scalp around the wound, but the hard cortical bone in the depression indicates that the injury was well healed and probably occurred many months to many years before death. This injury can be interpreted as a depressed skull fracture, but a very minor one. The bone of our braincase is designed to collapse, much like the bumpers of modern cars. It consists of a layer of spongy trabecular bone sandwiched between thin layers of hard, dense cortical bone. When the outer surface of the bone, known as the outer table, is struck, it can break inward, the shock being taken up by collapsing trabecular bone and thereby preventing fracture of the inner table. If the inner table is broken, its sharp edges may tear some of the many blood vessels that line the inner surface of the skull, leading to internal bleeding. This can put pressure on the brain and lead to unconsciousness or even death. The blow to Kennewick Man was absorbed effectively and, aside from giving him a temporary headache and minor scalp infection, probably troubled him little. How he received this blow, I cannot say with any certainty. Located as it is on the left side of his forehead, it could have been inflicted by a right-handed assailant. I have seen many such injuries in prehistoric collections. One 2,500-year-old population from the Columbia River, about a hundred miles downstream from Kennewick, had so many head injuries clustered on the left front quarter of the scalp that it was obvious that club warfare, or club fighting at least, had been commonplace. Conflict, while perhaps the most likely explanation for the injury, is certainly not the only one. He might have run into a low-hanging limb while chasing prey or might have struck his head on a rockshelter roof and been knocked to the floor. My skull bears a similar ding from doing just that in the days before occupational health and safety regulations required workers on archaeological digs to wear hard hats.

The injuries to the left arm and elbow are somewhat enigmatic and difficult to explain without a brief anatomy lesson. The elbow is an articulation among three bones: the humerus, which is the upper arm bone, and the radius and ulna, the outer and inner bones, respectively, of the forearm. The head, or proximal, end of the radius is shaped like a disk and the upper end of the ulna like a hook. The concavity of the ulnar hook articulates with a broad spoollike structure in the humerus, on which it rotates. When the arm is extended, the end of this hook, called the olecranon process, rests in a concavity in the back side of the humerus, called the olecranon fossa. This lower end of the humerus is shaped like a Y with the spoollike articulation held between its limbs. On either limb of the Y is a knob that serves as an attachment for the forearm and wrist muscles. On your own elbow you can easily feel the inner knob, which is the attachment for the muscles that flex the wrist. The long cylindrical shaft of the humerus is marked by roughened attachment surfaces for the shoulder and arm muscles.

Kennewick Man had abnormalities in the head of the radius and the olecranon fossa of the humerus. In addition, the ridges produced on the bone by the muscles of the forearm and shoulder were much less developed on the man's left side than on his right. A chip had been broken from the head of the radius, and new bone had formed in its place. The olecranon fossa on the humerus was also abnormally roughened and disfigured by many large and small pores. Hard new bone had built up in this area, indicating that inflammation or impact had damaged it. The chipped radial head made immediate sense to me: the man had fallen on his outstretched hand and driven the radius into the humerus, breaking a small chip of bone from the joint end. But this did not seem to explain the damage in the humerus or the apparent weakness of the left arm. For advice on diagnosis and as a check on other injuries to the skeleton, I turned to Dr. Christopher Kontogianis, an orthopedic surgeon I had been seeing lately for the increasing aches and pains that come with age. Trained at the New York University Medical School and with a residency at nearby Bellevue Hospital, he had a long-standing interest in sports-related injury. He also had a fascination with physical anthropology, which he had studied in a number of courses. I invited him over to my lab for lunch one Friday to give me a medical perspective on the pathologies in the Kennewick bones. We pored over the photographs and X rays. We began with a look at the elbow injury, which I hoped his expertise would help me interpret.

He observed that the radial head fracture would have limited the mobility of the elbow, particularly rotation and extension of the forearm. Nowadays, he told me, when people get such injuries, there is always some loss of the ability to extend the arm, which limits its range of motion. Usually with range-of-motion treatment, which entails using the arm as it heals, the loss can be kept down to 5 to 10 percent. Kennewick Man probably had to keep using the injured arm, so he was giving himself range-of-motion therapy. It is therefore unlikely that he experienced much loss of motion.

Dr. Kontogianis suggested that the damage to the olecranon fossa might have been caused by hyperextension of the elbow, possibly at the same time as the radius was broken. He suggested that it was also possible that the bone chip from the radius had moved around in the joint capsule, causing inflammation and remodeling of the bone.

The injury, however, seemed to have been more serious than a simple fracture and hyperextension. He noted that the medial epicondyle (the inner knob I mentioned earlier), which is the attachment point for all the muscles that flex the wrist, was much smaller on the left arm than on the right. That and the fact that the muscles in the left shoulder were so poorly developed suggested to him that the man had sustained the injury early in life. It is possible that pain in the elbow prevented him from using the arm, so the muscles there were poorly developed. Because the bones were the same length, though, the damage had to have occurred after the arm had reached its full length, or at about the age of fifteen.

This suggestion was corroborated independently by Jane Buikstra, a professor of physical anthropology at the University of New Mexico and one of the country's leading paleopathologists. Looking at the same photographs, which I showed her during a visit to her department in early 1999, she noticed a thin crack extending across the neck of the radius, just below the disklike head. The damage extended from the base of the healed chip and followed the contact between the epiphysis and diaphysis, indicating to her that the injury had taken place when the two growth centers had not yet fully fused, or in the middle teens.

I asked Dr. K. if the differences between the right and left arms could be due simply to handedness or to the extensive use of the atlatl, a stick used to propel spears. This was really playing to his strength, since differential use of one arm is common in many sports.

"No," he emphasized, "that's way too much difference to be behavioral. And too much for that radial head fracture. You have far more development of the forearm and shoulder on the right. That left arm was pretty weak. I wonder if there couldn't have been some additional damage to the arm, such as injury to the nerves that control the shoulder and arm. Didn't you say there were some broken ribs?"

There were in fact seven fractures in at least six ribs. When I had pieced them together on two occasions, I had been able, by reconstructing some ribs completely and locating others by process of elimination, to determine that the broken bones were at least two of the fourth, fifth, or sixth on the right and the third and at least two of the fourth through sixth on the left. The breaks had occurred in all cases between 2 and 4 inches (5 to 10 cm) from their articulation with the sternum. I was unable to assign the remaining breaks to a side, but one of them also came from the same area of the rib cage. The third rib, another break on the left side, and one unassigned fracture had healed together completely, but the two right ribs and one or two on the left side had not. They were healed, as indicated by hard cortical bone on what had been the fractured ends, but the separated segments had not rejoined, their broken ends instead tapering to smooth edges. Such unjoined but healed fractures are called pseudoarthroses, or false joints. Dr. K. looked at the rib photos, front and back.

"What an impact!" He shook his head. "That pattern of breaks is what we call a flail chest. We usually see that now when someone has been in a head-on collision and their chest has been driven into the steering wheel."

In a flail chest injury, multiple adjacent ribs are broken in two places each or near the sternum, where there is only flexible cartilage on the unbroken end. When the person tries to breathe in, the vacuum created by the diaphragm sucks the broken segment inward, because it is not attached to the rest of the chest wall. When he exhales, the pressure of the expelled breath pushes the broken segment outward. This constant flexing is what kept the ribs from healing together.

Flail chest, and particularly the break on either side of the sternum, called breastplate flail, are rare conditions in juveniles and youths. This is probably because the bones and cartilages are much more flexible in this stage of life, so it is unusual for ribs to break clean through as Kennewick Man's had. The condition is often fatal, owing in part to the fact that it reduces breathing efficiency and coughing effectiveness, thus lowering the oxygen saturation in the blood and allowing fluids to build up in the lungs. Once the condition healed, however, and Kennewick Man's body had adapted to the change in his breathing pattern, he was probably able to live normally. Judging from my own experience, however—I too have broken multiple ribs, including a complete break of a first rib—he would never have fully escaped the pain of the injury. The muscles between the ribs that are used in breathing, having been torn or severely bruised when the rib segments were displaced, would have developed scar tissue at the pseudoarthrosis, and deep breathing during exertion would pull against that damage. The result would have been a deep ache and sometimes sharp pain or a tearing or burning sensation.

We discussed what might have caused such a massive injury. A fall from a height or a kick from a large animal, such as a bison or elk, could have done it, we speculated. Both bison and elk are known to have lived in eastern Washington 9,500 years ago.

"I like the idea of a kick," Dr. K. concluded. "That could also have caused some damage to the nerves of his shoulder and diminished the use of that left arm."

We then turned to the most interesting of the injuries, the spear point in the right side of the pelvis. Again I brought out the photos, but this time there were the accompanying CT scans. The stone point could be clearly seen in both. At 2 inches (54 mm) long, .8 inch (2 mm) wide, and .25 inch (6 mm) thick, the large, sharp blade of volcanic stone was sandwiched between smooth cortical surfaces of the pelvis, just right of the sacroiliac joint. Windows in the bone opened to reveal the stone blade from the front and back, indicating that there had initially been a resorption of bone following the injury. Concentric bands of new, hard cortical bone could be seen on the front of the pelvis, where a large area of resorption was being filled back in. CT scans showed that a void remained between the stone and bone and that new, hard bone had walled off this void. At the upper edge of the window in the anterior surface, a broad channel marked the crest of the pelvis. To me it looked as if the bone had become infected when the foreign body—the spear point—had penetrated it. Judging from the extent of bone remodeling, the spear point had been in the bone for a long time before the man died, probably many years. Dr. K. concurred with my assessment and went on to enrich my understanding of the condition that had plagued Kennewick Man so long.

"This is a classic case of osteomyelitis," he announced. "What has happened is that this foreign body—the spear point—has entered the bone, bringing with it bacteria, probably *Staphylococcus aureus,* from the skin surface, causing an infection in the bone. The infection, and probably also the initial cut by the point, has shut off blood vessels that bring nutrition and oxygen to parts of the bone, causing the bone to die. The body had resorbed the dead bone—that's what caused the large void to develop there in the front surface—and was in the process of rebuilding with new bone.

"This guy was really hurting," he continued, flipping a CT scan cross-section onto the light table. "And you can see a little abscess pocket there, near the upper edge of the blade." He pointed to a small black circle walled by white areas of hard bone. "And there's another, near the outer bottom edge. A lot of dense bone has been laid down around the infection. His body is trying desperately to wall it off, but it could never succeed, not completely."

"One of the banes of orthopedics," he explained, "is getting rid of infected bone. To eradicate that infection, you'd have to clean out the wound, remove infected tissue, snip away the infected bone, and then use antibiotics to get rid of the infection. The usual regimen for osteomyelitis is three months of antibiotics, at least three to six weeks of which is intravenous. It's likely that nine thousand years ago it was a chronic draining wound."

"Draining how?" I asked. "You mean, draining pus from that void between the stone and bone?"

"Exactly. Chronic wounds, especially with a foreign body like that stone point, drain, heal over, fester, and then reerupt over and over again. See that channel there on the anterior surface above the window?" He pointed to the broad groove along the pelvic crest. "That's where it's draining off."

I recently spoke to a former rodeo rider who had suffered from osteomyelitis for many years. A bull had thrown him to the ground and gored him, leaving a small sliver of horn in the bone of his leg. For years, until he had the horn surgically removed, the wound had undergone a cycle of healing over, festering, erupting, and draining pus and blood down his leg.

"What he had," said Dr. K., "was chronic osteomyelitis that ate a big hole in his pelvis and was most likely draining out of the iliac crest area, about here." He grabbed my waist two inches from the right rim of my pelvis in that nonintrusive way doctors have. "What a mess."

I asked him if the condition would have been painful.

"With every step," he replied. "That wound is in the origin of the iliacus muscle [a massive muscle that works in opposition to the gluteus maximus; the gluteus extends the thigh, while the iliacus flexes it]. Every time he lifted his leg, with every stride, he was feeling pain from that old wound."

The angle of the spear point in the bone and the position of its rounded base, which was oriented slightly above the blade end and away from the body's midline, shows that the point entered from about 60 degrees to the right of front center and about 45 degrees above the horizontal, assuming the man was standing at the time. The position is such that he might have seen the spear coming at the last instant, twisting his torso to the left and arching his back in an effort to dodge the projectile. Another inch to the front and it would have severed major blood vessels, and he'd have bled to death in seconds. An inch to the rear, and it would have missed him entirely.

How he received the wound, we will never know. The two possibilities are accident and intent. He may have been struck by an errant spear while hunting, but unless the hunt entailed interaction with a large beast at very close quarters, it is unlikely such an incident could have occurred. Intent is more likely: someone tried to injure or even kill him. It could have been a member of an enemy group or an angry member of his own band. As we shall see later, early Americans suffered from many injuries, more than a few of them definitely or conceivably inflicted by their fellow men. (For this reason I speculated in the prologue that "Others'" had captured Kennewick Man's young wife and that he had nearly lost his life in his attempt to protect her.)

❈

The two remaining injuries were less exciting than blunt trauma to the chest and a spear wound, but they had the greatest likelihood of being related to Kennewick Man's death. I hurried to them, knowing that Dr. K. would have to be off soon. They were a damaged and healing area at the man's left temple and a chip off the right shoulder blade. I had a photo only of the head defect. The sharp image showed an area about .8 inch (2 cm) in diameter where the bone had an irregular appearance. The half of this lesion that was toward the front showed two star-shaped areas of porous new bone, what is called pericranial reactive bone because it is produced by the membrane, called the pericranium, that covers the skull. The posterior area lacked this new bone but showed exposed trabeculae beneath a flaky outer table. It looked to me like an area of infection.

"There are two kinds of osteomyelitis," Dr. K. told me as he began to explain the nature of this defect. "The spear wound was the chronic form; this is the acute form. Some soft-tissue infection has developed, something like strep throat, and the infection has clogged some of the small arteries to the bone, causing part of it to die. The new bone shows that healing was under way."

I checked the characteristics of this bone with clinical descriptions of osteomyelitis in the medical school library, and corroborated Dr. K.'s assessment of this head wound. Acute osteomyelitis of the skull includes the death of surface bone and formation of a flaky appearance, followed by healing when the blood supply is reestablished. The fact that the bone remained flaky in part of the lesion showed that the infection had still existed at the time of the man's death.

The damage to the right shoulder lacked any evidence of healing. A chip of bone .5 inch (12 mm) wide and .35 inch (9 mm) long had broken from the back rim of the shallow socket in the shoulder blade that articulates with the humerus. The color of the broken surface was the same as that of the unbroken bone, which meant that the damage had occurred at or around the time of death and not afterward.

Dr. K. suggested that this injury could have been caused by a shoulder dislocation of the kind caused when an individual falls forward on his elbow with the forearm flexed in front of the chest. The force of the fall drives the head of the humerus out of the socket, sometimes chipping the bone in the process. This is not the only possible explanation of the fracture, though. The bone might have been damaged after the man had died and his body stiffened. Forceful manipulation of the corpse, either by grieving relatives who were preparing him for the grave or by flowing water if floodwaters buried his body, might also have caused the fracture.

Dr. K.'s medical perspective helped me gain a sense of how the man had experienced his injuries, something paleopathologists don't address because it is thought of as overinterpretation. I see it, however, as humanizing the dead.

The remaining pathologies were simple. Kennewick Man had widespread but minor degenerative joint disease—arthritis—in his elbows, knees, lower back, and, most severely, his neck. The neck damage was greatest at the left occipital condyle, the articulation between the skull and the uppermost of the neck vertebrae, called the atlas. The left condyle had been pitted and polished by contact with the atlas because of degeneration of the joint cartilage. The polish was thus a result of bone-on-bone contact, which meant he may have heard a slight squeak when he nodded his head and probably experienced some minor pain. While the arthritic changes elsewhere in the skeleton were probably caused by normal wear and tear, the neck arthritis may have been a secondary effect of one or more of the man's major injuries. The blow to the head, the fall that broke the left arm, or the blow to the chest could have strained the neck, leading later in life to degeneration of the joints.

His teeth were healthy for a man of his age and time. There were no cavities, no severe abscesses, little tartar buildup, and only minor periodontal disease. They were heavily worn, but not inordinately so for an ancient hunter-gatherer, whose diet would have contained a lot of plant fiber and grit.

There is evidence, though, that his hearing was impaired. Both ear openings in the skull were almost completely blocked by benign bone tumors, which would have reduced his hearing by about 10 to 15 percent. This is not a severe hearing loss, but how these tumors develop is interesting and informative about the man's life. Gail Kennedy, a physical anthropologist at UCLA, has demonstrated that tumors of this kind are triggered by exposure to cold air or water. The tissues covering the bone in the posterior wall of our ear canals are very thin and provide almost no insulation against cold. Exposure to cold, especially cold water, which drains heat much more rapidly than does air, injures the pericranium in the auditory canal, causing it to respond by producing a profusion of new bone. Evidently, Kennewick Man spent quite a bit of time in cold water or experienced frigid winters with his ears unprotected. It is tempting to speculate that the infection in his pelvis, which probably caused fever at least while in its acute phase or phases, caused the man to immerse himself in the always cold water of the Columbia River as a palliative. At least as likely, though, was his probable lifestyle. The carbon isotope ratio of Kennewick Man's bone indicated that anadromous fish had accounted for about 66 percent of the protein in his diet. Fishing with nets or spears or constructing fish weirs in the river shallows would have exposed him to cold water on many occasions, leading to the development of his bone tumors.

✻

Although I have speculated in the prologue that Kennewick Man died by hypothermia and drowning while trying to bring down a fever, I cannot confidently say how he met his end. Cause of death is a question that a forensic anthropologist is usually unable to answer. We speak instead of manner of death (e.g., homicide, infection, blunt trauma) and are not always able to ascertain even this. There are at least three possible scenarios in this case that are indicated by the man's bones, with a fourth being illness or mishap, such as drowning, that left no physical trace. The three possibilities are septicemia (blood poisoning) from the chronic osteomyelitis in the pelvis, the infection that caused the acute osteomyelitis in the left temple, and the mishap that caused the shoulder dislocation. I am unable to say which, if any, of these was responsible.

Although the infection in the pelvis was well walled off from the body's other tissues with cortical bone and probably soft scar tissue, Kennewick Man was nonetheless at risk from it at all times. Medical texts state that during the years before antibiotics, a patient had about a 10 percent risk of contracting septicemia from such a chronic wound. Any tear in the scar wall could reinject bacteria into the bloodstream. It is this scenario that I have written into the prologue as fever following a fall on rocky ground.

The pathology that damaged the bone of the left temple is perhaps a better candidate, however. The skeletal manifestation of the disease, acute osteomyelitis, is often a symptom of nearby soft-tissue infection, perhaps a strep or staph infection in the nasal passages, pharynx, or sinuses. Such infections are serious and could easily have caused death in an older individual whose overall health had been compromised by many bodily insults. Most important, it was active at the time of death.

Also occurring at or around the time of death was the shoulder fracture. Certainly an injury of that sort could have been accompanied by soft-tissue damage and perhaps internal bleeding. It is possible, though, that this breakage occurred shortly after death. The lack of healing and the fact that the color of the break matches the color of the bone testifies to its occurrence at around the time of burial but does not allow us to assert that the injury occurred precisely at the time of death.

※

Such are some of the details of Kennewick Man's life and death. But what did he look like? By the spring of 1997, I had been asked this question countless times and had begun to search for someone or some group of people whom he closely resembled, so that I could provide the curious with a visual image. In looking at the skull, I could picture the face it had supported, but people without my background could not be expected to do the same. He had been a distinctive individual, with a long, narrow skull and a forehead that sloped gradually upward, reaching its highest point above the ear. His face, which was of moderate width, was strongly projecting, with high cheekbones, a prominent, high-bridged nose, a distinct, narrow chin, and a square jaw. After searching for weeks and no doubt annoying some people with my intense stares, I was getting nowhere. One person would have the right nose, another the right jawline or forehead, but no one put the pieces all together. Then one evening I was taking a break, watching a rerun of *Star Trek: The Next Generation*, and there was Patrick Stewart, who plays Captain Jean-Luc Picard. The resemblance was striking, although Stewart has a slightly wider forehead, broader chin, narrower jaw, and smaller nose. When asked about Kennewick Man's appearance by *New Yorker* writer Douglas Preston, I used Stewart as an image of Kennewick Man—as someone with a similar-shaped head and face.

This widely reported comparison elicited an unanticipated reaction. Other media took this statement to mean that I saw Kennewick Man as a European—a white man. But skulls of course have no skin color. I did not say Kennewick Man looked like a European, but rather that there was a modern European who looked like *him*. I was looking not at skin color but at the face produced by the man's bones. I wanted to do something to let the skull tell its own story.

The answer, I felt, was to devise a reconstruction or, more correctly, an approximation of the man's face using a cast of his skull as a guide. My sculptor friend Tom McClelland and I had talked about collaborating on such a project ever since the night Floyd Johnson had come for the skeleton, and the need to replace the Stewart comparison with something more accurate was now a further motivation. We did not get around to the daunting task, though, until spurred by documentary maker Ted Timerick of New York, who asked to film the entire process. In November 1997, we set to work, resolved to re-create the face by the most scientifically defensible method possible.

Facial approximation is always a combination of science and art. It is usually done by a sculptor with extensive training in anatomy, such as John Gurche of the Denver Museum of Natural History, or by a team consisting of a forensic anthropologist, who has the extensive anatomy background and ability to read clues from the bones, and a skilled sculptor. In our case, I had the anatomy skills and some sculpting ability; Tom would be the artist. But neither of us had ever attempted this before.

After reading everything available on the subject and viewing videotapes that illustrated facial-approximation artists at work, we decided to use a method named after the late Russian anatomist Mikhail Gerasimov. This method builds the face by first laying down muscles, then covering them with "skin," and thus results in a very lifelike face with relatively little subjective input from the artist. We wanted to avoid subjectivity as much as possible, given the level of scrutiny the Kennewick case was receiving.

We began our approximation of Kennewick Man by producing a complete plastic cast from the molds I had made of his skull. Along with this we laid out modeling clay, sculptors' wax, sculpting tools, uncut rods of rubber eraser material, anatomy books with photographs of skinned cadaver faces, photographs of bones with the muscle attachments clearly marked, and photographs of Ainu men.

The Ainu photos need some explaining. A facial approximation can be kept objective by following a strict set of protocols that allow the outcome dictated by the physical characteristics of the skull. The nose, for example, is approximately one and two-thirds times the width of the nasal opening in the skull; its forward projection is approximately three times the length of the bony projection below the nose added to the tissue thickness above the upper lip; and the corners of the mouth are at the lateral edges of the canine teeth. There are two points, though, where the decisions are entirely subjective: the form of the upper eyelid and the detailed characteristics of the lips. Because Loring Brace had observed that Kennewick Man had an Ainu appearance, we felt these people should be the ones to use as models for these two features. Besides, like most of the world's peoples, they had neither epicanthic folds, which give East Asians' and American Indians' eyes their distinctive look, nor Nordic folds, which are common in the eyes of northern Europeans. The Ainu seemed to exemplify, in their eyes and lips, the most common human form.

The final step, before the sculpting could begin, was to rebuild with wax any parts of the skull that were missing. I extended the bones of the nose to their apparent end point, built zygomatic arches—the bars of bone that extend from the cheekbone to the ear—and repaired the lower jaw.

With all in readiness, Tom and I said a little prayer: "Please don't let this man end up looking like Patrick Stewart!"

❁

To build a face by Gerasimov's method, I first studied the skull carefully, looking for asymmetries in the bone and scrutinizing the muscle markings. When muscles are used extensively, they cause buildup of bone at their points of attachment on the skull. Each muscle plays a different part in producing facial expression, so the pattern of more developed or less developed muscle attachments is evidence of the expressions an individual commonly used in life. As a people age, these expressions leave their mark in creases and wrinkles on the face, which give each person an individual identity. In Kennewick Man, two muscles in particular were well developed, one on the chin, called the mentalis, which pushes the lower lip up and out, and another on the cheekbone, called the levator labi superioris, which raises the upper lip. It appeared that the man had often held an expression of discomfort. As John Gurche remarked later when I showed him the skull cast, "This guy cried a lot."

I then built the nose and placed the eyeballs. The nose was huge because of the immense spine at its base; it seemed extreme, but we were following protocols and did not wish to deviate from them to create what we thought a "normal" nose should look like.

On the skull, we then placed sections of eraser at each of twenty-one bone landmarks. These erasers were cut to the average thickness of soft tissue, which was once measured in cadavers by anatomists and more recently measured in live subjects using modern medical imaging techniques. These thicknesses vary by sex, ancestry, and the physical health of the individual. At the time of our work, thicknesses had been published for Europeans (or whites), African Americans, and Japanese; there were no data for American Indians. Since our man was of unknown heritage, we chose not to pigeonhole him by using data from a single group. Assuming he had descended from some Eurasian stock (i.e., from the landmass now called Europe and Asia), we averaged the Japanese and European measurements for males. In reality there was little difference at most points; only at the cheekbone, the tip of the chin, and the corner of the jaw did our average diverge from either original group by more than 2 millimeters.

Tissue markers in place, we began to lay down the muscles. As I was the team anatomist, this task fell largely to me, and I spent nearly twelve hours painstakingly building and positioning seventeen muscles on each side of the face, from the oval sphincters that surround the mouth and eyes and the massive muscles that close the jaws to the delicate muscles that manipulate the corners of the mouth and wrinkle the brow and nose. Once these were in place, the face had already taken on a human look, albeit a macabre one.

By the end of the second day, we had reached the moment of truth, ready to put flesh over the muscle and let the face emerge. My neighbors, who had been following the Kennewick story from the start, joined us, creating along with Ted Timerick and my wife, Jenny, a gallery of sorts. We rolled out even thicknesses of clay and began to lay them on the face, making the surface even with the tissue thickness markers but being careful not to mask the topography created by the muscles. It was very much like laying a rug on a bare floor and had a similar transforming effect. Tom and I labored together. Both having reached the stage where we need reading glasses but didn't want to admit it, we had our glasses off and were so close to the face that we could see only a small portion at a time. We had just finished getting the face covered and were about to begin work on the eyes and mouth when my neighbor Kent piped up, "Why, it's Jean-Luc Picard!"

Once the clay skin was in place, we moved to the details, I shaping the eye, and Tom the mouth. Then, to alleviate the alien look of the face, I gave the man ears, using Tom as a model. After some refinement, Kennewick Man took on the distinctly human look of a smooth-faced young man. We had completed our "technically correct" model, and now it was the artist's turn.

Over the next several months, Tom worked to age the face, first poring over photographs of people from around the world to see how they aged, then sitting at a mall and studying the faces of people passing by. He wanted to get the patterns of wrinkling and drooping just right for a person with Kennewick Man's facial structure and expressions. He found especially useful a movie that featured Clint Eastwood and Ed Harris. Yes, they are white, but they have the same narrow chins, square jaws, and hollow cheeks as Kennewick Man, and their aging faces showed us how such faces wrinkle—deeply in one or two lines behind the corner of the mouth.

To this knowledge, we added the evidence from Kennewick Man's injuries and facial muscles. A scar now marks the skin over his head wound, and his face shows the weariness of a middle-aged man in chronic discomfort. We gave him no hair or beard and kept the eyes the color of the olive green clay and the skin the gray of fine plastilina. To choose a hair form or skin color would have been to arbitrarily assign him to some "race," which was exactly what we had been so careful to avoid. If we had given the eyes a color, it would have been brown, in keeping with our vow to base all subjective decisions on the human norm. His skin would be light brown as well, which was probably the skin color of our first fully human ancestors.

Everyone seems to see something different in our approximation. Besides the inevitable but overreaching comparisons to *Star Trek*'s captain (another bald man with a big nose), many people saw a likeness to folks they knew. One of my assistants saw her French grandfather, another his rancher uncle. Native American activist Vine Deloria saw Sauk chief Black Hawk, and the Umatillas saw Chief Peo Peo Mox Mox of the Walla Wallas. In fact, Kennewick Man resembles a lot of people and none, because he comes from a time before the modern geographic groups by which we so tenaciously try to categorize ourselves had come into being.

So who was Kennewick Man? He was a relatively tall fellow of medium build with a big nose and, for his time, a fairly advanced age. He had a stiff neck that squeaked and a left arm perhaps weakened by an injury suffered in his youth. As he breathed, some of his ribs were sucked in and pushed out, and any exertion that caused him to inhale deeply caused a dull, tearing pain around the old scars. It hurt to lift his right leg, and an old spear wound would ache from time to time. He oozed pus and fluids from an opening near his waist, which to top it all off, probably made him smell bad. His was a hard life indeed.

But he did not live it alone. He was surely a member of a social group that loved him dearly. How but by their care could he have survived two near-fatal wounds? While he convalesced, his people medicated, fed, and protected him.

7

A Place in Time

KENNEWICK MAN LIVED—or at least died—in a part of eastern Washington State known as the Columbia Basin. Although Washington calls itself the "Evergreen State," the Columbia Basin is anything but green. With only six inches of rain a year to moisten its sand dunes and water its pastures, it is one of the driest places on the continent, kept that way by the high Cascade Range that lies between it and the moisture of the Pacific Ocean. Yet through it, incongruously, flows the Columbia, the largest river in western North America south of the Yukon. As one might expect, this water was the source of most life in this parched land. Walking away from the river in any direction one saw, before irrigation, only olive green sagebrush and dried white-yellow bunchgrasses, punctuated here and there by the white crescents of sand dunes. Dune fields stretch north and east, blending into hills of fine windblown silt, called loess, which merge into the wooded foothills of the Rocky Mountains. West and south are low, treeless ridges, and far in the distance are the forested volcanos of the Cascade Range.

The first evidence of human beings in this region dates to the end of the last glacial epoch, between 13,000 and 14,000 years ago. During this time, a dry tundra of grasses, sedges, and cold-adapted sagebrush grew throughout eastern Washington and down the Cascade and Rocky Mountain chains. Mammoths, giant bison, camels, ground sloths, horses, and caribou had all lived here, and by the time people first appeared, the mammoth and bison, at least, remained along with other large animals, such as elk, deer, and bighorn sheep that still exist. Icy rivers created broad outwash channels where the Columbia is now.

People of two cultures occupied the region at this early time, but very few sites bear witness to their presence. One culture was the Clovis, which dominated America from about 13,400 to 12,800 years ago. Long identified, perhaps incorrectly, as a big-game-hunting culture especially fond of mammoths, Clovis is distinguished by fluted spear points and a technology not unlike that of the Upper Paleolithic cultures of Europe and northern Asia. A spectacular cache of immense Clovis spear points and knives was discovered in 1991 at the Ritchie-Roberts Site, about a hundred miles north of Kennewick, but no homes of these enigmatic people have ever been uncovered in the western United States.

The earliest campsite in the region is at least as old as Clovis but represents a very different cultural pattern, one that Roy Carlson of Simon Fraser University has labeled the Intermountain Stemmed Point Tradition. Extending from southern British Columbia far into the Great Basin of Nevada and Utah and into the Central Valley of California, this culture includes spear points with long, tapering stems, bola stones, enigmatic stone crescents, tiny, eyed needles, and an assortment of composite fishing implements, probably including nets. The Stemmed Point Tradition is typically associated not with big game but with rivers, lakes, and inland streams—that is, with fishing.

The early part of the postglacial, or Holocene, epoch (which includes the last 11,500 years) was a time of warmer summers and colder winters than we experience in the Columbia Basin today. Around 11,000 years ago, the glacial tundra gave way to a rich grassland. Finally free of the torrent of ice melt, the rivers stabilized, but because they were draining from glacially denuded hills the rivers were silt-choked and created broad floodplains of fine soil in the now-obsolete meltwater channels. By at least 9,500 years ago, salmon had begun to recolonize formerly ice-covered watersheds. Bison and oversized elk still roamed the grasslands of the Columbia Basin, but mammoths had become extinct.

Three cultural—or more properly, technological—traditions are distinguishable in the Pacific Northwest at this time. East of the Cascade Mountains, in the area that includes the Columbia Basin, the Stemmed Point Tradition persisted. The meager archaeological record of this time shows that people lived by a well-developed seasonal round of gathering food at the best locations. There are fishing stations at falls, hunting camps in the interior basin, where bison and elk were hunted in the spring, and winter camps in the river canyons. The technology and pattern of annual movements both show a high degree of planning for the food quest, similar in some ways to that of the later Eskimo peoples of the Arctic.

Along the southern coast of British Columbia we see the progressive spread of a technology known as the Pebble Tool or Old Cordilleran Tradition. The tools of this technology are much more limited and less formalized than those of the Stemmed Point Tradition, consisting largely of leaf-shaped knives and spear points, heavy cutting tools made from river cobbles, and smaller tools made from chips struck off those cobbles. The tiny needles and complex composite implements—bolas, fishing gear—of the Stemmed Point Tradition are rare or lacking. In all likelihood, this technology was equally complex but relied more heavily on implements made from hide, fiber, and wood, materials that decompose rapidly in most environments. Thus, the Pebble Tool Tradition left much less of a tool kit behind for future archaeologists to ponder. Simon Fraser's Carlson believes this tradition was adapted to coastal resources, especially salmon. If we rely on radiocarbon-dated sites alone, the Pebble Tool Tradition first appeared around 10,700 years ago on the mainland opposite the upper end of Canada's Vancouver Island. By 10,000 years ago, it occupied the lower Fraser River near the city of

Vancouver, B.C., and soon after spread southward down the coast, reaching the lower Columbia River by 9,000 years ago.

Farther north, beginning around Prince of Wales Island and the Queen Charlottes, people used a technology that placed a heavy emphasis on microblades—thin, narrow, razor-blade-like flakes of stone set in rows to make a cutting edge. But otherwise their culture resembled that of the Pebble Tool Tradition. This technology extended into Alaska, where it is called Denali, and throughout eastern Siberia, where it is known as the Dyuktai. To some, myself included, the Pebble Tool Tradition appears to have developed from this technology, which it closely resembles.

Between 9,500 and 8,800 years ago, the Columbia Basin climate became progressively drier. Grassland was replaced by a sagebrush steppe in the northern and eastern parts of the basin, and the central basin near Kennewick became only sparsely vegetated. The rivers, which at this time drained only thinly forested mountains and arid plains, dropped and ceased flooding. Great fields of sand dunes formed, blowing onto the now-stable floodplains and out across the basin to the northeast. Lower stream flows and warmer water meant poor salmon productivity; the desiccated plains could no longer support bison, and elk became few. This aridity would persist for nearly 3,000 years, punctuated only by a brief moist interval around the time of the eruption 7,700 years ago of Mount Mazama, the volcano that now holds Crater Lake, Oregon.

By 8,800 years ago, the Pebble Tool Tradition had fully replaced the Stemmed Point Tradition in the Columbia Basin. Gone from archaeological assemblages are the stemmed spear points, bolas, fine needles, crescents, and grooved net sinkers, replaced by leaf-shaped points, a cobble tool-and-flake technology, and net weights made from unmodified, paired stones. Locally, this new tradition is known as the Cascade Phase of prehistory and the leaf-shaped spear tip is the Cascade Point. Sites of this period lie along the rivers nearly everywhere there are geologic deposits old enough to contain them. Each was occupied for no more than a few weeks or months, probably because the food supply was so sparse that it was readily depleted. Gone was the well-developed seasonal round. Throughout this and the preceding period, the human population remained small, and individual bands were probably under constant threat of extinction.

After 6,000 years ago, as the climate improved, human population rose. The climate became progressively cooler and more moist after 4000 B.C. and underwent a series of wide fluctuations at about 2,000-year intervals. The forests advanced, and salmon and big game again flourished. People settled in houses dug partway underground in the most favorable locations, from which they foraged for whatever the newly enriched landscape had to offer until its resources were depleted, then moved on. On the upper Columbia River, people settling into the pit houses may have been descendants of the Pebble Tool peoples, but archaeologists working on the smaller Snake River, at the southern edge of the Columbia Basin, see a cultural discontinuity. A short period of cold climate caused local populations to collapse around 3900 B.P., and when people again appeared, it was with a distinctly new culture. On the upper Columbia River, these new people probably moved south from Canada, where they had followed salmon runs up the Fraser River some 1,000 years before, and gave rise to the Salish-speaking groups of which the present-day Colville tribe is an example. The immigrants to the Snake River were probably from the Penutian language stock, which many linguists believe expanded out of the deserts of Nevada and eastern California and ultimately became the modern-day Yakamas, Umatillas, Nez Percés, and Wanapums. Life continued much like this until European contact, except for a long period of famine between 2,500 and 2,000 years ago, when the populations were again reduced drastically and a new cultural pattern emerged from the rubble.

Where does Kennewick Man fit into this regional sequence of environmental and cultural changes? To be sure, this question must be asked of every new archaeological find. But in this case the question takes on greater importance because Kennewick Man differed so markedly from the modern Indian peoples of the Columbia Basin.

His distinctiveness raises the real possibility that at least one of the cultural changes I described above entailed not only a change in how people behaved, as I had long believed, or what language they spoke, but also a change in who they were biologically. Because the discovery had such significant implications beyond its value as one of the most intact early skeletons ever found in North America, extra effort had to be taken to confirm Kennewick Man's age and place in cultural time. Three elements are important to this effort: the skeleton's geological source or context, any cultural context he might have had, and additional radiocarbon dates on the skeleton itself.

Ordinarily, archaeologists and paleontologists establish the geologic context of a skeleton by directly observing the strata that enclose the bones, and the cultural context by noting the artifacts lying among the bones, the physical attitude of the body in the soil, and any mortuary treatment of the body. Mortuary treatment may include such processes as cremation, dismembering, defleshing, or painting of the corpse or the cleaned bones.

In Kennewick Man's case, both geologic and cultural context were unusually difficult to establish because the skeleton had been completely eroded from its resting place. To further complicate the situation, there were apparently no artifacts with the body except for the spear point, which we can assume was not associated with his bones through any intent on his part or that of his loved ones. We could not observe the skeleton's placement and associations but had to determine indirectly where in the soils of Columbia Park he had formerly lain at rest.

There were four central questions: From what geological stratum had Kennewick Man eroded? Had he been interred there by his people or as the result of some natural process? What was the age of the deposits in which he had been buried or of the surface from which he had been interred? Was this age consistent with the radiocarbon date, and were both consistent with the age of the spear point found in his pelvis? All these questions can be approached in a rational, straightforward manner but proved decidedly difficult to answer for both technical and political reasons.

Technically, it was possible to compare the soil that was cemented to the skeleton with each stratum in the eroded riverbank beside the skeleton and thereby establish the origin of the bones. I had collected some of the soil from the bones when I had them in my possession, keeping not the soft soil but the cemented clumps of sand that fell away as the bones dried (the soft soil, after all, could have adhered to the bones as they lay in the reservoir muck and would have provided false information about the skeleton's source). I had also, in November 1996, made a drawing of the stratigraphic sequence at the site and had taken a series of samples from the locality. The place I chose for the stratigraphic study was a concave bank approximately 7 feet (2.1 m) directly inland from the place where the skull and larger bones had been found, probably the place from which the soil containing the bones had slumped into the reservoir.

The bank contained two distinct strata. The upper stratum consisted of windblown sand without any internal layering. The river had deposited the lower stratum, and it included many distinct water-laid (alluvial) layers of fine sand and silt. The skeleton had to have come from somewhere in one of those deposits. I sent the samples of soil from the bones and samples of the riverbank to Alan Busacca, an expert on the Pleistocene soils of the northwestern United States at Washington State University, whose task it was to determine precisely the size characteristics of each sample. To ensure that no bias entered the analysis, I designated each sample by only a letter until after the lab work was completed. The analyst thus did not know which of the samples came from the bones, and this made the result more reliable.

Busacca's staff analyzed the soil and found that the uppermost layer of the river-laid stratum was an excellent match for the soil from the bones and that the bone sample did not match the wind-deposited unit. I conveyed my findings to the Corps of Engineers but cautioned that this was a single analysis of one set of samples and needed to be replicated. That replication was attempted in 1999 by Gary Huckleberry and Julie Stein of the government's study team. Analyzing soil texture and chemical composition using a wide array of techniques, they too found that the skeleton appeared to come from the uppermost 20 inches (51 cm) of the alluvial unit.

Was the radiocarbon age of the bone corroborated by the geologic position of the skeleton? In 1997, we sought to answer this question and to gather additional information about the processes by which both the skeleton and the sediments surrounding it had been deposited. Tom Stafford, Rob Bonnichsen, Gary Huckleberry, and I requested an ARPA permit from the Corps of Engineers for detailed study of the site. Together we had more than 150 years' experience in archaeological geology and the prehistory of western North America. We sought to clean the naturally cut riverbank, describe and sample it, and excavate at least one trench perpendicular to the bank to understand the three-dimensional characteristics of each stratum. We would welcome tribal participation, of course.

Huckleberry requested the permit in August, but it was not until November that we received an answer. The Corps had sent the request to the five Indian tribes for comment, as ARPA regulations require, and received two responses. The Nez Percés wanted the permit denied because of what it labeled bias on the part of the investigators, although how we might be biased in a geologic study was not stated. The Umatillas responded with a permit request of their own, which read very much like ours. In true bureaucratic form, the Corps would not decide between the proposals or grant the first one received, as would have been normal, but decided instead to field its own geologic team from the Waterways Experiment Station in Virginia. Our team and the tribe would be allowed to participate in a limited way.

The resulting expedition went into the field the first week in December. The Corps team was led by Lillian Wakeley, who, gracious and capable as she was, had no experience in archaeological or historical geology. Her geologists not only had no previous experience with the high-energy rivers of the West but seemed remarkably out of date in their field methods. The two archaeologists, although competent in their own right and clearly desirous of doing good scientific work, had no prior knowledge of the region's prehistory or geology.

They came to the field with orders from General Ballard, national commander of the Corps, to answer only one question: Did Kennewick Man predate 1492 and therefore fall under the government's interpretation of the term "Native American"? The Umatilla tribe fielded a crew, but they simply did manual labor for the government team, conducting no studies of their own. To this assembly were added our research team and non-Indian observers for the Corps, the Justice Department, and each of the five tribes.

Our work was tightly constrained and constantly scrutinized by the Corps, various observers, and Umatilla tribal members, who kept a video camera trained on us much of the time. The Corps would not allow us to clean even a few millimeters of soil off the eroded riverbank to expose the geologic strata, a standard practice that would have contributed greatly to our understanding of how the skeleton had come to rest. We were not permitted to excavate our perpendicular trench, nor even to take one-inch-diameter soil cores from the intact floodplain as a poor substitute. All we could do was inspect ten 20-inch-wide (50-cm-wide) strips of the bank that the Corps team had chosen and cleaned off along 1,150 feet (350 m) of the Columbia Park shoreline. Only four of these strips were near the site of the skeleton find. The reason we were given for these constraints was that "the tribes consider this site sacred," apparently because Kennewick Man (which they were now calling "The Ancient One") had been found there.

Despite the limitations, we were able to describe the geology of the selected spots and take more than a hundred soil samples. The Corps took other samples, some of which were used by Huckleberry and Stein in their 1999 analysis. From this information, we were able to narrow down the geologic age of the floodplain by noting its relationship to other geologic deposits in the neighborhood and by radiocarbon-dating the sediment layers themselves .

There are at least five ancient natural terraces in the Kennewick vicinity. The highest two consist entirely of gravel capped by wind-blown sand and were left behind by catastrophic glacial floods. They are, therefore, older than the last of these floods, which occurred about 14,700 years ago. The second terrace down, which is formed of deposits laid down in a cut eroded into the first terrace, contains volcanic ash from the 13,100-year-old eruption of Glacier Peak, another Cascade Range volcano. Columbia Park is on the next lowest and therefore second-youngest terrace, where we found a layer of Mazama volcanic ash in the upper, windblown stratum, which means the river-laid layers beneath it are more than 7,700 years old. Therefore, the stratum that contained Kennewick Man *must* be older than 7,700 years and younger than the 13,100-year-old Glacier Peak ash of the second terrace.

This conclusion and my original radiocarbon date on Kennewick Man were corroborated in January 2000, when the Interior Department obtained a second date on the skeleton of 8,410±40 radiocarbon years. This calibrates to 9,500 actual years old, and is virtually identical with my original result.

The final geologic question had to do with whether Kennewick Man was buried by his family or by nature. I considered two hypotheses. If the skeleton had been buried intentionally, the excavators of the grave pit would certainly have intersected many soil layers, mixing them when they refilled the hole. Thus, if the body had been buried intentionally, the soil should not match any single stratum. If, on the other hand, natural processes—in this case limited to flood—had buried the body, the soil adhering to the bones would be expected to match only one layer: the one that had engulfed the body. Sediment analyses seemed to support the natural-burial hypothesis, since the bone soil linked closely with only one stratum in my analysis and at least the uppermost 20 inches (50 cm) of alluvium in Huckleberry and Stein's work. Twenty inches would be a very shallow grave.

There are certain characteristics of the skeleton that seem to contradict the natural-burial hypothesis, though. First, the bones were in an excellent state of preservation, which we would not expect if they had lain close to the surface, where chemical and physical weathering processes would have damaged them. Second, the skeleton showed no signs of scavenging by coyotes or other carnivores, which it might if it had lain on the surface for many days or months before being covered by flood sand. Physical anthropologists Jerome Rose and Joe Powell, who worked with Huckleberry and Stein on the government's study of Kennewick Man's bones, contend that these two facts show that the bones are from a grave. Powell and Rose also saw reddish coloration on some bones, which they interpreted as ocher, a pigment often seen in the graves of early modern humans throughout America and much of the world.

Completeness and lack of damage, however, indicate only rapid burial after death; they do not speak about the *agent* of burial. Also, the fact that the layer that matches dirt from the skeleton is thin in the portion of the bank we were allowed to analyze does not mean that it was uniformly thin elsewhere on the floodplain. When a flood passes over a vegetated landscape, it does not leave behind a thin, even layer of new soil. Anywhere the water is slowed, such as behind bushes or in shallow depressions created by rodents, badgers, or wallowing wildlife, more sediment is laid down. Kennewick Man may have been washed into just such a sediment trap and been covered by one or more feet of mud. Unfortunately, the Corps's restrictions prevented us from learning how variable in thickness the flood layers at the site had been.

Pollen that I obtained from the layer that matched the bone soil showed that sediment traps probably existed on the site. Grass was the most common of the pollen grains I was able to find, but there was also a large amount of sagebrush. The brush could have snagged a floating body, and its branches and the corpse could have trapped additional sediment. As for the presence of ocher, none of us who looked at the skeleton, except Rose and Powell, has seen any indication of red pigment, but if the red stains can someday be sampled, further analysis may prove the presence of ocher. Until then, we cannot be sure whether there is pigment or whether the red color came from a form of alga that is common in the Columbia River. The question of whether Kennewick Man was buried by his kin or by nature thus remains unresolved.

My colleagues and I had hoped that it might be possible, through further geologic studies at the site, to clarify the question of how Kennewick Man came to rest, but our efforts were again stymied, perhaps permanently. On December 23, 1997, four days after the limited joint geologic study ended, the Corps announced that it would soon award a contract to construct "bank protection features" at the Kennewick Man site. The Corps intended to drop earth and rocks on the shoreline by helicopter, cover them with sand, lay down coconut-fiber logs and coconut-fiber matting, cover them with sand, and plant trees. Its explanation was that it needed to prevent more bones from washing out and guard the site from looters. We were incredulous and immediately protested to the court, the media, and Congress. Rob Bonnichsen complained, "They haven't allowed us to give the site the kind of rigorous study it deserves, and now they're going to bury it."

The Corps's reason for the action was entirely specious. Kennewick Man had been completely washed out, and there was no evidence that any other skeletons existed at the site. I was particularly concerned that more parts of the skeleton might lie in the fine mud along the shore and would be crushed by the attempt to "protect" them. I had found an additional rib fragment on the first day of the geologic study, and more parts of hands, feet, and ribs were still missing. Some of them might help me confirm which ribs had been broken and therefore better interpret the nature of the man's injuries. The only thing the Corps was protecting the site from was us scientists.

Congress stepped in. Congressman Hastings and Senator Gorton first protested, doubting the need to act so soon and questioning the Corps's fiscal responsibility in spending money on this work when they claimed they lacked the $60,000 needed to complete a congressionally mandated transfer of Columbia Park to local ownership. The Corps continued with its plans, however, and by mid-March had awarded the construction contract to a firm from the Nez Percé Indian Reservation. The Washington State Historic Preservation Office and the National Advisory Council on Historic Preservation approved the action. Gorton and Hastings lost patience and inserted language in an emergency federal appropriations bill blocking the Corps from "any action to stabilize, cover, or permanently alter" the shoreline of the site unless a court ordered the action to protect the site's scientific value. The bill passed both houses of Congress, and on March 31, with earth and logs stockpiled at Columbia Park and the helicopter idling, the Corps announced it was backing down.

A few days later, Congress went into recess before Senate-House conferees worked out their differences on the bill. The Corps, acting on directions that, according to *The Philadelphia Inquirer,* came all the way from the White House, seized the opportunity and buried the site. I had walked the shoreline one last time a few days before construction began and found more bits of human bone, confirming my fears that more of Kennewick Man was there to be found and had certainly been destroyed.

❋

Although we were unable to complete a thorough geologic analysis of the site, we had been able to corroborate the skelton's age. But what about Kennewick Man's *cultural* context? This, as I said, was particularly problematic, since we had no evidence of his people's mortuary practices—even if he had been buried ceremonially—and there were no associated artifacts that could be thought of as the man's possessions. The spear point in the pelvis was a clue to someone's culture, but whose?

From the part of the point that can be seen through the bone windows, I could tell it was made from a gray igneous rock and had serrated edges and a narrow, nearly straight base. This was confirmed by the CT scans, which show a leaf-shaped implement with a slightly rounded base and broken blade. In comparison with other projectile point styles in the region, it is identifiable as a serrated form of the Cascade Point, which can be linked to Carlson's Pebble Tool Tradition.

Here's where the story gets interesting. My friend and sometime collaborator Virginia Butler of Portland State University has recently reinvestigated the Road Cut Site at The Dalles, Oregon, one of the

Will Thomas found the Kennewick skull near the point marked by the arrow. Most of the rest of the skeleton lay scattered in the soft mud between the arrow and the large tuft of grass at lower right.

Kennewick Man's bones lay scattered on the beach among chunks of naturally cemented soil. The fragment shown here is the lower segment of the right femur.

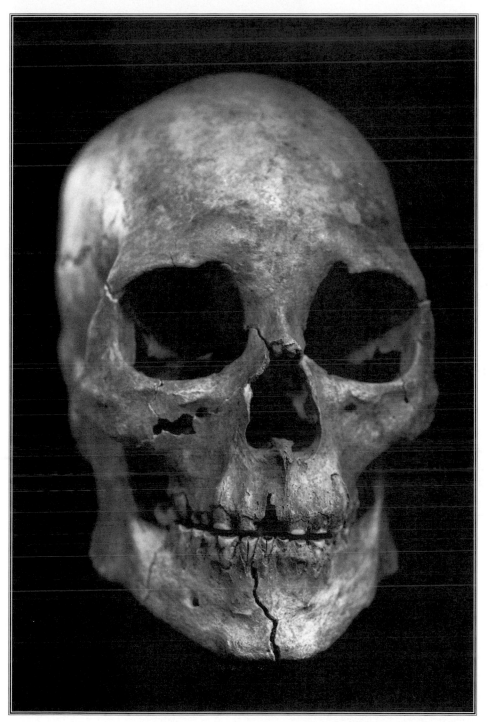

Frontal view of Kennewick Man's skull.

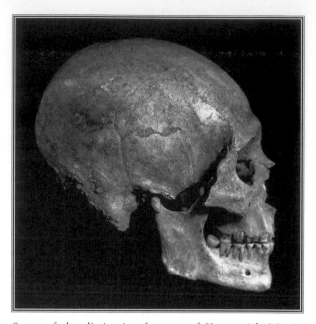

Some of the distinctive features of Kennewick Man's skull can be seen in this profile view, including the prominent chin, projecting nose, and placement of the face far forward of the braincase. It is also apparent from this perspective that the lower rim of the eye socket is slightly behind the upper and that the opening for the right ear is almost entirely enclosed by bone.

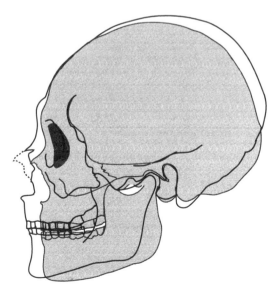

Profile outline of Kennewick Man's skull superimposed on the skull of a Northwest Indian (shaded), with both oriented in the standard Frankfurt horizontal and with the ear opening used as the point of reference. Among the major differences are the forward placement of the face in Kennewick Man, his high-bridged nose, and the more lightly constructed lower jaw with its prominent chin.

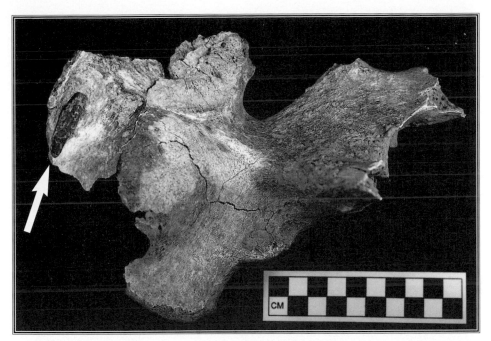

A stone spear point (indicated by arrow) was found embedded in Kennewick Man's pelvis. The angle of the arrow shows the direction of entry. Evidence that the skeleton was male can be seen in the deep, rounded notch at top center; in females this notch has a much wider angle.

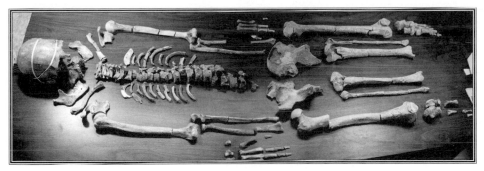

After weeks of returning to the beach at Columbia Park, the author had assembled the nearly complete skeleton of a relatively tall man. In addition to the bones shown in this composite photograph, there were more than 200 small fragments, mostly from ribs, vertebrae, and the pelvis. (Composite photo from original photgraphs by Floyd Johnson)

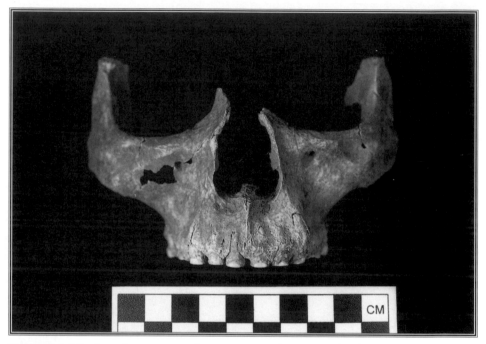

Kennewick Man's teeth were severely worn, as can be seen in this front view of his upper jaw. Only a thin strip of enamel remains on his incisors, which were worn nearly to the gum line.

This close-up of the spear wound shows the stone blade (a), a large crescent-shaped area of new bone that was built up after the initial infection (b), and the channel through which the isolated chronic infection drained (c).

A re-creation of Kennewick Man's face was produced by first gluing measured tissue-thickness pegs to a cast of the skull, and then by building up the overlying muscles. Once this was completed, a clay skin was laid over the muscle, as sculptor Tom McClelland is doing here on the left side of the face.

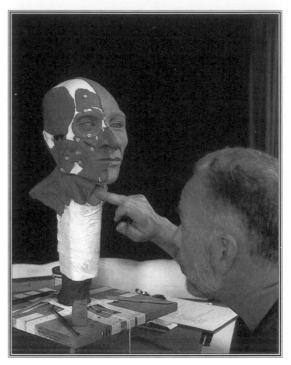

Archaeologists Rob Bonnichsen and Gary Huckleberry describe sediments at the Kennewick Man site during the brief geologic survey allowed by the Corps of Engineers. We were permitted to study only a few 2-foot-wide sections of the riverbank, which the Corps selected and marked with plastic tubing.

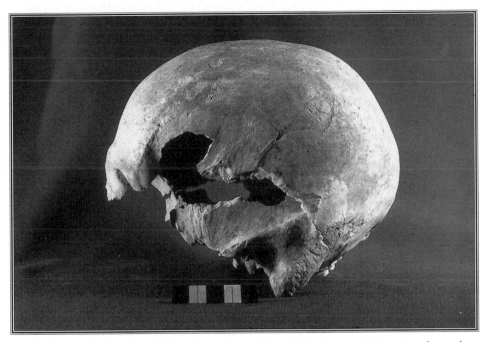

During an inventory of skeletal collections at Central Washington University, the author observed that this skull bore many resemblances to that of Kennewick Man. Nicknamed Stick Man, it proved to be nearly as old and also to differ markedly from modern Indian people.

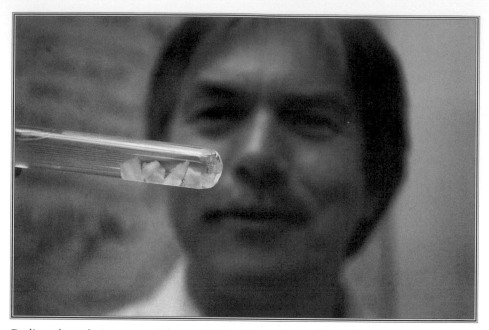

Radiocarbon dating expert Thomas Stafford examines collagen from Stick Man before preparing samples for dating. This small amount of material was enough for two radiocarbon age determinations and studies of carbon and nitrogen isotopes.

Physical anthropologist Richard Jantz measures an ancient skull using an electronic 3D digitizer. The measurements were used in our study of how Kennewick Man and Stick Man compared physically with modern peoples.

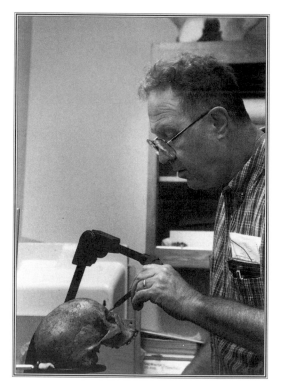

An Ainu man from Urap village, Hokkaido Island, Japan, photographed by Romyn Hitchcock. U.S. National Museum Annual Report for 1890, Plate LXXXV. (Courtesy of the National Anthropological Archives, Smithsonian Institution)

Because the skull of the 10,700-year-old Spirit Cave mummy was still covered with dry skin and hair, scientists used a CT scan to digitally produce this replica, which explains the gridlike pattern on its surface. The original mummy and skull models are in the Nevada State Museum.

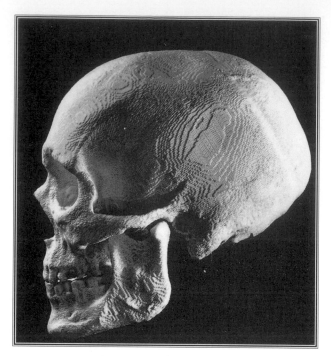

Deep beneath the floor of Horn Shelter, Texas, Frank Watt and Al Redder discovered the skeletons of a middle-aged man and a twelve-year-old girl, nestled together in a single grave. (Photo courtesy of Al Redder)

The author prepares the skull of the Horn Shelter male for casting. Casts make it possible for many people to study a specimen, but they can never be a complete substitute for the original bone.

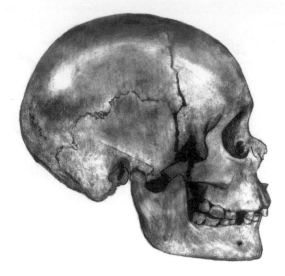

Buhla had a short face and a prominent nose. As with other Paleo-Americans, her face, the part of her skull containing upper jaw, cheekbones, and nose, is placed far forward, almost in front of her braincase. (Drawing by Jamie Claire Chatters)

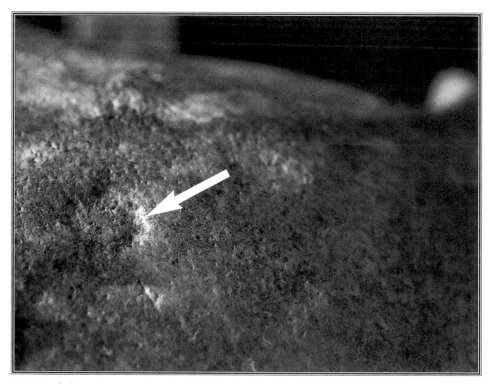

Many of the Paleo-American males had serious injuries that left traces on their bones. Shown here at left of center as a circular dimple (indicated by arrow) is a healed depressed fracture in Stick Man's skull.

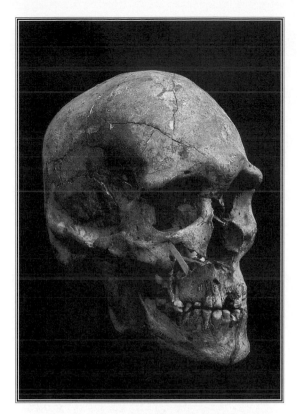

The middle-aged male from Horn Shelter has one of the most robust skulls of all Paleo-Americans, with a prominent brow and very distinct muscle markings on the jaw and face. His narrow skull and short, narrow, forward-positioned face exemplify the Paleo-American males.

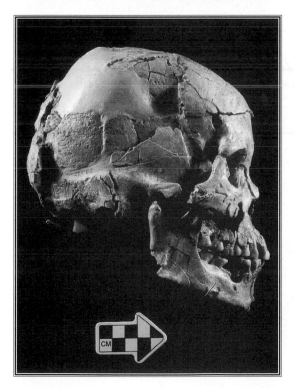

Paleo-American females were slight of build with narrow faces and marked prognathism (forward thrust of the tooth row). This skull is that of "Leanne," a twenty- to twenty-five-year-old female whose crushed 11,500–12,000-year-old skeleton was found at the Wilson-Leonard site, near Leander, Texas. (Photo by author, courtesy of the Texas Archaeological Research Laboratory, University of Texas, Austin, and the Texas Department of Transportation.)

Brazilian anthropologist Walter Neves, right, has found that the most ancient South Americans resemble Australian Aborigines and Africans more closely than modern American Indians or northeast Asians. Here he works with his student Max Blum, comparing a group of ancient skulls from the Lagoa Santa region with the cast of Kennewick Man.

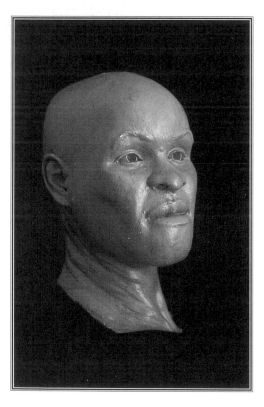

This bust of Luzia (Lapa Vermelha), created by Richard Neave of Manchester University, Great Britain, demonstrates how much ancient Brazilians resembled modern Australian Aborigines and Africans. (Photo courtesy of Mark Davis)

most ancient archaeological sites in the Pacific Northwest. In its deepest levels, the deposit contains bola stones, stemmed projectile points, and pieces of composite bone implements, and can thus be assigned to the Stemmed Point Tradition. Above these are a series of strata assignable to the Cascade Phase. Butler dates the beginning of the Cascade component at 9,000 years ago, a few centuries after Kennewick Man's death. The Cascade Phase was firmly established in the Columbia Basin shortly thereafter.

Given the coincidence of Kennewick Man's demise with the period of changeover between two cultural traditions, we are left with some rather important questions: Was the change in traditions accompanied by a population replacement, or were the local stemmed point makers acculturated by the newcomers? Which tradition did Kennewick Man belong to? Was the spear thrown by a member of his own ethnic group or by a member of another, competing group? Was the wound inflicted intentionally or by accident? With the information in hand, I can offer no answers, only a few thoughts.

Accidental wounding seems unlikely because of the angle of entry (from the right front) and the depth of the wound. Kennewick Man probably saw the spear coming and tried to dodge it, which indicates he was facing his assailant. The depth of penetration—more than 2 inches (51 mm)—indicates that the weapon came at a high velocity and was almost certainly propelled by an atlatl, or throwing stick. This seems to rule out a ricochet, since impact with another object before the spear struck the victim would have slowed its flight considerably.

If thrown intentionally, the spear could have been cast by a rival in Kennewick Man's own social group or in a ritual battle between bands of his own people. Some peoples in the New Guinea highlands, as documented in the anthropological film *Dead Birds*, settled disputes in this way. Two armies would stand facing each other at a distance and fling spears and arrows until someone was injured. Then the fighting would stop. The fact that Kennewick Man did not die from a wound that must certainly have brought him down and left him temporarily defenseless indicates either that his compatriots fought off the assailants or that his wounding effectively ended the squabble.

There are indications that the spear injury was not Kennewick Man's only battle wound. While the rib fractures are likely to have been caused by more force than another man could inflict, at least without martial arts training, the small skull fracture could have been inflicted by a right-handed foe. Multiple healed battle injuries, however, could also result from either interethnic warfare or ritual battle and might even lend greater support for the latter, since they would indicate that conflict was not a life-and-death issue.

It is tempting to take Kennewick Man's extreme dissimilarity from modern American Indians as an indication that he was a member of a population that became extinct or was genetically swamped by newcomers to the region. This could argue for his allegiance to the people who produced the Stemmed Point Tradition, or to one or another of the later cultures that have been supplanted in the Columbia Basin over the past 9,000 years. To know whether or not this is true, we would need the remains of many more individuals from before and after each cultural change. As Alan Goodman of Hampshire College wrote in an article criticizing me for using the word "Caucasoid" in reference to Kennewick Man, it is possible that this skeleton was merely an unusual individual in an otherwise ordinary American Indian population. We simply do not have other skeletons with which to compare him. Or do we?

8

Kennewick Man's "Brother"

IN JULY 1996, while waiting for Katie MacMillan to evaluate Kennewick Man, I had spent some time casually inspecting the laboratory shelves that surrounded her. Central Washington University was beginning a NAGPRA-required inventory of skeletal remains and sacred objects in its possession, and the shelves were lined with human skulls awaiting description. For the most part, these remains had come from the state of Washington and were well documented, but one counter held a diverse array of material. Staring from the enameled surface in tidy rows were modern forensic cases that had never been successfully identified, culturally deformed and red-stained skulls from Central America, the skull of a Roman soldier, and a braincase identified as having come from a cave in Australia. One specimen in particular drew my attention because of its remarkable similarity to Kennewick Man. It was a light tan, faceless skull of a large male with the same long, narrow, flat-sided braincase and the same constricted forehead. The face, had it been preserved, would, like Kennewick Man's, have been placed far forward, almost in front of the brain. The nose, though broken away, appeared to have been high-bridged and projecting. Looked at in frontal view, the brows of

163

the two skulls would have had almost identical patterns of notches and perforations. From behind, they both had two sets of muscle attachment lines placed high on the skull and unusually shaped. Except for this new skull's high, rounded forehead, the two skulls could have come from brothers. When Katie finished her inspection and confidently announced, "Caucasian male," I remarked offhandedly, waving in the general direction of this new skull, "Well, in that case, you have another one right over there on the counter."

❄

After the early radiocarbon date came in on Kennewick Man, CWU Anthropology Department head Steven Hackenberger and I began to wonder about this similar skull and began to study it in detail. All that remained was the braincase, but it was in near-perfect condition and provided a surprising amount of information. Completely obliterated sutures showed that the man had been between forty and sixty years old. At some point during his long life he had suffered a small skull fracture to the right side of his crown that had healed completely, leaving a circular depression about .3 inch (8 mm) in diameter. There was also a distinct smear of red ocher covering much of the left side of the head. The uneven distribution of pigment, combined with a deposit of natural cement inside the same side of the skull, indicated that the head had been lying on its left side in the grave. With the head in this position, water moving downward through the soil had flowed over the right half of the skull, washing away any ocher that might have been there but leaving it on the underside of the skull where the water could not reach. Carrying carbonate from rainwater and the overlying soil, the moisture had pooled in the lower side of the cranium, where it had slowly been drawn out by plant roots, leaving the carbonate behind.

Curious to know whether this man too was ancient, we scraped together the money to send a small sample of the skull to the University of California, Riverside, for dating. Our curiosity was rewarded when the age came back as 8020±50 B.P. To confirm this date, we had Thomas Stafford run a second pair of bone samples from the same portion of the skull and received affirmation of the skeleton's great age in dates of 8110±50 and 8140±50 B.P. Corrected to calendric ages, these results averaged just over 9,000 years. This man *was* from the same era as Kennewick Man. It thus appeared that we might have not one unusual-looking northwesterner in the early postglacial period, but two. And they were the only males of that age for which reasonably intact skulls existed.

There was just one problem, and it was a big one: we had no idea where the skull had come from. There was no number on the skull, no record of where or when it had been found, or who had donated the skull to the college. Given the sources of the skulls that were sitting with him on the counter, he could have been from anywhere in the world. Hackenberger queried the departmental faculty, with no luck. Even the retired professors had no recollection of how or when the cranium had come to be housed at CWU.

The lack of provenience was serious, because, great age or no, if we could not link the skull to a geographical location, this man would be a scientific nonentity. We could not even determine if NAGPRA applied, let alone whether the individual might be affiliated with some modern tribe. He even had no name other than the designation "DO1" assigned during the inventory process. After I reconstructed the partially broken cranium, he acquired the nickname "Toothpick Man" for the method I used to hold the fragments together. Hackenberger felt, however, that someone might find that label offensive, so we modified it to "Stick Man." If the man was truly from the same area as Kennewick Man, the name had special meaning. To the Wanapum band, the Stick People are mythical beings who inhabited the Columbia Basin before the Indians. The name probably refers to real predecessors, because it can also be translated as "Stick Shower People"—"shower" also meaning "to throw"— and may refer to the use of the atlatl to cast spears. (The atlatl was largely abandoned for the bow and arrow nearly 2,000 years ago, which is more than long enough in the past for its users to have acquired mythical status.)

Armed with a small grant from the university's foundation, we set out to locate Stick Man's place of origin—to provide him with that essential provenience. It seemed a quixotic endeavor from the outset; there was just so little to go on. In fact, the only evidence we had other than his similarity to Kennewick Man was about four table-spoons full of soil that coated the inner surface of the skull, held there by the calcium carbonate cement. We gently scraped this out, split it up, and sent small samples to various experts for analysis. It wasn't much to work with, but if the soil contained minerals or fossils specific enough to one geographic region, we might be able to confirm at least the general area from which the man had come. One sample went to Washington State University soil scientist Alan Busacca, who would measure particle sizes and identify the mode of deposition. Another went to geochemist Nick Foit at the same insti-tution, in the hope that he might find volcanic ash that could be iden-tified as having come from a specific volcanic eruption. We sent the remaining sample to Linda Scott Cummings, a paleobotanist in Golden, Colorado, who extracted pollen and opal phytoliths—the silica casts that form in the leaf and stem cells of many plant species. In addition, hoping that ancient DNA would be able to provide a hint about the continent of origin and, if that continent was North America, to add to the pitifully small database on the genetics of early North American peoples, we sent tiny samples of bone to the University of Michigan and University of California, Davis, for analysis.

✹

After many months of waiting, we finally began to receive the results late in 1998. Busacca identified the soil from the inside of the skull as fine, windblown material called loess, which blankets many regions of the world where large, sediment-laden, flood-prone rivers once flowed. Most of the great breadbaskets of the world—eastern Eu-rope, central China, and the Great Plains—boast deep, extensive beds of loess. So do parts of central Alaska and eastern Siberia. So does the Columbia Basin, where Missoula floods and glacial melt-water left fine soil exposed to the wind. The calcium carbonate in the skull ruled out some of these areas. It could be precipitated only in a semiarid-to-arid environment with soils that were chemically basic. This ruled out Alaska and Siberia, where bone rarely survives in postglacial soils, the better-watered parts of eastern Europe, the eastern Great Plains, and China but left the other areas as possibilities. *If* the loess was from the Columbia Basin, its size would be a further hint as to its location. The farther loess is carried from the source river, the smaller its particles become. In this case, the loess particles were the right size to have come from one of six subbasins centering on the Tri-Cities, an area of about 6,000 square miles.

Volcanic ash might have helped us narrow down the skull's source. If the ash could be identified as belonging to one of the volcanoes in the Cascade Range, we would at least be certain that the skull had come from the Northwest. Because some of those eruptions spewed ash over fairly limited areas, we might have been able to reduce our 6,000-square-mile area of loess to a more manageable size. Glacier Peak, for example, scattered ash over the northern parts of the loess zone, while the Pleistocene ash deposits from the Mount St. Helens eruption tended to be confined to the south. The presence of ash from Mount Mazama, although younger than the skull, would at least have narrowed the source to the Columbia Basin. Volcanic ash was no help, however, as Foit's first inspection of the soil revealed none.

Plant phytoliths tended to confirm what the loess indicated and to give one additional hint. As confirmation, they showed that grasses had been the dominant plants in the ecosystem where Stick Man had been buried and that the grasses had been subject to frequent periods of drought. This applies to most of the areas indicated by the loess data, particularly in the early postglacial period, but it does rule out river floodplains and some higher-elevation portions, where grasses would have been better watered. The *kinds* of grasses present were also instructive. Many phytoliths were from species that, in the Columbia Basin at least, grow only near moist or alkaline soils, such as stream banks or the flats around seasonally dry lakes. Globally, these same plants tend to occupy hotter, drier habitats. Stream channels can be found throughout loess areas, however, so this information by itself added nothing new.

Pollen looked promising at first. It was surprisingly abundant and well preserved, and it seemed to fit reasonably well with the age of the skull. Most of the grains came from grasses, which were abundant during the early Holocene epoch in the Columbia Basin. As I scanned the microscope slides that contained the sample, I became increasingly excited that we would be able to narrow the location. Then came disappointment. Among the grasses were the distinctive pollen of plantain, an introduced weed, and a few grains of black walnut and elm, neither of which is native to northwestern America. The skull still contained a small amount of cemented soil, so I rinsed it in distilled water, scraped it out, and tried again. This time there was no pollen. The grass and tree pollen had apparently blown in from the hay-growing valley that surrounds the university and told us nothing about the vegetation of the skeleton's source. Despite some initial success, the geologic work had been a disappointment. After many analyses, we still could not be certain that the skull even came from North America, let alone the vicinity of Kennewick Man.

The DNA also looked promising at first; then it too fizzled. Analysts at both universities saw indications that DNA was preserved in the bone, but something prevented it from being duplicated. If it could not be duplicated, it would not be abundant enough to measure. Ironically, the chemical that seems to have been blocking the replication proved to be one of the keys to the geographic puzzle. Needing to know what the blockage might be so that it could be eliminated, I contacted Tom Stafford to see if he could provide any insight. A geochemist, Tom keeps impeccable records at every stage of the carbon dating process. If there had been some odd characteristic of the bone, he would have taken note of it.

"Well, yeah," he said, "there was something odd about that bone. When we boiled the collagen in acid, it smelled like rotten eggs. Stunk up the whole lab."

That might be the answer. There was an excess of sulfur in the bone, probably in the form of calcium sulfate, also known as gypsum. With that realization, everything fell into place. Sulfur could be the DNA blockage, but, more important, the presence of gypsum indicated the kind of environment the skull had come from. Gypsum becomes concentrated in the highly alkaline waters of ephemeral (periodically dry) lakes that have no outlets. The skull must have been buried in or near the bed of such a lake. In the Columbia Basin, only two of the subbasins identified as sources of the loess in the skull contain such lakes, one of which is so high in gypsum that it is even named Sulfur Lake. Both areas lie east of the Columbia River and north of Kennewick. The chloridoid grasses Linda Cummings had found to be so abundant among the phytoliths grow on the salt flats around such lakes! If we could be sure Stick Man was from North America, we would have his source narrowed down to an area of only thirty by sixty miles, a veritable pinpoint on a global scale.

Evidence of a North American, and even Columbia Basin, origin came through another by-product of the radiocarbon dating process. The ratio of carbon 13 to carbon 12, described as the per mil (parts per thousand) difference from that of seawater, was very high: –14.5. The carbon 13 value of –14.5 meant that, like Kennewick Man, this individual had gotten a high percentage of his protein—about 70 percent—from marine sources. Of the great loess regions of the world, only the Columbia Basin is rich in marine protein, primarily in the form of salmon and steelhead trout that migrate up the rivers each year.

This was exciting, but we needed to be sure. I asked Foit to make one more attempt to find volcanic ash in the skull soil. He agreed, and in the spring of 2000 I received an excited e-mail from him. He had found ash, lots of it, and it was a near-perfect match to pumice from the 13,100-year-old eruption of Glacier Peak. This ashfall has been mapped by geologists, and its distribution just overlaps the northeastern Quincy Basin, narrowing Stick Man's probable source to an area of no more than twenty by thirty miles. We had him! Stick Man was from the same time, the same area, and maybe even the same population as Kennewick Man.

✹

Now there were two ancient individuals from the central Columbia Basin, both of whom appeared to be very different from modern Indian people in the same ways. Rather than being an unusual member of an otherwise typical Indian group, Kennewick Man was probably a typical member of a very distinct population. It could be argued that both of these men were atypical, but that stretches credibility. When any population is sampled randomly, the greatest likelihood is of selecting—or in this case finding—a typical individual; they are, after all, most common. Very unusual members of a population are rarely selected—or found—because of their rarity. To illustrate, let's say individuals such as Kennewick Man occurred in a given population at a frequency of one person in a thousand (which is probably an overestimate in that none of the thousands of late prehistoric American Indian skulls resemble his). The chance of selecting him at random with a single try is also one in a thousand, which is well within the realm of possibility. The chance of finding two people like him out of two consecutive selections, however, is the product of the two probabilities, that is, one in a thousand times one in a thousand, or one in a million.

✹

If the ancient people of the Columbia Basin did not resemble Indians, whom did they resemble? An answer to this question might bring us closer to understanding where Kennewick Man came from.

In my initial analysis of Kennewick Man, when I had necessarily assumed him to be a recent inhabitant of the Columbia Basin, I had described him on the basis of a general set of physical characteristics as being more like Europeans than like American Indians. When later asked by the press if he had been a European, I would correct them, saying that he merely had Caucasoid-like characteristics; American Indians tend to have what are known as Mongoloid characteristics. I published a short note to this effect in the *Anthropology News,* the widely read newsletter of the American Anthropological Association. To me this was an important observation: contrary to expectation, the inhabitants of North America had *not* always closely resembled American Indians. What, I wondered, could explain this difference? Could it be that the peopling of the Americas had been a more complex process than we once had thought?

To others, however, such notions were anathema. To many, I was suggesting by my use of words that Caucasians (which they reduced to Europeans, although "Caucasian" refers to most people from central Asia, India, the Middle East, and North Africa as well) had occupied North America before the Indians. As Adeline Fredin of the Colville tribe said in an NPR radio interview, "You have this person standing up and saying, 'Look, we have a Caucasian,' and you have an automatic opposition." Vine Deloria, author of such Native American manifestos as *God Is Red* and *Red Earth, White Lies,* called me a "public relations genius" who had deliberately introduced the idea that Kennewick Man was a Caucasian to undermine Indians' claims of primacy in America and to suggest that white people had been pushed out by the Indians. Perhaps encouraged by the words of Deloria and his compatriots, white supremacists did indeed take up the idea, suggesting on their Web sites that Indians had killed off their kin at an earlier time. Even some members of my own field, caught in the late-twentieth-century quicksand of political correctness, referred to my use of what they called the "C-word" as racist science. I should have known, they chided, that the use of such a word would elicit a negative reaction. Alan Goodman of Hampshire College even implied in an article in *Anthropology News* that I was in league with the supremacists.

But hindsight has shown me that "Caucasoid," however innocently used, was not a good choice of words. It drew racist reaction from both the Native American and white supremacist camps, as well as criticism from my colleagues and the media, and it distracted attention from the main scientific observation: *that this early person is different from what we expected him to be.* Now, with two ancient individuals sharing similar physical characteristics, this observation had become a pattern in need of explanation. If we could find people elsewhere in the world, in the present or the past, who shared the characteristics of Stick Man and Kennewick Man, we might be able to formulate hypotheses about the place from which at least their portion of the early American population had come.

When we first looked at the Kennewick skeleton, Katie MacMillan and I were working in a forensic anthropological paradigm. Starting with the assumption that this man was modern, we were trying to place Kennewick Man into one of the common groups of people found today in North America, groups that are referred to by the labels "Caucasoid," "Negroid," and "Mongoloid" and that in common parlance are designated "whites," "Africans," and "Asians." Native Americans fall into the last group. Latinos usually show characteristics of two or more of these main groups. People of these three broad groups, largely because they evolved from our common *Homo sapiens* ancestors in widely separated geographic regions, tend to have distinctive skulls and teeth. An experienced forensic anthropologist can assign an unknown skull to one of these groups with 85 percent accuracy, based solely on surface observation. This ability is valuable, because a forensic anthropologist's purpose is nothing more nefarious than to determine who a dead person is so that the deceased can be returned to grieving kin and, in the case of murder, the killer can be brought to justice.

The practice has come under fire from people such as Alan Goodman, however, because it uses racial terminology developed in the nineteenth century for an entirely different purpose. Races were then seen as distinct groupings of human beings who had different capacities for learning, civilization, emotional expression, sexual behavior, and so on. It is bad science to use such terms, say the critics of forensic anthropology, because the idea of human races has created injustice in America and elsewhere, and we all know that races don't exist.

Anyone accustomed to filling out census forms or to recognizing fellow citizens as African American, Native American, and the like may wonder at this last statement. But in a biological sense, it is true. Taxonomists, biologists whose role it is to categorize the living world, divide a species into subcategories on the basis of the degree to which geographically separate populations of that species share common genes. If geographic populations differ genetically from one another by more than 30 percent, they are considered subspecies or, in older terminology, races. The large human populations traditionally called races, however, differ from one another by only about 15 percent, and the range of variation among individuals in each of these populations is greater than the average difference between them. Hence, the groupings Mongoloid, Caucasoid, and Negroid should not properly be thought of as races. The distinctions we impose on our species are therefore arbitrary and have more social import than biological meaning in a taxonomic sense. The physical differences on which they are based are superficial and, in the words of C. Loring Brace, merely "kinship writ large." This does not, however, negate the facts that human populations do differ from one another to some degree and that those differences, however minor, are an aid to physical identification.

✹

Partly in reaction to changing ideas about the concept of race and partly because increasing human mobility has brought together an ever wider array of humanity from throughout the world, physical anthropologists have begun to devise new ways of distinguishing among people based on their skeletal features. The old method of superficial observation, called by the important-sounding name "anthroposcopy," relies heavily on subjective impression and experience. It works fairly well when the peoples occupying a region, like early-twentieth-century America, differ markedly in their cranial morphology. But when the human variety increases, due to immigration (as it has in places like New York or Los Angeles), distinctions are blurred, and an observer's ability to distinguish among the larger range of peoples declines. There are a few anthropologists, such as Doug Owsley of the Smithsonian, who have such broad experience that they can readily distinguish among many human populations on the basis of observation alone, but few if any of us have come into contact with the *full* range of human variation. To accommodate changing conditions, forensic anthropology needed new, more accurate means of distinguishing among diverse peoples, means that were not based on oversimplified racial categories.

❁

The solution was to use mathematics or, more specifically, multivariate statistical techniques. When we subjectively categorize things, be they skulls, living people, fruits, or any other entity, our brains take into account many variables of shape, size, proportion, texture, and color and process them simultaneously. The brain recognizes a pattern within this mass of data, devises a classification scheme, and groups individual specimens accordingly. The conscious mind makes use of these categorizations but may be only dimly aware of the reasons for the grouping. We may be able to identify some of the criteria our brains are using to make distinctions, but probably not all of them. In large part, we simply feel that members of the groups "look different." This "intuitive" grouping is what experienced forensic anthropologists such as Owsley use as an initial step in identifying people by ethnic group. What multivariate analyses do, aided by powerful modern computers, is to replicate what the human brain does; it compares dozens of measures simultaneously to determine a pattern of groupings among the things being measured.

There are three main differences between the statistical approach and the intuitive one. First, the statistical approach is explicit, while the intuitive approach is much less so. That is, multivariate analyses work only on the data provided to the computer and, once the analyses are completed, can tell us which features are being used to distinguish among the groups. The second difference, which strengthens the scientific validity of the grouping, is that once the data are entered, the analysis minimizes the effect of a scientist's cultural loading—that is, his or her prejudices or preconceptions. Finally, the results of statistical analyses are replicable. That is, whereas two scientists doing visual assessments may disagree about the affiliation of a skull because they place a different emphasis on different cranial features, by using the statistical approach they will achieve the same or very similar results.

The data used to identify unknown individuals statistically include multiple measurements of the skull, measurements of the teeth, and observations of discrete characteristics of the skull and teeth, such as the positions and numbers of small openings (called foramina) in the skull or the roots of a tooth. Skull measurements, called craniofacial morphometrics, are currently the most widely used, perhaps because they assess the skull as a whole and thus most closely mimic the traditional method of intuitive observation. This system of measurement was pioneered in the mid-1970s by W. W. Howells of Harvard University, who sought a non-race-based means of accurately assigning skulls to their populations of origin. He devised a set of sixty-one measurements, including maximum length and breadth of the skull, breadth and height of the eye socket and nasal opening, and distance from the ear opening to a series of points around the profile of the skull. Each measurement is explicitly defined and usually identified by such universal landmarks as the intersections between sutures. Howells measured more than 2,500 skulls of males and females drawn from twenty-eight geographically restricted modern human populations from around the world. Analyzing his measurements with multivariate statistics, he found what intuition had been telling anthropologists for decades—that populations from different parts of the world were grouped together: Africans clustered with Africans, Australians with Australians, and so on. He also had a high degree of success identifying the geographic region from which additional populations and individuals came. Using this method, we can compare fossil skulls, such as those from the Cro-Magnons site in Europe or the Zhoukoudian site in China, with modern populations to determine which, if any, of the modern groups most closely resemble them and therefore might be their closest living relatives.

Howells's methods have been refined by Richard Jantz, who, along with his student Steven Ousley (a relative of Doug Owsley, but with a different spelling of the surname), has developed a computer program called FORDISC. This program, which is now publicly available, uses a series of measurements from an unidentified skull to estimate which group of human populations the unknown specimen most likely belongs to. One limitation of the program is that it will always assign an unknown skull to the best match among the group of populations with which it is compared. For example, if a Japanese skull were compared with only Tasmanians, Hawaiians, Zulus, and Austrians, FORDISC would identify one of these four populations as the most likely source. For the sake of discussion, let's say it identifies the skull as Austrian. To surmount this limitation—FORDISC uses only a little more than two dozen populations for comparison out of the many hundreds that exist, so there is a good chance that an unknown skull is not related to any of them—Jantz added a second measure to show the degree to which the individual would be typical of each of the compared groups. Our Japanese skull, for example, would probably prove to be atypical of all four of the control groups, which would discourage us from identifying it as Austrian. Such a result would mean, of course, that an unknown individual probably does not come from any of the test groups.

This craniofacial morphometric approach is highly effective, but it has been criticized in some quarters as a throwback to nineteenth-century racial anthropology, which used measurements such as the volume of the braincase (known as cranial capacity) to argue that some peoples—particularly Europeans—were more intellectually gifted than others. The comparison is a specious one. The two approaches both use measurements of the skull, and even some of the same measurements, but for entirely different purposes—one to identify the dead and the other to justify racist thinking. The criticism is like condemning heart surgery because knives are often used to commit murder.

Critics further assert that variations in skull form are not primarily genetic but are subject to mechanical stresses and that skulls don't retain characteristic forms for any great length of time. This may be true for the mandible, which is primarily a tooth holder and attachment for massive muscles and therefore changes shape with heavy use or tooth loss, but it does not appear to be true of the cranium. J. H. Relethford of SUNY Oneonta has shown that human populations exhibit about the same degree of variation in craniofacial morphometry as they do in their overall genetic makeup, about 15 percent. Therefore, he concludes, craniofacial form is largely genetically determined. Loring Brace and his collaborators demonstrated this in an extensive morphometric study of Egyptian people that covered ten thousand years. They found that despite extensive changes in climate and adaptation, the ancient occupants of Upper Egypt had always been more similar to modern Nubians and ancient Lower Egyptians to peoples of Europe and the Mediteranean. Howells's finding of geographic clustering among peoples on the basis of measurements is further evidence that cranial morphology is largely genetic.

❈

I first ran a multivariate statistical analysis of Kennewick Man while visiting Walter Neves, a flamboyant Brazilian physical anthropologist who has conducted the most extensive studies of ancient human skeletons in South America. Working with his right-hand man, Max Blum, we compared the data from Kennewick Man with data from eighteen human populations that Howells believes encompass nearly the full variability of the human species while showing the smallest amount of recent intermarriage with other peoples. We also added the Ainu, the aboriginal people of Japan, because of Brace's assertion that Kennewick Man's skull resembled them. We found that when size and shape were both considered, Kennewick Man came closest to the Polynesian Moriori of the Chatham Islands in some respects and to the Ainu in others. American Indian populations were distant. When we took size out of the equation and looked only at proportional relationships among the measurements, Kennewick Man was unlike any modern people in one set of characteristics, but in another he was closest to the Ainu, the Easter Islanders of Polynesia, and two European populations. American Indian groups were again among the most distant, along with Australians and Africans.

As a check on this analysis, I asked Richard Jantz if he would run my measurements using his more sophisticated statistical system, which would compare the unknown skull with Howells's entire worldwide database. He, too, found that Kennewick Man was unlike any modern people but closest to the Moriori and other Polynesian groups. Europeans were among the most distant, along with Africans. American Indians and northeast Asians were intermediate.

A third set of analyses was done by Joseph Powell and Jerome Rose, who conducted the government's Kennewick Man analysis.

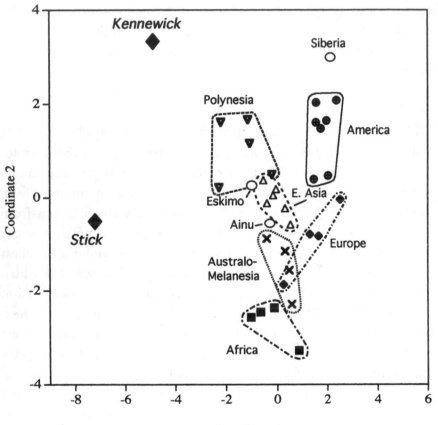

This graph compares Kennewick Man and Stick Man with males from modern-world populations according to two computer-derived dimensions based on measurements of the braincase. The horizontal axis is dominated by the forwardness of the face and length of the skull (inversely represented), whereas the vertical axis is most influenced by skull height and breadth.

Working with a complete set of measurements taken directly from the skull, they compared Kennewick Man first with Howells's data, then with a different set of measurements taken by Japanese physical anthropologist Tsunehiko Hanihara of Japan's Saga Medical School. The advantage of using Hanihara's data was that he had studied a wider range of human groups in Asia and North America, including American Indian groups from the northwestern United States. Altogether, Powell and Rose's analyses compared Kennewick Man with 330 human groups. If Kennewick Man had close kin somewhere in the world, this analysis should have found them. But the result was the same: Kennewick Man was atypical of any modern people. Again, he was closest to Polynesians and the Ainu and unlike American Indians and Europeans.

❋

Jantz and I conducted a similar analysis of Stick Man. This effort was limited, of course, by the fact that we had only the braincase, which restricted comparisons to only about one fourth of the total range of measurements and left us with no information on teeth and little on discrete cranial characterstics. Working only with cranial morphometrics, we obtained the same result whether we used Jantz's measurements or mine. Stick Man had the greatest morphological similarity to Polynesians. Among the closest groups were the Easter Islanders and a Hawaiian population from Oahu. American Indians were the peoples who were the *least* similar. Most important, however, is the fact that someone with Stick Man's characteristics is highly unlikely to be found in *any* modern human population.

We then ran an analysis including both Kennewick Man and Stick Man to see if they differed from modern peoples in similar ways (see graph on page 178). In a two-dimensional graph that compares the two mathematical functions that the computer has found to be most useful in distinguishing among human groups, we can see that all modern peoples are forced by Kennewick Man and Stick Man into a tight cluster at the right-hand side of the graph, while the two fossil skulls occupy the left-hand side. Note that American Indian populations are located farther away from the two ancient Columbia Basin dwellers than any other group. Kennewick Man and Stick Man, however, are positioned far enough from each other that it is possible they could have come from two separate local populations. I suspect, though, on the basis of their similarity in genetically determined discrete characteristics, that they come from different bands or tribes who formed part of a larger, regional population.

✹

Discrete characteristics of the skull and teeth provide a second line of evidence for relationships between human populations. Discrete traits are visually distinguishable characteristics that vary from person to person and breeding population to breeding population. In the bone of the skull, they include such things as the presence, completeness, and number of foramina (the small openings in bone through which nerves and blood vessels pass), notches, bone spurs, and extra bones formed in the sutures between major bones of the skull. In the teeth, they include the numbers of roots and cusps on molars and premolars (bicuspids), the shape of grooves between the molar cusps, and the presence and degree of development of enamel buttresses on incisors and canines. These characteristics are thought to be, and in some cases have been proven to be, genetically determined. For example, one of the factors that led me to see Stick Man and Kennewick Man as alike was the shape of the upper rims of the eye sockets. Each had a partially formed notch above the eye, to the outside of which was a small foramen. They differed, however, in the position and number of foramina in the parietal bone (the pair of large bones that make up the top and upper sides of the skull). Kennewick Man had only one foramen on the right side, while Stick Man had two on each parietal bone (a very unusual characteristic). Within a breeding population, we expect such genetically determined traits to be expressed in approximately constant frequencies through time, providing there is no selective advantage to one or more of the genes that cause a trait to be formed. Discrete dental and cranial traits can therefore be used to determine how closely related two human populations are or to which population an individual is most likely to be related.

Powell and Rose conducted a statistical analysis to compare Kennewick Man with two groups—American Indians and everyone else—on the basis of his discrete cranial traits. The result was that there is a 99.98 percent chance that Kennewick Man was not American Indian.

They went on to consider discrete dental traits, taking into consideration only eastern Asian and American Indian dental characteristics. Their reason for doing this was that dental anthropologist Christy Turner, author of the controversial book *Man Corn,* has divided these peoples into two groups on the basis of their teeth. The north Asians—North Chinese, Koreans, Japanese, Siberians—and modern American Indians he calls Sinodont, or "Chinese-toothed." He defines this group as having high frequencies of several characteristics, including shovel-shaped incisors (incisors with enamel buttresses down both edges of the inner surface, giving the tooth a broad, shallow, U-shaped cross section), winged upper central incisors (winging is a rotation of the tooth such that the outside edge of the tooth projects forward), single-rooted upper first premolars and lower second molars, three-rooted lower first molars, and small or congenitally absent third molars (wisdom teeth). The second group he calls Sundadont, for the place of its presumed origin in Sundaland, an Ice Age subcontinent formed when lowered sea levels exposed the continental shelf around Indonesia and Southeast Asia. Sundadont peoples have, among other characteristics, low frequencies of incisor shoveling, winging, two-rooted upper first premolars, two-rooted lower first and second molars, and standard-sized third molars. Southeast Asians, Polynesians, and the Ainu of Japan are classified as Sundadont.

Being able to assign Kennewick Man to one or the other of these groups would go a long way toward clarifying his origins, since he

shares so little craniofacial similarity to any modern-day human beings. Unfortunately, Sinodonty and Sundadonty are *population-level*
designations. That is, they denote patterns of genetic expression of
groups, not *individuals.* Nonetheless, it is possible to suggest, on the
basis of his dental traits, to which group Kennewick Man most likely
belongs.

During my initial analysis, I observed only that Kennewick Man
had the characteristics common to the Sundadont peoples—two-
rooted upper first premolars, two-rooted lower first and second molars, full-sized third molars, and unwinged incisors. Powell and Rose
took this one step further and analyzed these observations statistically, testing the similarity of this man's dental features to Sinodont
and Sundadont populations as a group. Their results corroborated
my impressions: Kennewick Man had a 48 percent chance of belonging
to a Sinodont—that is, American Indian or north Asian—population. That's a high probability, but it is overwhelmed by the likelihood that he came from a Sundadont group: a whopping 94 percent.

Thus, craniofacial morphometrics, dental characteristics, and discrete traits of the skull all pointed to the same conclusion: Ken-
newick Man and Stick Man are identifiable neither as northeast
Asians nor as American Indians. They have the closest affinity to
Polynesians and the Ainu. These findings do *not* mean that Stick
Man is a Hawaiian or an Easter Islander—that would be absurd,
since neither place was colonized by human beings before 3,000
years ago—nor does the analysis mean that Kennewick Man is an
Ainu or Polynesian. What it does mean is that the Polynesians, the
Ainu, and the early people of the Columbia Basin might be de-
scended from the same parent population. But who might that be?

❂

The Ainu are the vestiges of a hunting-gathering-fishing people who
occupied the northernmost islands of the western Pacific, including
Hokkaido, the northernmost island of Japan, and the Kurile Islands
and Sakhalin, which are now controlled by Russia. Before they inter-

married heavily with their Japanese and Siberian neighbors, the Ainu were a physically unique people. Whereas their neighbors had flat faces, epicanthic folds, yellow-brown skins, brown eyes, thin, straight black hair on their heads, and virtually hairless bodies, the Ainu (who are now nearly gone as a physically distinct people because of intermarriage with Japanese) had short faces, high-bridged, prominent noses, no epicanthic fold, light skins, sometimes gray eyes, dense, wavy-to-frizzy hair on their heads, and unusually hairy bodies. They were considered by physical anthropologists of the late nineteenth and early twentieth centuries to be a Caucasoid people, and there has been endless speculation about historical ties between them and Europeans.

Before rice farmers from Korea emigrated to the Japanese islands around 300 B.C. and gave rise to the modern Japanese, the islands were occupied by a culture known as the Jomon, after the cord-marked pottery that the people produced. The Jomon culture appeared first in the archaeological record of Japan, and perhaps in neighboring Primorye (coastal Siberia to the west of Japan), at around 15,000 years ago and seems to be one of the few cultural traditions anywhere in the world that continued with little interruption for more than 10,000 years. These people lived by a combination of hunting, nut gathering, and fishing in the highly productive Japanese archipelago, occasionally flowering into large societies with extensive trading relationships both internally and with the Asian mainland. Some of the Jomon had a fully maritime adaptation, catching deep-sea fishes and even hunting whales from open wooden boats. Following the arrival of the Yayoi, as the Japanese rice-farming culture is known, the Jomon progressively changed as a result of both acculturation and conquest, finally being confined, after around 900 A.D., to Hokkaido, Sakhalin, and the Kurile Islands to the north. The Ainu are believed to be the last identifiable vestiges of this ancient people.

Polynesians would seem at first to have little in common with these unique people, but the two groups may be descended from similar ancestors. Polynesians occupy the island chains of the central and eastern Pacific, including the Marquesas, Hawaii, Samoa, New Zealand, Tonga, Easter Island, and many others. Relative newcomers on the scale of global history, they are Asian peoples who set forth in large outrigger canoes from somewhere in southeastern Asia about 6,000 years ago, carrying dogs, chickens, pigs, coconuts, and taro. They progressively colonized various islands, first the already occupied lands of Indonesia and Melanesia and later the uninhabited volcanic atolls of the Pacific, where they lived by a combination of animal husbandry, fishing, and horticulture. Their homeland has been traced to somewhere on Taiwan or the adjacent coast of south China, which is not terribly far from the southernmost islands of Japan. They are a big-boned people with relatively small faces, light brown skin, and wavy-to-straight brown-to-black hair. Physical anthropologists have long noted that Polynesians share some characteristics with Asian, Australian, and European peoples. Brace has conducted craniofacial morphometric studies of Asians and Pacific Islanders and found that the Ainu, their Jomon ancestors, and the Polynesians form a single group that he calls the Jomon-Pacific cluster. Together they appear to be remnants of a population that inhabited coastal eastern Asia in the later Pleistocene, before the advent of rice agriculture and the consequent rapid expansion of northeast Asian peoples.

Thus it is not surprising that if the early inhabitants of Washington's Columbia Basin would resemble Polynesians somewhat, they would also resemble the Ainu, assuming that morphometric likeness is a reflection of genetic similarity. What is surprising, in fact the most striking finding of the Kennewick Man and Stick Man studies, is that not only does neither of them resemble American Indians or north Asians, but they differ significantly from *all* modern human beings, despite the fact that they were clearly members of our species. This marked distinction between past and present led me to wonder what might have happened to the descendants of Kennewick Man and Stick Man. Seeking answers to this question, I gathered as much information as I could find on all ancient Americans who predated 7000 B.C., visiting, when I could, the institutions that housed their remains and studying their bones directly. What I learned told me a great deal about who these ancient people may have been, both as members of groups and as individuals, and how they lived their lives.

9

Who Were the
Paleo-Americans?

MY INTRODUCTION TO America's most ancient human fossils actually began one winter evening in 1965, when my father, who operated a radiocarbon dating laboratory at Washington State University, brought home a shoebox half full of bone fragments. A graduate student in geology, Roald Fryxell, had submitted the collection to the radiocarbon laboratory for dating, but my father had refused to fulfill the request. A former anatomy professor, he knew at a glance that the bones included bits of human skull, and it was against his principles to destroy human bone. Besides, the rather primitive dating methods of the day would have entailed destroying the entire assemblage and also were unlikely to provide a reliable age estimate. With the permission of the archaeologists in charge, he had brought the bones home, thinking that I might reassemble the fragments and learn something useful about human skeletal anatomy in the effort.

Fryxell had collected the bones that summer while supervising a bulldozer he had hired to excavate a deep trench at the foot of the Marmes Rockshelter archaeological site. Worked by Doc Daugherty between 1962 and 1964 as part of a massive reservoir salvage operation, the site had been unusually fruitful, revealing an intermittent record of human habitation that had begun nearly 11,000 years ago. Human skeletons had been plentiful, although poorly preserved, and it was the skull of one of those that flashed through my mind when I first set eyes on Kennewick Man. Fryxell, the geologist on the project, wanted to know how the strata in the rockshelter connected to deposits in the floodplain some thirty feet below. As the dozer blade scraped beneath rockfall from the cliff face into smooth water-laid sand, a small bit of burned bone nearly ten feet below the modern land surface had caught his eye. Could this, he wondered, be food refuse from a still older campsite? Returning that November, he and Daugherty recovered a small collection of both burned and unburned bones, which they submitted to my father's laboratory.

Over the next year and a half, the bones stayed in a closet in my room, to be periodically lifted down from the shelf and scattered upon the table. Working as with a complex, incomplete jigsaw puzzle, I eventually managed to assemble three patches of partially burned human skull between two and three inches in diameter, but I was unable to fit them to one another. About the time I graduated from high school, the bones went back to the university, but it was almost another year later when excitement finally erupted. Fryxell had again taken an interest in the ancient bone fragments and gone back to the site to confirm their stratigraphic position. Working with a student crew, he had recovered additional bone fragments in place, and a visiting Polish physical anthropologist had been able to add them to the original three portions to assemble a large portion of a human skullcap. Now that he had worked out the complex geologic history of the site, Fryxell was convinced, even without the radiocarbon date, that the bones must be between 9,000 years old and the age of the last glacial floods, which we now know to have occurred about 14,700 years ago. This would make them the oldest human remains yet found in North America.

It often happens that the best find is made just before a dig ends, and this was no exception. The Corps of Engineers' Lower Monumental hydroelectric dam was scheduled to flood the site in less than nine months. Daugherty went into emergency mode. Packing the reconstructed skull of "Marmes Man" in a cotton-lined box, he traveled all the way to Washington, D.C., to plead for funds. Working his friendships with powerful senators, he was hugely successful. By early summer, a massive excavation effort was mounted. Over the summer and well into the cold of winter, crews of student excavators opened a great pit in the floodplain and exposed much of what remained of the deposits in the rockshelter floor.

The effort was rewarded beyond anyone's imagining. The team found more of Marmes Man, all right. Her shattered bones, including more of the skull, part of a mandible, and bits of ribs, vertebrae, and limb bones were scattered over an ancient floodplain surface that dated to nearly 9700 B.C. Yes, "her," for Marmes "Man" had been a young woman, and she was not alone. Altogether, the crew uncovered charred fragments of at least nine more people, including five adults, a teenager, and three children. Marmes Rockshelter, it seems, had been an ancient crematorium. Parts of three more skulls appeared in the fine soil of the floodplain; Marmes II, which consisted of parts of the frontal bone and four teeth from a six-year-old child; Marmes III, a tooth and part of the skull of an adult male; and three bits of a fourth adult skull named Marmes IV. Among them, but uncertainly associated with any one of them, were found stemmed spear points, tiny bone needles, and an amulet made from the foot of an owl, to which had been wrapped two fresh stone flakes.

After helping to strip off the overburden of the floodplain, another young student and I were assigned to work inside the rockshelter, in what were believed to be younger deposits. Because everyone thought the most ancient skeletons were being found in the floodplain, we felt we had been exiled to the less important work. We were wrong. After weeks of scraping our knuckles on tons of sharp basalt roof fall, we were rewarded with a discovery at least as significant as the skull fragments down below. In the fine dust among shattered stones lay a cremation hearth nearly ten feet in diameter. In it were the badly burned remains of three adults, an adolescent, and two younger children. They were largely unrecognizable, but the left side of one child's face remained reasonably intact, a single tiny visage from the distant past. With it lay two halves of a huge stemmed spear point and a lump of red ocher about the size of the child's fist.

The patterns of burning showed us something about the mortuary practices of these ancient people: the bones had been largely, if not entirely, clean of flesh before being cremated. When bones are burned with flesh on them, the fire burns much hotter than it does when the bones are defleshed and dry, and it burns from both inside the bone and out. The fat inside the bone—the marrow—particularly acts to fuel the flame. As a result the bones not only char but appear to almost melt, becoming severely misshapen. Wavy cracks appear in the surface, and the bones shatter along them. When dry, the bones char and break into rectangular fragments, but they do not warp. The Marmes bones were not warped, although one of the children was quite thoroughly burned. Further evidence of defleshing before cremation came in the form of small cuts on a fragment of leg bone. Although Grover Krantz, who arrived at Washington State University that fall, at first saw the scratches as evidence of cannibalism, he later came to see ritual cleaning of the bones as a more likely explanation.

Despite the magnitude of the discoveries, the skeletal remains themselves offered little information. From them, we learned a bit about the mortuary practices of these early people and the fact that for a time around 11,700 years ago, Marmes Rockshelter had been a traditional place to burn the dead. Beyond that, however, there were only a few hints. We learned the ages of most of the people and the sexes of a few, but little else. With careful study, one might eventually have been able to extract data on a few genetic traits from the jaws and teeth (and of course today we could do DNA analysis), but that was about it.

✦

The experience of recovering what were then some of the earliest known Americans impelled me toward a degree in physical anthropology, but not toward the study of our continent's early immigrants. There seemed to be little promise in that. The conventional wisdom of the late 1960s still followed the dictum of the imperious Aleš Hrdlička, longtime curator of physical anthropology at the Smithsonian Institution. Back in 1937, Hrdlička had gone to great pains to justify his opinion that the aboriginal peoples of America had always resembled modern American Indians. Despite the suggestions of such men as Thomas Newman of the University of Indiana and T. Dale Stewart, who succeeded Hrdlička, that a long-headed people appeared to have preceded the more recent American Indians, Hrdlička's position held sway. In fact, Grover Krantz seemed to be influenced heavily by this view. After analyzing the cremated fragments from Marmes Rockshelter, he declared them to be proper round-headed Mongoloids, despite the fact that not one adult skull was complete enough for a single measurement. With the answer to the question "Who were the first Americans?" seemingly known, what, I wondered, would be the point of studying ancient skeletons?

Even if the prevailing view had not been so dominant, there were simply very few ancient human bits to work with. The Arlington Springs, California, man consisted of three broken limb bones. Midland Man from West Texas was little more than a skullcap. There were a few claims of old skeletons in Florida and California, but the dating was equivocal. Of reasonably intact skeletons that seemed securely old, there were only five: from Browns Valley, Sauk Valley, and Pelican Rapids in Minnesota, Gordon Creek in Colorado, and Tepexpán in Mexico. And these people merely *seemed* to be old. A means of accurately dating bone that would have confirmed or refuted claims of antiquity without using large parts of the skeletons themselves had not yet been devised. Nobody wanted to destroy an important fossil just to see how old it was. So that is where the field stood, with little change, for the next twenty-five years. Or so I believed.

❁

The discovery of Kennewick Man reawakened my interest in America's most ancient inhabitants, and I set about learning all I could about them, traveling to study as many as possible and conferring with the people who had discovered them and those who had analyzed and dated them. I found that a great deal had changed since 1968. For one thing, new analytical techniques have revitalized the field. I knew, of course, that radiocarbon dating had improved to the point that only a tiny scrap of bone or a piece of tooth is needed for age determination. DNA can be extracted from old bone—even the partially charred bits from Marmes Rockshelter—and data on diet can be gleaned from bone protein, the plant phytoliths embedded in people's teeth, and the patterns of growth in their bones. But what really reawakened the field was the realization by those who have taken the time to look carefully, such as Gentry Steele, Joe Powell, Doug Owsley, Richard Jantz, and Walter Neves, that the early Americans might not have been who Hrdlička thought they were.

What makes these new technical developments all the more meaningful is that many new discoveries have been made. At the turn of the twenty-first century, we have found enough remains of ancient Americans to draw some tentative conclusions—or, more cautiously, to advance some hypotheses—about who they were, how they lived their lives, and how long those lives were. New dating techniques have eliminated most of the individuals who topped the list in the late 1960s—Midland "Man" (actually a woman), who was once thought to be very ancient, may be no more than 8,000 years old, and the Sauk Valley skeleton is only about 5,000. But they have conferred antiquity on others, such as Stick Man, the Spirit Cave mummy, and remains discovered in Grimes Burial Shelter and at Wizards Beach, that were never even suspected of being old. As of early 2001, the number of confirmed individuals between 9,000 and 13,000 years old had grown to just thirty-nine individuals from twenty-six sites (see map on page 192). That is still only four fossils per thousand years, but the number continues to grow almost yearly as museums scramble to study the human remains in their collections before all are claimed by Indian tribes under NAGPRA. Even more exciting is the fact that the skeletons of more than one third of those thirty-nine individuals are complete enough that we can understand them as individuals. Each tells a story—in fact, two stories—one

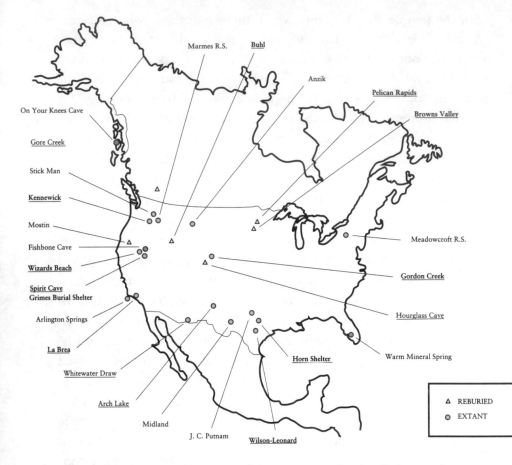

In North America, remains of thirty-nine people who died more than 9,000 years ago have been reported from twenty-six sites. Sixteen individuals shown here (underlined) include more than half-complete skeletons (there are two each at Whitewater Draw and Horn Shelter) and even fewer (in boldface) have nearly complete skulls. Skeletons—especially the more complete ones—are rapidly being claimed for reburial.

about the long-ago dead and another about the discovery and discoverers themselves. Some of the stories are tragic, some uplifting, some a bit of both. Three of the most important and engaging are those of the Spirit Cave mummy, the double burial from Horn Shelter, and Buhla.

❋

Spirit Cave, located about sixty miles east of Reno, Nevada, was one of a series of caves excavated during the first half of the twentieth century as part of an archaeological salvage program of the Nevada State Parks Commission. The program was instituted because artifact collectors and guano miners had been wreaking havoc in Nevada's dry caves, and the loss of potential knowledge, not to mention excellent museum specimens, had become alarming. These caves held a significant number of antiquities. Dry and protected, they contained not only the remains of stone tools and bone artifacts of the same type as those found along ancient lakeshores throughout the West, but also a rich array of the perishable manufactures—sandals, baskets, nets, snares, spear shafts—that make up the bulk of human material culture but so rarely survive the ravages of time.

In August 1940, Sydney and Georgia Wheeler, who made up a salvage team working out of Fallon, Nevada, decided to investigate a small rockshelter near Grimes Point. They had passed by it several times that summer but had not found it very interesting because of its size. After walking a mile over hot, bare desert, they entered the overhang and decided to do a couple of small test excavations to see if the shelter held any promise. Georgia began a small pit near the back wall, while Sydney explored a small side chamber. Almost immediately, Georgia's search was rewarded. A foot below the surface, under a layer of stones, she uncovered a bundle of disarticulated human bones. They were wrapped in a small piece of a finely woven blanket made from the strong red fiber of Indian hemp, a perennial that occupies seasonally moist ground in many parts of the West. She collected the blanket but reburied the few bones, then continued digging. Beneath the first bundle, surrounded above and below by layers of sagebrush, lay a second, larger one about 4 feet (1.2 m) long.

With the help of some locals, the Wheelers lifted this second bundle from the ground, unopened, and took it back to their motel for unwrapping. Inside they found something remarkable. Beneath an outer twined mat made of tules and hemp cord were two more of the woven hemp blankets. These had been wrapped around a human body and sewn together at the ends. The body was that of a man in his middle forties, clothed in a unique style of moccasins and remnants of a robe twined from thin strips of rabbit skin. He lay on his right side, knees partly drawn up, as if sleeping. And he was not mere bones. Yellowed, dried skin clung to the left side of his chest, and patches of slightly wavy black hair still sprouted from his desiccated scalp. Even his large intestine remained.

In another area of the shelter, Georgia later discovered a cremation pit containing charcoal and scattered bits of burned human bone. At the back of the pit, resting against the rockshelter wall, were two flat, side-opening shoulder bags made from the same type of cloth as the man's blanket, lying one atop the other. They were filled with cremated bone. Later analysis by Doug Owsley showed that the two bags contained parts of the same person, a young woman of around seventeen to twenty-one years of age. Cut marks along her jaw may indicate that her kin, like the Marmes people, had cleaned her bones of flesh before ritually burning her remains.

The Wheelers returned with their finds to Carson City, where archaeologists at the Nevada State Museum proclaimed them to be only about 1,500 to 2,000 years old. Who could conceive of something so well preserved being much older? A special box was built for the mummy, and he went into storage for more than forty years. For much of that time he literally lay beneath the desk of Don Tuohy, the museum's curator of anthropology.

Then, in 1994, the museum began a collaborative research project with Erv Taylor of UC Riverside, a project designed to show the value of reexamining museum collections using new scientific techniques. Erv also wanted to know if it was possible to get accurate radiocarbon dates from hair, so he was especially interested in the museum's several mummies. One of those he chose was the Spirit Cave mummy. He ran dates on the man's bone, hair, and matting and was astounded to learn that the man had been dead not just 2,000 years, but nearly 10,700. Further tests on a shred of blanket from the small bundle and bits of one of the shoulder bags that held the cremation showed them to be nearly as old.

Like the Marmes discovery, this revelation kicked off a flurry of activity, funded in part by the Nevada State Legislature. Specialists, including Owsley, Turner, Steele, Jantz, and Powell, examined the mummy at the museum's invitation, learning about the man's physical characteristics, life history, and even his last meal. Amy Dansie, the museum's anthropologist, became interested in the unusual fabrics from the cave and had radiocarbon dates run on other examples of the fine woven hemp. This exploration revealed that all the examples of the cloth were older than 10,000 years and resulted in the discovery of two more ancient skeletons in the museum's collection: a child of about nine and an adolescent male of seventeen years of age, both from Grimes Burial Shelter, not far from Spirit Cave.

The research team learned that the Spirit Cave mummy had been a slender man in his early forties who had stood about five feet five inches (165 cm) tall. Residues from his large intestine revealed that he had last dined on water parsnip and small minnows, eaten whole. His injuries, although less numerous than those of Kennewick Man, were nonetheless serious. He had a small healed fracture and two ruptured disks in his lower spine, two healed fractures in his right hand, and a fractured skull. The skull fracture was suspicious. Located at the left temple and marked by a small, shallow circular depression from which two small cracks radiated, it may well have been inflicted by a right-handed human assailant. The dead man had probably suffered this injury only a few days before he took his last breath, for the break had just begun to heal, as shown by the tiny bridges of bone that had just begun to reach across it. Suspicious as it was, however, the fracture may only have contributed to this man's demise. The real cause might have been considerably more mundane than homicide—three of his teeth had large, active abscesses, pointing to blood poisoning as at least a contributing factor.

As interesting as these observations were, Jantz and Owsley's analysis of Spirit Cave Man's skull topped them all. His face was short, narrow, and placed strongly forward, like those of the ancient pair from the Columbia Basin. The cheekbones did not flare, as do those of modern American Indians and northeast Asian peoples, but, like those of Kennewick Man, slanted outward gradually toward the ears. Like Stick Man, he had a prominent forehead with only moderate brow ridges and a long, narrow braincase. Using multivariate techniques and the Howells database of worldwide human skull measurements, Jantz and Owsley found that this man, too, was outside the range of variation of any modern human populations. He was most similar to the medieval Norse and the Ainu. It would be helpful to learn what his DNA might tell us, but requests for analysis have been denied by the Bureau of Land Management, which administers the desert from which he came. The Fallon Paiutes demanded that he be turned over to them for reburial, despite the fact that archaeology, linguistics, and their own oral traditions say that they have occupied western Nevada for only about 1,000 years. That demand was denied in 2000.

❈

The Wheelers were professional archaeologists, but many of North America's early skeletons have been discovered not by professionals, but by responsible laymen. Foremost among those were Frank Watt and Al Redder of Waco, Texas, who discovered an 11,200-year-old double grave in a site called Horn Shelter Number 2.

Al Redder and Frank Watt were avocational archaeologists, which, they would tell you rightly, is a far cry from being artifact collectors. Frank Watt was a printer who, since 1934, had been an active member of the Texas Archaeological Society and editor of its respected *Bulletin*. In the early 1960s, although he had previously retired from active fieldwork, he took young Al Redder under his wing to teach him proper scientific archaeology. By 1967, when they received permission from owner Herman Horn to excavate in a large limestone overhang beside the Brazos River, they were a crack team. Starting by establishing control points in the shelter roof, they laid out a grid of five-foot squares and began carefully excavating, in natural stratigraphic layers. At the base of every layer, they stopped and mapped in the contents of the floor; they drew profiles of each pit wall; they screened all excavated soil, keeping all bones, stone chips, and artifacts in carefully labeled bags. No professional could have done a better job at the time. Many were less thorough.

They worked almost every weekend when weather permitted and were bountifully rewarded. The site contained layer after layer of artifacts and campsite debris from the Paleo-Indian period (the time before 7000 B.C.), associated with the remains mostly of fish, shellfish, turtles, and small mammals. Then, in 1970, more than 14 feet below the modern shelter floor, Watt and Redder discovered a pile of limestone slabs that did not look like natural roof fall. Lifting the stones and clearing away the fine, cemented soil that lay beneath, they discovered a poignant sight. The skeleton of a middle-aged man lay on his left side, his head resting on a stack of turtle shells, his knees drawn up, his hands placed near his chin. Nestled snugly against his back, her head nearly touching his, were the bones of a twelve-year-old girl, perhaps his daughter or very young wife.

The excavators were alarmed. They knew that if word of this discovery got out, they would have collectors from all over Texas rummaging through the shelter. This grave would surely be disturbed if not destroyed, as would all their careful excavation work from the three previous years. Working continuously through an exhausting weekend (Watt was by now eighty-one), they exposed the skeleton and drew a map of the grave's contents. Then, taking advantage of a natural travertine deposit that had cemented many of the bones together, they removed the bodies in blocks to be painstakingly excavated in the safety of Watt's home. They scraped together the soil from around the bones and took it also, and later sifted it through a fine-mesh screen for bone fragments and grave artifacts.

The man's relatives had provided well for him, placing more than a hundred offerings with him in the grave. In addition to the turtle shells and a tennis-ball-sized lump of red stone for producing ocher pigment,there were tools for manufacturing hunting implements: stone-chipping tools of deer bone and antler; two wrenches for straightening spear shafts, also of antler; two sandstone slabs for shaping bone or shell; and a large oval flint knife. All of these things had been laid at his head. Around his neck were four canine teeth from a dog or a wolf and more than eighty beads made from shells of marine snails brought in from the Gulf of Mexico. Except for a scattering of beads that had probably been relocated from their original position near the man, the girl had only a tiny bone needle, placed near her waist, where it may have been kept in a pocket or carrying bag.

The man, who was between thirty-five and forty-four years old when he died, was small and muscular, standing about 5 feet, 5 inches (165 cm) tall and weighing around 150 pounds (68 kg). His upper body was especially well developed, perhaps more than those of any of the other ancient American males found; flanges on his forearm bones tell of a powerful grip, and ridges in his upper arm show massive shoulder strength. In many respects he is the least Indian-like of the ancient males. His skull is long and narrow, with a deep chin, a relatively narrow upper face, a massive, overhanging brow, close-set eyes, and a depressed nasal root. His nose, low and very broad, probably had a rather bulbous look in life. Although he is much more robust than the man from Spirit Cave, they are similar in appearance.

His body may have been sturdy, but his teeth were in terrible shape. All were heavily worn, some had been broken off, and a few were missing. His incisors were rounded from being used as tools, perhaps to strip fiber or sinews. Like Spirit Cave Man, he too had large, active abscesses at the time of his death, one of which had penetrated into his sinus cavity and might have contributed to his demise. Relatively free of injuries compared to some of the other males, he nonetheless had a fractured and arthritic left foot and appears to have broken his left clavicle early in life. In other ways, his life was harder. Multiple Harris lines—the temporary growth interruptions that develop as mineral deposits in the limb bones of growing children—told of a life of frequent privation or illness. Harris lines could not be read in the girl's deteriorated bones, but her teeth showed multiple growth interruptions that would indicate the same sort of life as the man had led when he was a child. She too appeared to have some sort of sinus infection. This evidence of infection and frequent malnutrition may give us a hint about the cause of these people's simultaneous deaths: infection made worse by starvation, perhaps during an unusually harsh winter.

Frank Watt and Al Redder kept the Horn Shelter discovery secret for fear of attracting collectors to the site. After Watt's death in 1981, Al Redder published their findings and has since made them available for scientific research. Now retired himself, he has dedicated himself to cataloging the collections he and Frank Watt made, hoping that someday "real" scientists can gain the full benefit of what he has found.

Such dedication is rare, but recognition of a responsibility for preserving vestiges of the past is not. Many of the finders of early skeletons have been construction workers, farmers, or foresters. In fact, my studies showed that 75 percent of the remains, which include most of the best-preserved individuals, have been discovered by chance. For example, the Anzik skeletons in Montana—really only fragmentary parts of two young children—were discovered after a rancher, while moving earth to develop a watering tank for his stock, exposed a cache of ancient tools. The Minnesota woman, also known as Pelican Rapids, was uncovered by laborers digging a pipeline trench. Guano miners turned the remains from Grimes Burial Shelter over to the Nevada State Museum. Several individuals have been found in gravel pits, including the Browns Valley skeleton from Minnesota and Buhla, one of the most ancient individuals yet discovered in this hemisphere. Her case is yet another of initially mistaken identity.

On the morning of January 18, 1989, Jim Woods and Phyllis Oppenheim of the Herritt Museum in Twin Falls, Idaho, were on their way to the nearby town of Buhl to look at a bone. They weren't overly excited by the prospect. Archaeologists frequently receive calls from citizens who have found suspicious-looking bones, and as often as not they turn out to be modern animal bones. Still, we always look. Jim and Phyllis worked in a fossil-rich area and on occasion had been rewarded by part of an extinct camel or horse, so they hoped for something interesting.

At the Buhl High school, they were met by Loretta Burkhart, a special education teacher, whose husband had found a large limb bone while supervising a rock-crushing operation at the local gravel pit. He had retrieved the bone from the conveyor belt just before it had fallen into the crusher's maw, she said, and suspected it was human. This supposition had been supported by the science teacher at Mrs. Burkhart's school. Woods immediately knew that the science teacher had been right. The bone was a human femur. According to Idaho state law, he quickly put in a call to Tom Green, who was then the Idaho state archaeologist. Green asked Woods to check the site to see if any other bones were left in geologic position at the gravel pit and to get back to him with what he learned.

Upon arrival at the pit, Woods asked the quarry crew where the bones had been found and was directed to "over there where we've been digging this morning"—a chasm about half the size of a football field covered with fresh tracks from the front loader. The two archaeologists searched the walls of the pit to no avail and were ready to give up when, near the very edge of the excavation, Phyllis spotted something white about the size of a thimble, 13 feet (4 m) below the modern surface. Careful excavation revealed a piece of the mandible, and soon other bones—vertebrae, ribs, and bits of hands—appeared, scattered along the wall of the pit. Woods called Green and returned to ponder the best way of recovering the skeleton.

The situation was precarious. The soil around the bones was a loose, dry, wind-deposited sand dotted here and there with melon-sized boulders. Near the surface, though, where moisture had seeped into the soil, the ground was frozen solid. Fine soil had sloughed away from under this icy mass, leaving an overhanging precipice weighing several tons. The warm afternoon sun was starting to thaw the ice, and vibrations from the earth-moving equipment in the gravel pit were loosening the unconsolidated sand and gravel. At any moment, the overhanging ice might come crashing down, crushing the skeleton and burying anyone who was standing near it. They had to work quickly to expose and remove the bones, while stones and sand rained steadily down upon their heads. (At one point a 3-foot block of frozen ground gave way, crushing their archaeological screen and narrowly missing the excavators themselves.)

The bones lay in a jumble near the base of a steep gravel bank. In one place was the skull; 4 feet (1.2 m) away sat the mandible in a cluster of disarticulated ribs and vertebrae, all still firmly held in the soil. In all, the bones were scattered over an area at least 2 feet (61 cm) wide and 6.5 feet (2 m) long. They must once have covered a much larger area, because many parts of the skeleton, including the left arm, the pelvis, and most of both legs, were already missing, presumably crushed by the machinery or taken home as souvenirs by the highway crew. Among the bones were a freshly made stone knife, a new needle, the baculum (penis bone) of a badger, and another unrecognizable object of bone. There was no evidence of a burial pit, although the soil above the bones remained intact and would have revealed one had it existed. Nor was there evidence of rodent burrowing or any other disturbance of the soil after the body had been buried. The windblown soil, they concluded, must have built up too rapidly for rodents to have colonized the exposed site until long after the body was deposited there.

Woods and Green, who by this time had arrived from Boise, found this geologic situation curious and seemingly at odds with other evidence. The skeleton consisted of the skull, fifteen ribs, eight vertebrae, most of the right arm, the right femur, much of both hands, and parts of one foot. The bones were in near-perfect condition, lacking mineral deposits and showing no signs of weathering or scavenger attack. Clearly they had been buried quickly, but how? The lack of use wear on the knife and needle seemed to suggest that they had been made specially for the grave; the knife even lay directly beneath the cranium, as if placed there intentionally, like the offerings that had been found in Horn Shelter. But the idea that the body had been buried intact was contradicted by the scattered placement of the bones. The cranium had been moved away from the other bones, and its front teeth had long ago fallen out into the nearby soil. How, the team wondered, could these lines of evidence be reconciled?

Green and his collaborators left the question open, but there are two ways the bones might have come to rest as they did and still be in nearly perfect condition. The body may have deteriorated in place, on the ground surface, over the space of a year or more (scavengers do not find all bodies), while windblown sand gradually covered the bones. Or, the burial might have been secondary, that is, of the bones of a person that had been partially or completely cleaned of flesh before being laid to rest on the surface or with a shallow covering of sand scooped from the slope above. In this scenario, the bones and artifacts might have been scattered by gravity down the bank of the gravel bar.

Whatever her means of burial, Buhla, as the skeleton came to be known, had been a young woman of seventeen to twenty-one years who stood approximately 5 feet, 2 inches (157 cm) tall. She had a short face that was placed well forward under her braincase, a low nose with a hooked bridge, and a distinct overbite. Her bones were stong and healthy, but, when x-rayed, her femur showed fifteen Harris lines, evidence of many periods of hunger during her youth and childhood. The lines were so regularly spaced that hunger seems almost to have been an annual event—starvation brought on by winter to a people who were unable to find enough food and had not yet learned how to lay away food stores for the shortage they knew would come. Her teeth showed a similar tendency to hunger in a single enamel hypoplasia that had developed when she was about five and a half years old. There might have been more hypoplasias earlier in her life, but, except for her freshly erupted third molars, her teeth were heavily worn for one so young (as badly as those of Kennewick Man, who was twice her age). Extreme wear is evidence of grit in a diet that must have consisted of foods heavily processed with stone grinding implements. The carbon isotope composition of her bones bespoke a diet rich in meat with a smattering of salmon taken in summer from the nearby Snake River. Perhaps, Green speculated, her people had dried the meat and pounded it into a pemmican, like that eaten by the historic Plains Indians.

Buhla looked young, not only in her degree of maturity but also in geologic time. As Harrington had thought with Spirit Cave Man and

I with Kennewick Man, Green and Woods felt that her good condition and lack of mineralization meant that she had died no more than 8,000 years ago. Following Idaho state law, which requires that every ancient skeleton be turned over to whichever Indian tribe historically occupied an area, Green contacted the Shoshone-Bannocks at the Fort Hall Indian Reservation. When told of his estimate of the skeleton's age, however, the tribe's leaders were not interested in taking immediate possession. They knew the traditional story of their people's relatively recent arrival in Idaho and were convinced that Buhla was not one of theirs. They therefore agreed that the skeleton could be kept for study at Idaho State University and that a rib and half a humerus could be sent to Erv Taylor of UC Riverside, who had offered to radiocarbon-date them for free, time permitting. Taylor found the protein in the bone to be too poorly preserved and was unable to obtain a date. And that is where things sat for two years.

Then, in 1991, a new tribal administration reversed the Shoshone-Bannock position and demanded that the bones be turned over to them for burial. To obtain some sort of age estimate, Green quickly had a bone shipped to Beta Analytic, a commercial lab in Florida, and soon received the surprise of his career: Buhla dated to 10,675±95 B.P., or approximately 12,800 years ago. Amid demands for immediate return of the bones, Green raised some money to have the artifacts and teeth cast and flew Todd Fenton, a graduate student, up from the University of Arizona to conduct an analysis of the bones. Fenton took photographs, made a few measurements, and, basing his assessment only on selected characteristics of the skull, proclaimed the skeleton to be that of a typical American Indian. Then the Shoshone-Bannocks took Buhla to Fort Hall and buried her. There was no opportunity for a second analysis to confirm or refute Fenton's findings on the oldest intact human fossil yet found in North America.

❈

From each of these ancient individuals we have learned the tale of one life. Buhla often experienced hunger in her youth and died when only a young woman, perhaps lying alone in the sand at the base of a bluff, never to be found by her kin. The man from Horn Shelter was a maker of hunting tools, whose people left his manufacturing implements with him in the grave. He had lived long, but, like Buhla, he had led a difficult existence, not only feeling extreme hunger but experiencing painful injuries to his foot and clavicle and breaking many of his teeth or losing them to infection. A girl, perhaps his nearly grown daughter or young wife, did not outlive him and rested beside him in death. Spirit Cave Man's people were accomplished weavers, perhaps as accomplished as any North Americans before or since. They were not big-game hunters but fishermen and collectors of roots. He had been severely injured, perhaps during an altercation with another man, shortly before he died. Each single story is fascinating in its own right, and each gives us a glimpse of what it was like to live in North America so long ago. But our picture of ancient Americans is patchy, like the image we might see of a movie projected onto a tattered screen with gaping holes. It is frustratingly incomplete.

Of the thirty-nine people older than 9,000 years whose remains have come down to us thus far, the majority are too fragmentary to do much more than hint at the sex or age of the deceased. These include the ten cremations from Marmes Rockshelter; the bits of two children found at the Anzik site in Montana; a foot and clavicle from Fishbone Cave, Nevada; a vertebra and part of a pelvis from Warm Mineral Spring, Florida; three long bones from the Arlington Springs site off the California coast; skull fragments from Meadowcroft Rockshelter in Pennsylvania; and pieces of ribs, vertebrae, and arm bones from the Grimes Burial Shelter teenager. In fact, so little remains of twenty-three of the skeletons that not much of a personal nature can be learned from them. Of the remaining sixteen skeletons that are at least half complete, only eleven—five males, five females, and a child—include complete or nearly complete skulls. Only two complete, well-preserved skeletons have ever been found: Spirit Cave Man and Kennewick Man. It is, therefore, only when we look at all the stories together that we can start to fill in the gaps in the image and begin to sense the experiences of our predecessors. The story we see in the lives of the individuals who have been found thus far tells us about the health, stature, injury, life span, and burial practices of these ancient people.

✹

The first thing archaeologists learn when they encounter a very ancient skeleton is the manner of burial or, more inclusively, the manner by which the corpse was disposed of. Evidence clearly indicates that at least twenty-three of the thirty-nine individuals were ceremonially treated at death. Thirteen, such as the Horn Shelter pair, the Pelican Rapids girl, and a woman from Gordon Creek, Colorado, were buried, and eleven, from Marmes Rockshelter and Spirit Cave, were cremated. Most of the burials were of intact bodies (primary burials), but the upper bundle in Spirit Cave and the child from Grimes Burial Shelter were apparently bundles of bones (secondary burials). Some of the cremations also appear to have been skeletal when they were burned. Many bodies, however, simply lay where they had died, like Buhla, or were carried off by predators or scavengers. An adolescent female from La Brea, California, may have been caught in a tar pit; Buhla's scattered bones suggest that she merely lay on the surface; a man found deep inside Hourglass Cave, Colorado, may simply have gotten lost in the cavern.

Grave offerings are uncommon. In addition to the many items left with the Horn Shelter male, there was a cache of finely made spear points with the man from Browns Valley, knives with Buhla and the Gordon Creek woman, needles with the Horn Shelter girl, Marmes I, and Buhla, and shell and a bone implement with the Pelican Rapids girl. The most common offering found with many of the graves in the center of the continent, however, is red ocher. The skeletons found at Gordon Creek, Anzik, and Browns Valley, as well as a young woman from Arch Lake, New Mexico, and possibly Stick Man, were coated with it or placed in graves lined with it. The Horn Shelter grave and one of the Marmes cremations contained raw lumps of the pigment.

Burial practices seem to be geographically patterned, although the pattern is not entirely clear. Primary burials—those of intact bodies—are largely in the Great Plains and adjacent Southwest, where they are associated with cultures descended from the Clovis pattern. Burial with ocher occurs largely in this area, with Stick Man and one Marmes cremation being the exceptions. Cremation and secondary burial or disposal with neither burial nor cremation is the norm in the Great Basin and Northwest, where they are associated with the Stemmed Point Tradition.

❀

When we look at the skeletons themselves, one thing that is immediately evident is that children experienced frequent, or at least periodic, episodes of extreme deprivation. We can say this because of the evident record of nutritional stress in the Harris lines in the long bones and the lines of poor development (hypoplasias) in the tooth enamel. Adults may also experience such difficulties, but their fully developed bodies create no record of the events. Early life is, however, recorded in bones and teeth, and the record remains readable well into adulthood, until the bones have been completely remodeled and the teeth are worn to the gum lines.

I have been able to inspect four sets of long-bone X rays: from Buhla, the Horn Shelter man, the Minnesota girl from Pelican Rapids, and Kennewick Man. All show repeated Harris lines except for Kennewick Man, and he was old enough that any lines would have been expunged by the process of bone removal and rebuilding that is always under way in our skeletons. Harris lines form in the bones of people who are generally well nourished but undergo episodes of food shortage. In Buhla's case, the periodic lines probably tell us that she went hungry about the same time every year, probably during the winter. Therefore, Buhla's bones indicate that food storage was not a major part of her people's survival strategy. The same appears to have been true of at least some of the others.

Dental hypoplasias have been found in about half of the more complete individuals, including Buhla, Kennewick Man, and the young girls from Horn Shelter and Pelican Rapids. The two teen-agers show repeated interruptions of tooth growth. In an analysis of dental health among the earliest Americans, Joseph Powell and Gentry Steele found that such interruptions occurred between 2.5 and 5 years of age and most often at about 3.5 years. Because nutritional stress often occurs at the time a child is weaned, these hypoplasias may simply be telling us that children were not weaned until they were about three and a half years old. This has some import for understanding the reproductive success of mothers, as we shall see shortly.

Differences in the reliability of a food supply may have led to some differences in stature among the Paleo-Indians. The seven men for whom stature can be estimated—from Browns Valley, Horn Shelter, Hourglass Cave, Spirit Cave, Wizards Beach, Gore Creek (British Columbia), and Kennewick—stood between 5 feet, 3⅔ inches (162 cm) and 5 feet, 8 inches tall (173 cm), with an average height of about 5 feet, 5⅔ inches (166.7 cm). The men from the northwest part of the continent—Gore Creek, Wizards Beach, and Kennewick—were uniformly taller than the men from the Great Plains and the Southwest, with an average height of just over 5 feet, 7 inches (170 cm). The men from the South and East are all less than 5 feet 5 inches (165 cm), averaging 5 feet, 4½ inches (164 cm). They show little difference in robustness, however. In the legs, the males became more robust with greater height, which is to be expected, as with a constant body build, the legs are called on to support proportionately more and more weight as a person gets taller. There is more variation in the upper body, though. Kennewick Man, who was the tallest, had a much less developed upper body relative to his size, perhaps because of his extensive arm and chest injuries, than Horn Shelter Man, one of the smaller men. The man from Wizards Beach was also powerfully muscled.

The women—at least the four for whom stature can be estimated—averaged 5 feet, ½ inch (153.7 cm). Buhla and Wilson-Leonard were 5 feet, 2 inches (158 cm), the woman from Gordon Creek, Colorado, 4 feet, 10 inches (148 cm), and the Pelican Rapids teenager about 5 feet even (152 cm). In general, they appear to have been quite slight of build, especially the very thin Minnesota and La Brea adolescents.

Life was hazardous, particularly for the males. Kennewick Man, with his fractures of the skull, rib cage, arm, and shoulder, had been injured the worst, but some others had it nearly as bad. The Spirit Cave mummy had fractures of the skull, hand, and spine. The man from Wizards Beach, although incomplete, showed what was interpreted as a systemic infection that had caused new bone to form on his limb bones. A similar condition is visible on one of the deteriorated femurs of the Browns Valley man. The Horn Shelter man had foot and clavicle fractures. Stick Man and the Marmes III man had minor skull fractures. Kennewick Man and the teenage male from Grimes Burial Shelter had suffered stab wounds. Altogether, eight of the twelve males show signs of serious injury or major nonoral infection. Injury in 67 percent of the men is a remarkably high proportion for hunting and gathering peoples. In fact, in a study of 209 skeletons from southern France, who died from 10,000 to 100,000 years ago, Mary Brennan, a New York University doctoral student, found just five fractures, only two of which were in anatomically modern humans.

A few years ago, Thomas Berger, a student at the University of New Mexico, and his professor, paleoanthropologist Eric Trinkaus (now at Washington University in St. Louis), conducted a study of injury patterns in Neanderthals, who more commonly show signs of physical trauma. They wanted to compare the anatomical distribution of injuries in their study population with those of modern humans from various cultures, hoping for some insight into the behavior of Neanderthals. They had samples of city dwellers, rural Americans, and ancient subsistence farmers but had a particularly difficult time finding a hunter-gatherer population for comparison because traumatic injuries were so rare for that lifestyle. To get enough injuries to make their comparison worthwhile, they had to use a skeletal population of more than 1,200 individuals and still had fewer than 100 injuries among them.

What Berger and Trinkaus learned may help us understand the

lives of the earliest Americans. Berger and Trinkaus found little resemblance between the injury distributions in Neanderthals and the
modern human groups used for comparison—until they compared
the Neanderthals to participants in one of the modern world's most
dangerous occupations: rodeo riding. The patterns were nearly identical. Both the Neanderthals and the rodeo cowboys had numerous
injuries to the head, arm-shoulder complex, and trunk, and few injuries to the hands or lower limbs. They concluded that the Neanderthals had engaged in particularly close interaction with large,
dangerous animals, presumably not for entertainment but simply to
eat. They lacked the technology for propelling spears from a distance
and were thus forced to confront their prospective dinner—horses,
bison, woolly rhinos—from the length of a spear shaft. Hazardous
duty.

When I compared Berger and Trinkaus's data to the pattern of injuries from the most-ancient Americans, the result was the same. Injuries to the head, arm, and trunk predominate, just as they do in
rodeo cowboys and Neanderthals. This is not to imply any connections between the earliest Americans and Neanderthals nor to
suggest that Paleo-Americans possessed only a middle Paleolithic
hunting technology. The deeply embedded spear in Kennewick Man's
hip shows that their technology included the atlatl, an Upper Paleolithic innovation. But if these men were hunting with atlatl-thrown
spears, why were they severely injured so often?

One possible explanation is that they were indeed coming into
close quarters with large, dangerous animals. But if so, what animals
might those have been? Perhaps the answer is hinted at by the spear
wounds in Kennewick Man and the Grimes Burial Shelter teenager,
and by the positions of minor skull fractures in others.

The Grimes Burial Shelter teenager is represented by only a few
bones, but one of his ribs bears strident testimony to the manner of
his death. Two cuts mar its upper edge, one cut still containing tiny
chips from the obsidian blade that made it. The two cuts show that
this injury was no accident. After stabbing him the first time, the
young man's assailant pulled out his blade and stabbed at least one

more time, leaving bits of the obsidian blade behind in the injury. The wound shows no sign of healing, which led Doug Owlsey, who made the discovery, to give the skeleton the nickname "Paleo Homicide." The wound in Kennewick Man's pelvis had healed, but its position and depth are also indicative of an intent to do bodily harm.

And what about the head wounds? People can injure their heads accidentally in many ways—by slipping on ice or loose rocks on hill slopes, walking into tree limbs, and the like—but the pattern of head injuries on these early males is intriguing. First of all, it is only on males that we see skull fractures. None of the females found thus far is so afflicted. Second, the injuries are all located toward the front of the skull. This rules out the slip-and-fall scenario, since this accident is most likely to injure the back of the head. Third, three of the four injuries are on the left side, the side that would be struck by a right-handed assailant who was facing the victim. The number of cases is still very small, but the pattern suggests that the large, dangerous animals with whom these fellows were interacting violently may have been other men.

This is something that just doesn't make conventional anthropological sense. Conflict is not supposed to have been part of the idyllic life of the early hunter-gatherer with a nomadic lifestyle and the low population densities we believe these people to have had. In his seminal work *Man the Hunter,* and in a 1998 address at the international Conference on Hunting and Gathering Societies in Osaka, Japan, University of Toronto anthropologist Richard Lee described nomadic hunter-gatherers as having lived in small bands with egalitarian political systems and little propensity for interpersonal violence. When they developed conflicts, he asserted, they just lived apart until the anger subsided. This image of an innocent life, held up in stark contrast to the crowded, strife-ridden inequality of civilization, has become an image of Eden Lost to the overly stressed modern Western society. Of course, like all ideals, this one was rarely realized. Some of the simplest, most dispersed societies known to anthropology—the peoples of Patagonia, some Australian Aborigines, and the Fayu of lowland New Guinea—were also among the most violent, perhaps in part because their low densities made it unnecessary to develop formalized means of conflict resolution. Individuals simply worked out their differences directly.

Whatever the reasons for injury and violence, most of the ancient males of North America lived relatively long lives. More than half of the thirteen adolescent or adult males whose ages have been determined, including those from Spirit Cave, Wizards Beach, Horn Shelter, Hourglass Cave, Kennewick, and a male from the J. C. Putnam site in Texas, lived into their late thirties or early forties. Stick Man was around fifty. Five males were younger, but three of them had met with fatal accidents. In addition to the Paleo Homicide, the twenty-three-year-old from On Your Knees Cave in southeast Alaska died about 10,500 years ago, apparently killed, or at least eaten, by a bear. The thirtyish man found at Gore Creek was buried nearly 9,000 years ago by a landslide. Still, the average age at death for males who had survived early adolescence was thirty-two to forty years.

Women did not fare so well. Their remains show few bone-damaging injuries or infections (only the Minnesota girl has a healed fracture, in one of her ribs) but this may be because they did not live long enough to accumulate the signs of wear and tear we see on the men. Their average ages at death, not including the probably premenarcheal girl from Horn Shelter, were between 18.8 and 23.3 years. Only two women, from Gordon Creek and Whitewater Draw, Arizona, appear to have been older than twenty-five, and none reached what we would now call middle age. The number of individuals is small—only nine—but as I said earlier, we expect that our random sample of ancient people is more likely to be telling us about normal conditions, not unusual ones. I have no idea what killed them, but infections—of the bladder, or related to childbirth—are perhaps strong possibilities. It is also possible that the technology of these early peoples placed a disproportionate amount of physical stress on the women. Moving camp frequently, carrying equipment and a young child, cannot have been easy for mothers in the societies of early America.

The relative youth of the women is shocking, not only in the lives not fulfilled but in the implications this fact holds for the viability of early American populations in the regions from which the ancient skeletons come. One of the tenets of the conventional model of how the Americas were peopled is that as few as a hundred people may have migrated south of the glacial ice around 13,200 years ago and multiplied so rapidly in the Eden they discovered that within 500 years the entire hemisphere was populated, if sparsely. If we assume that the lives of the first-arriving people were comparable to what we find in the fossil record of their presumably immediate successors, this scenario seems unlikely.

To explore the issue, I contacted Michael Crawford, a demographer at Kansas University who has an interest in America's earliest history, and gave him the particulars of the case. Before I disclose his assessment, a bit more information is in order. First, eight of the most ancient American skeletons are those of children, ranging from 1.5 years for the 12,000-year-old Anzik child to the eleven- to thirteen-year-old Horn Shelter girl. Except for the Anzik baby, all died after the age of four. This threshold age is important because the enamel hypoplasias indicate that the typical age of weaning was about 3.5 years. A long period between birth and weaning limits a woman's fertility, because as long as she is nursing her child, her hormones do not allow her to resume a normal menstrual cycle and she remains largely infertile. Thus the average weaning age plus nine months, or about 4.25 years, must have been the average spacing between births. A wide birth spacing is a good adaptation for mobile hunter-gatherers, as it relieves a woman of the burden of having to carry more than one small child at a time. Given the thirty people for whom ages have been estimated, this means that seven, or nearly one fourth, of the children who lived past the age of weaning died before they reached reproductive age. If the average woman reaches menarche at about age fifteen (physically active and poorly fed women tend to reach puberty significantly later than do girls in sedentary, well-fed modern America) and lives to be only 23.3 years old, and if she bears one child every 4.25 years, she will bear an average of only 2.8 children. If one fourth of these die between weaning and adolescence, she can expect to produce only 2.08 future members of her society during her lifetime.

I posed this scenario to Michael Crawford, and his response was entirely predictable, although colored by extreme caution because of the very small sample we were working from.

"You're not going to people the Americas with that level of fertility!" he exclaimed. "They're barely replacing themselves."

Either we are not seeing a representative sample of the Paleo-Indian population, especially the female contingent, or these early populations were extremely vulnerable. With marginal fertility rates, they would have been vulnerable to famine induced by environmental fluctuation or change (to which their long bones and teeth attest), vulnerable to competition from neighbors or immigrants who had even slightly higher fertility, vulnerable, in fact, to extinction. The early death of the females may give us a strong hint as to why the features of Kennewick Man and Stick Man did not persist among aboriginal Americans to the present day. It may also be one of the reasons why the level of conflict among males seems to have been so incredibly high: it is possible that they were competing fiercely for a limited pool of eligible and healthy mates.

✵

In the physical characteristics of these people, there are both commonalities and differences. In general, the females are small and gracile, with narrow, moderate to long skulls and small faces. They are often moderately to markedly prognathous, that is, their jaws project forward relative to their chins and the upper portions of their faces. Modern peoples who share this characteristic are many African peoples, Australian Aborigines, and some indigenous peoples of the Philippines, to name a few. Minnesota Woman and the crushed female skull from the Wilson-Leonard site in Texas exemplify this tendency. The males have long, narrow skulls, moderately narrow faces, and small mandibles when compared with recent American Indians but lack the prognathism seen in the females. Among both sexes, the midface—the area between the upper teeth and the brow—is placed strongly forward, in some cases to the extent that almost the entire upper jaw sits in front of the brain when the skull is in the Frankfurt horizontal. In this respect, Buhla and Kennewick Man are the most extreme, Spirit Cave Man the least.

In their bodies, these people tended to be relatively gracile, especially the females, although with the aforementioned tendency for greater robustness of the leg with increasing stature. What I found most surprising in reviewing the data on skeletal measurements, however, was that, at least for the males (no female skeleton possesses both tibia and femur), the tropical proportion of femur and tibia—the high crural index—is the norm. Of the five males for which this characteristic could be measured—those from Browns Valley, Horn Shelter, Spirit Cave, Wizards Beach, and Kennewick—only Spirit Cave Man had a lower crural index. His leg proportions were more those of someone from the middle latitudes, such as a modern European from the Mediterranean. None of the men had the relatively short tibia found today among Arctic peoples. If the first colonizers of America came across the frigid wastes of Siberia and the Bering Land Bridge, and if their ancestors had spent very many generations in that environment en route, they would have experienced strong natural selection in favor of shorter limbs. The fact that they had not evolved that adaptation to Arctic cold, which is found today in Eskimos and the Sami reindeer herders of Scandinavia, is particularly instructive. There are several possible explanations: a longer limb may have had a selective advantage in their nomadic lifestyle, especially for chasing game, that overrode the need for compactness of body. They may have possessed an adaptation to cold that emphasized high metabolism and constant movement rather than energy conservation. Or—and I find this hypothesis the most intriguing—their ancestors may not have spent many generations in the Arctic before arriving in America.

✵

So who were these people, and where did they come from? The "who" question usually means what kind of people, what ethnicity, what "race" did they belong to? Of course, as I noted earlier, the accepted answer to this question for many years was that they were indistinguishable from modern American Indians and sprang from the peoples of northeast Siberia and north China. Kennewick Man, Stick Man, and the Spirit Cave mummy, as we have seen, do not resemble modern American Indians or north Asians. The evidence is mounting that the earliest North Americans were a distinct people, or perhaps several distinct peoples, who cannot easily be linked to modern American Indians. In this sense, the old label "Paleo-Indian" that has been used for these people, after the name given by Frank H. H. Roberts in 1922 to a stone tool technology found at Folsom, New Mexico, may be misleading. A less presumptuous term, one that neither assumes nor denies a direct linkage between the earliest Americans and their historic successors, would be "Paleo-American."

Gentry Steele and Joseph Powell, in a series of papers published in the mid-1990s, were the first scholars in the late twentieth century to demonstrate the differences in cranial shape between the Paleo-Americans and modern American Indians. They were not, however, the first to take note of these differences, as they recently wrote in a compendium of papers entitled *Who Were the First Americans?* edited by Rob Bonnichsen. Some physical anthropologists were aware of the difference as early as the 1920s, but the idea had been subdued in the intervening years by a change in the scientific paradigm.

During the early half of the twentieth century, as I mentioned, there were two schools of thought on the origins of American peoples. Aleš Hrdlička held the position that the American Indians were not a particularly variable people and that this lack of variability could be attributed to their descent from one recently immigrated ancestral group. Indeed, they shared many characteristics, especially soft-tissue and biochemical characteristics such as brown eyes, straight black hair, brown skins, epicanthic eye folds, and blood types. They had these characteristics, as well as large, broad, relatively flat faces and high, flaring cheekbones, in common with peoples of northeast Asia, such as Koreans, Japanese, Chinese, and Siberians (then known collectively as Mongoloid peoples). Even ancient skeletons such as the Minnesota woman, Hrdlička insisted, did not differ in any significant way from modern Sioux women living in the vicinity of her discovery.

In counterpoint to Hrdlička, a number of scholars, most notably Joseph Birdsell of UCLA and Georg Neumann of Indiana University, saw a high degree of variability among aboriginal Americans. Embedded in a paradigm that sought to pigeonhole people into discrete categories (as was Hrdlička), they saw as many as ten cranial "types" in the Western Hemisphere. Taking into account the fact that some of the types occurred more often in older archaeological sites (including what were then thought to be the most ancient Americans) and among peoples who had historically inhabited marginal environments, Neumann felt that these types could be reduced to two main groups, who had migrated into the Americas sequentially. The Paleo-Amerinds, who were distinguishable by small faces and long, narrow skulls, had come first. They had later been replaced by the Ceno-Amerinds, who, like northeast Asians, had large faces and round braincases. The Ceno-Amerinds, behaving like an advantaged colonizing population, had occupied the better environments of the hemisphere, relegating the Paleo-Amerinds to harsher environments and the continental margins, such as Tierra del Fuego. Birdsell thought he could identify the people from whom the Paleo-Amerinds had sprung: the long-headed late-Pleistocene people found in the Upper Cave at Zhoukoudian in northern China, site of the well-known Peking Man discoveries. Noting the similarity between the large Upper Cave male, known as 101, and Cro-Magnons of Europe, he hypothesized that the first Americans had sprung from a "proto-Caucasoid," European-derived population that had once spanned the Eurasian continent from western Europe across the steppes of southern Russia and Siberia.

Around midcentury, as physical anthropology turned its attention away from categorizing people and toward understanding the processes by which human populations change, Neumann's and Birdsell's ideas were repudiated. Rather than seeing human variability in terms of immutable "races" and "types" that moved about the landscape, colonizing and commingling, scholars had begun to realize that human differences were the result of evolutionary processes. Such concepts as mutation, natural selection, genetic drift, and gene flow became the basis of understanding human diversity and sequences of historical change in the human form. The population, not the individual, became the unit of study. Unfortunately, this drew interest away from the earliest American skeletons because, as many authors wrote in their descriptions of new discoveries, there weren't enough specimens to analyze in a meaningful way. A 1971 article on the Gordon Creek female is a case in point. In it, David Breternitz and his colleagues wrote, clearly in reference to the ideas of Neumann and others, "[I]t seems desirable for archaeologists and physical anthropologists to be more concerned with other biocultural aspects of early man and to leave the problems of morphology and 'racial mixture' until such a time that sufficient data are available to justify statistical analysis of human variability among early North American Indians." Efforts to understand the origins of American peoples thus turned away from the fossil record and toward the genetic characteristics of the living.

If they did not have enough fossil material to understand history from its beginning using the population paradigm, anthropologists would invert the process and attempt to understand America's human story from its modern end point. Studies of blood groups, serum proteins, and more recently DNA markers have all been aspects of this approach, and they have made valuable contributions. Christy Turner's work on genetic variation in teeth, which I alluded to earlier, is a good example. Based on the frequencies of expression of certain dental characteristics that he felt were genetically determined, Turner grouped Asian peoples into a southern, Sundadont pattern and a northern, Sinodont pattern. Placing all American populations into the Sinodont category, Turner further broke them down into three subgroups, the Paleo-Indian, the Eskaleut, and the Dyuktai. He traced the Paleo-Indians, which he saw as the first American immigrants, to the Lena River basin of south-central Siberia because, like early skeletons from that region, they shared some dental characteristics with Europeans. He derived the Eskaleuts from the Amur Basin of southeasternmost Siberia and believed they arrived in the Americas second. The final group, the Dyuktai, he identified with the latest Paleolithic culture of northeasternmost Asia. In his analysis he had studied a few purported Paleo-American skeletons, which he saw as Sinodont, but most of these proved later to be much younger than the skeletons described earlier in this chapter and even so were not as closely related to his other Sinodonts as he claimed (Kennewick Man, as we saw, seems to have been from a Sundadont population). Like Birdsell before him, Turner traced his Sinodonts to the Upper Cave skeletons of China, but unlike Birdsell, who had envisioned a link between the the Upper Cave skeletons and Europe, Turner thought these people had evolved from earlier human progenitors in Southeast Asia. In the work of linguist Alan Greenberg and geneticist Steven Zegura, he found support for his tripartite colonization process, and it become the standard view of how the Americas were populated.

There is one major problem with attempts to understand America's peopling from its most recent inhabitants, however: the biological history of humankind is not linear. That is, not everyone who lived in the past has descendants alive today. A relative few progenitors account for the majority of humanity, because of natural selection's giving advantage to the multiplication of the most favorable genetically determined characteristics, and to random processes such as genetic drift, which include historical accidents—floods and famines, for instance—that remove entire genetic lines from existence. As Michael Crawford points out in his 1998 book, *The Origins of Native Americans: The Evidence from Anthropological Genetics,* there have been severe "genetic bottlenecks" in the millennia since the first people arrived in the Americas, not the least of which were the catastrophic epidemics that accompanied European colonization in the sixteenth century A.D. and afterward. In metaphorical terms, human evolutionary history is not a slender tree with just a few branches, all of which are still alive. It is, more accurately, a dense bush, and most of the branches on that bush are dead. To understand the history of humanity, whether in the Americas or elsewhere, it is essential to follow that history from its starting point, the trunk of the bush. Only then will we be able to distinguish the dead ends from the live ones and to give a place in the grand narrative to peoples who may no longer exist. The best way to work from the starting point is to pay close attention to what fossils can tell us. We will thus go there first, then see what additional insights genetic data can provide.

❈

In 1990, armed with powerful new statistical tools and the calculating power of computers, and stimulated by work that had recently been conducted by Walter Neves on ancient South Americans, Steele and Powell reexamined North America's human fossils. They began by comparing only four individuals—the Browns Valley and Sauk Valley males from Minnesota and the Gordon Creek and Pelican Rapids females—with today's peoples in terms of eight measurements of the skull and face. They worked first with individual measurements, then with pairs of measurements, such as face length and width and nose length and width. Then they conducted multivariate analyses using all eight measures together. They found that in terms of single dimensions, the Paleo-Americans rarely differed significantly from modern peoples. That is, they were fully modern humans in every sense. However, on the occasions when they did differ significantly, the populations they differed from were usually American Indian. In two-dimensional comparisons and multivariate analyses, Steele and Powell found that the Paleo-Americans were distinct from American Indians and northeast Asians and were closer to south Asians and Europeans. They differed from modern American Indians and northeast Asians in having longer, narrower skulls, shorter, narrower faces, and higher, narrower eye sockets, much as described earlier in this chapter.

Ironically, Steele and Powell were seeing the same pattern that Neumann and his contemporaries, using their outmoded typological methods, had identified—the ancients had longer heads and smaller faces—and they were making their observations on some of the same skeletons. At the time Steele and Powell began their studies, the collection of intact Paleo-American skulls had improved little from what it had been in the 1950s. Then, for better or worse, the flurry of research activity stimulated by the need to comply with NAGPRA changed all that, adding new individuals, identifying others as too young, and removing some from scientific scrutiny forever through reburial. By 1996, when Kennewick Man was discovered, radiocarbon dating of museum collections had more than doubled the number of known Paleo-Americans, although it removed the Sauk Valley skull from the list of the truly ancient and showed the Minnesota woman to be almost too young to be included in this exclusive group. Multivariate analyses that included Spirit Cave Man, the Wizards Beach Man, the La Brea female, Buhla, Kennewick Man, Stick Man, and another presumably ancient skull from Warm Mineral Spring, Florida, continue to support and amplify Steele and Powell's findings. Time after time, in studies by Jantz, Owsley, and Neves as well as Steele and Powell, Paleo-American skulls from North America have been found to differ from those of northeast Asians and American Indians and to be outside the range of modern human beings—*all* modern human beings. There is just one exception: Wizards Beach Man could be a typical member of several modern American Indian populations, but he is most typical of the medieval Norse and would not be out of place among other Europeans and Polynesians. Most of the others, such as Kennewick Man and Stick Man, come closest to Polynesians or the Ainu but some are morphologically closest to Europeans, Australians, Eskimos, and even Africans.

Each reported analysis that I had seen compared two or three males and one or two females at a time to other peoples. To see what would happen if we looked at all the males together, I asked Dick Jantz if he would assist me with an analysis of measurements I had taken on the Kennewick, Stick, Wizards Beach, and Horn Shelter skulls and a stereolithograph (precise computer-produced replica) of the Spirit Cave mummy, as well as data on the Browns Valley man that David Hunt of the Smithsonian had taken. (I had attempted to measure the Browns Valley skull itself, but the first time I flew to St.

Paul to study it, it was out being cast. By the time I returned, it had been reburied—just four days earlier.) We first compared all six individuals to the populations in Howells's database—on the basis of the braincase only, since Stick Man lacks a face—then eliminated Stick Man from the group and compared the facial *and* skull measurements of the remaining five individuals.

When we did this analysis, we used the computer to organize the skull measurements into new composite dimensions that most clearly separate the individuals or groups being compared. When completed, the analysis produced a measure of the mathematical distance between all the sets of skulls; the more alike two skulls or groups are, the shorter is this statistical distance. In this analysis we were comparing this group of skulls with the skulls in Howells's database to see which groups were most and least alike.

This kind of statistical investigation produces different results depending on which groups are included in a comparison. So each time a new individual or group is added that differs from those already in the analysis, a new pattern of distance relationships is found. Despite this characteristic variability, the results we got were comparable to what others had obtained. The Browns Valley, Kennewick, Stick, and Wizards Beach skulls were closest mathematically to Polynesians. The Spirit Cave skull was closest to Europeans, and the Horn Shelter skull, although very far from any group, was closest to Africans, Australians, and Polynesians. Wizards Beach Man could be a member of many modern populations, but none of the others was even remotely typical of any recent ethnic group.

The graph shown on the opposite page, which displays the results of the comparison of the five skulls, maps peoples according to the two principal dimensions that the computer decided were most useful in distinguishing among them. The first dimension, along the horizontal axis, is most strongly influenced by several measurements for facial forwardness and the length-to-width relationships of the nose and eyes. The second dimension, on the vertical axis, correlates to the length-to-width ratio of the skull, the height of the nose, the height of the eye sockets, and the length of the parietal bone of the

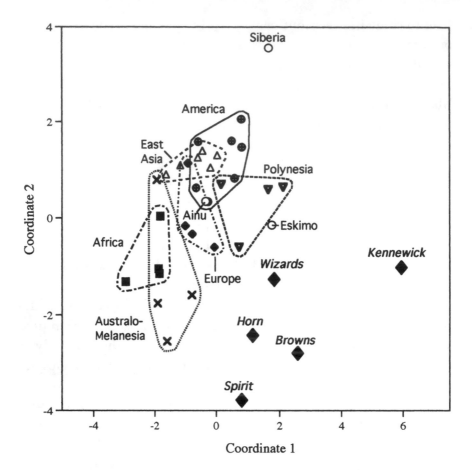

In this comparison of the most complete Paleo-American males with males for modern populations, the horizontal, computer-derived dimension is influenced mainly by facial forwardness and the shape of the nose and eye openings (positively this time), and the vertical dimension is controlled mainly by the skull's length-width ratio and the height of the nose and eyes. Note how modern peoples are forced into a cluster at left by the very different Paleo-Americans.

braincase. The ancient American skulls are scattered in the lower-right quadrant of the diagram, and all other peoples are in a clump near the center and left, in discrete but overlapping groups. This pattern, which has been observed over and over again in analyses by other researchers, probably tells us something about the historical relationships among peoples.

First, American Indians and north Asians form a closely overlapping group in the upper center, a pattern that highlights their close genetic relationship (which has been demonstrated by genetic studies of the living), and they lie opposite the ancient Americans, farther away than Polynesians, Eskimos, some Europeans, the Ainu, and even some Australian and Melanesian peoples of the southwestern Pacific. Assuming that skull form is significantly influenced by genetics, an assumption that seems to be validated by the close grouping of peoples by geographic region, this suggests that the north Asian and American Indian populations are more related to each other than either is to the earliest colonizers of North America.

Second, the skulls of recent members of our species are more like one another than they are like those of the ancient Americans, raising the possibility that modern peoples are closely related, that is, that they have continued to share genes, albeit indirectly in the case of such groups as Africans and American Indians or Europeans and Aboriginal Australians, since they diverged from a common ancestor.

Third, the skulls of the ancient Americans are statistically scattered more widely than those of the modern groups. Although this may be due in part to the fact that they are individuals whereas the modern points represent *averages* among large numbers of individuals, at least two of the early men, Spirit Cave and Kennewick, are different enough from each other to be from distinct populations. When we added Stick Man into the group, he was so distinct that the only population he could have been part of was Kennewick Man's.

Other studies have also shown that the Paleo-Americans were surprisingly diverse. In an analysis that included the ancient skulls from Nevada, California, and Minnesota along with several possibly ancient individuals from Nebraska, Jantz and Owsley observed that the oldest individuals formed two geographically demarcated groups. One group, from the northwestern plains, included the Browns Valley man, the Minnesota woman, and a suspected early skull from Lime Creek, Nebraska. The second group included other possibly ancient Nebraska specimens plus the Wizards Beach skeleton from Nevada and an approximately 8,000-year-old individual from Oregon that

Jantz and Owsley believe on the basis of overall appearance to be very Indian-like. Spirit Cave Man occupied a position midway between them. These groups, Jantz and Owsley observed, were so different from one another that they were highly unlikely to have been from the same parent population but probably were the descendants of distinct peoples who had migrated separately to the Americas.

Working since the late 1980s on ancient skeletons from South America, including large collections from Sabana de Bogot, Colombia, and the Lagoa Santa region of Brazil, Walter Neves and his colleagues have been coming to similar conclusions. When they compared their collections with Howells's data on skull shapes, they found that South American skulls were unlike those of American Indians or Asians but were very similar to, and in fact would not be out of place among, Australians or Africans. This was particularly true of the oldest individuals, Lapa Vermelha IV (affectionately dubbed Luzia, after Lucy, the female *Australopithecus afarensis* from Africa), a female dated to around 10,600 B.C., and Santana do Riacho I (SR-I), a male from 11,400 B.C., both of which were older than most, if not all, human skeletons from North America. This finding, they believed, demonstrated that "non-Mongoloid" people had been the first to colonize America. There had been four migrations, they contended, not just the three proposed by Turner: first came the non-Mongoloids, who they believe came out of Southeast Asia, followed by Turner's Paleo-Indians, Eskaleuts, and Dyuktais.

In February 1999, I visited Neves in his lab at the University of São Paulo to teach his students how to cast ancient skulls and get a look at one of the skeletal collections from the Lagoa Santa region. When I saw the collection of nearly forty skulls believed to be between 9,000 and more than 11,000 years old, I could see why Neves and his colleague Hector Pucciarelli had found such a morphological similarity to Africans and Australians. The skulls were long, narrow, and flat on top, with very short, prognathous faces and wide, low-bridged noses. These are all characteristics common today among many sub-Saharan Africans, although this does not necessarily mean that the early Brazilians were Africans.

To explore the relationships between northern and southern Paleo-Americans, Neves, his student Max Blum, and I pooled our data and ran a statistical analysis comparing SR-I and Kennewick Man with worldwide skull data. Would they group together as the North American skulls had? The result was just as Neves expected: the two Paleo-Americans, North and South, came out on opposite sides of the modern human spectrum. Kennewick, the younger by more than 4,000 years, was nearer the peoples of Polynesia and southern Asia; SR-I was closer in shape to the Africans and Australians. Neves and Blum conducted a similar analysis using Luzia and Buhla, with the same result: morphologically, at least, the North and South Americans were different peoples.

In the summer of 1999, to evaluate the proposition that America had been colonized in multiple early migrations, Joseph Powell and Walter Neves conducted another analysis that pooled a large number of North and South American fossils. Again, as Jantz and Owsley had observed, the Paleo-Americans, South and North, as well as those from various regions of North America, were too morphologically different to be considered members of the same populaton. In his research on the dental characteristics of ancient Americans, for which he analyzed more than six hundred skeletons older than 2,000 years, Powell had made similar observations. Contrary to Christy Turner's hypothesis, he concluded that the first Americans cannot be classified as Sinodonts, nor are they strictly Sundadonts. In fact, they show a higher proportion of both Sinodont and Sundadont characteristics than are found in the modern peoples of Asia and America. In addition, they have high frequencies of some characteristics, such as the Carabelli cuspid (a small projection on the inner surface of the upper first molar), that are more common today in European populations. They also show a higher degree of variability in tooth form than do the modern populations with which Powell compared them. That is, they are more variable than all modern American Indian groups combined. This too could mean that the Paleo-Americans were made up of more than one founding group. The evidence seems to be mounting that this was indeed the case.

Joe Powell has an alternative viewpoint founded on the principles of population biology. Jantz and Owsley, he suggests, are falling into the same trap as did the typological thinkers—Neumann and Birdsell—in believing that America's early peoples must have retained the physical characteristics of their forebears during their migrations and did not change once they arrived in the Americas. The early differences, he asserts, could be explained by evolutionary processes (called microevolution on this short time scale) acting on what he refers to as a hypervariable founding population—one with many different alternative genes for the same physical characteristics of teeth and skull. In other words, all the Paleo-Americans *could* have been descended from one founding group.

❄

Biological evolution is often oversimplified to mean simply Charles Darwin's theory of natural selection. That theory contains two main components, the random generation of variability, which we now know occurs through genetic mutation, and the nonrandom influence of environment on the reproductive success of the different variants mutation has produced, or natural selection. Through the latter process, characteristics that enable one individual to produce more offspring than its peers will become increasingly common in later generations. In addition to these basic Darwinian processes, evolution also operates through genetic drift and gene flow.

Genetic drift, like mutation, is random. Through drift, characteristics that are not being strongly selected for or against may increase or decrease strictly by chance, especially in populations that remain small for long periods of time. The most extreme manifestation of genetic drift is called the "founder effect." When a small number of people leave their native land and begin a new colony, they are highly unlikely to carry in their DNA a representative sample of the genetic diversity present in their parent population. The colony they found, if it grows rapidly, will therefore not contain the same genetic variability as the parent population and may appear different from it even though the two groups are closely related. The blood types of the ABO group provide a good example.

Let's begin with a population whose members carry all three alleles, or gene variants, for blood groups A, B, and O. A small group of people sets out to found a new village that is too far removed from the parent population for intermarriage between the two to continue. Purely by chance, the founder group possesses only the alleles A and O. If the new colony grows rapidly and stays large, its descendants are likely not only to retain both of the alleles they arrived with but also to express them in about the same proportion as the founders did. The resulting difference between the parent and daughter populations is called the founder effect. If the new colony does not grow, however, but remains small, random change is likely to occur as accidents and catastrophes, for example typhoons or epidemics, eliminate parts of the colony, changing the relative proportions of the alleles. Eventually, it is likely that only one allele, probably whichever one was originally more common—let's say O—will remain. This is genetic drift, and it can, over time, produce radical differences in the characteristics of peoples who are descended from a common ancestor.

Gene flow is the movement of genes between populations through intermarriage. It can increase the genetic variability of both participating groups. One population does not exert an undue genetic influence over the other unless the two are unequal in some way, especially in size. In the absence of social barriers to mating, gene flow will tend to have a disproportionately greater effect on small populations than on large ones. The process is somewhat analogous to diffusion in chemistry in that flow has a greater influence on the smaller population than on the larger one. Say that after many generations, our small type O colony reestablishes contact and the exchange of mates with its parent population. Mates entering the colony from the parent population may reintroduce the A allele and introduce the allele for type B, thus restoring genetic diversity to the colony. The trickle of type O folk to the much larger parent population, however, will have little impact on the prevalence of blood types there.

✳

Powell suggests that the high degree of diversity seen in the skulls and teeth of the Paleo-Americans, as well as the differences between the peoples of North and South America, although significant in a statistical sense, may be due largely to the founder effect, gene flow, and natural selection. The Americas, he posits, may have been peopled by a small but highly variable colonizing population. As this population grew, small groups separated from their parents and established secondary colonies, which in turn divided into new colonies until people occupied most of the Western Hemisphere. Each time a daughter colony separated from a larger group, its genetic makeup would have been influenced by the founder effect. These daughter colonies became isolated from one another by geographic barriers, cultural barriers, or merely distance and, where their populations remained small, diverged from one another through genetic drift and unequal degrees of gene flow. Mutations occurring in one regional population and not spreading by gene flow to all others would further diversify people's physical characteristics.

This argument has merit, but it seems to suffer from a flaw— namely, the idea of a highly variable *founding* population. Such a population would be one with a large number of alleles of each gene. Founding populations are typically small and, as mentioned earlier, contain only an incomplete sample of the genetic diversity of their parent populations. They are, therefore, usually less variable than their parent groups. A founding band derived from related hunter-gatherer populations that were themselves small and scattered, and thus strongly subject to the founder effect and genetic drift, is unlikely to have been genetically diverse to begin with. A highly variable founding population, especially in the context of America's colonization, is almost a contradiction in terms. I say "almost" because a founding group that drew from multiple genetically distinct parent populations in the land of origin—perhaps small, diverse bands that commingled in the cold expanse of the Arctic just before their entry into the Americas—could have been hypervariable. This is possible, but a simpler and therefore logically better explanation is that more than one of these diverse peoples managed to find their way to the Americas by the same or different routes.

❖

Whether the Paleo-American fossils can be said to represent one immigrant group or many, three key questions remain: Why don't the Paleo-Americans resemble modern American Indians or northern Asians? Where did the Paleo-Americans come from? And why do American Indians and northern Asians now closely resemble each other?

To the question of why Paleo-Americans do not resemble American Indians, answers have been offered from both the political and the scientific perspectives. The politicians, such as Native American historian Vine Deloria, Jr., and and politically oriented anthropologists Alan Goodman and David Thomas, have asserted that Kennewick Man and the other old fossils look different from modern Indians because "Nine thousand years is a long time; why shouldn't we expect them to be different?"

There seem to be three possible scientific explanations, founded securely in the principles of biology. Walter Neves sees separate colonization events; Joe Powell is more comfortable with evolutionary processes, especially genetic drift; and Gentry Steele suspects that both processes were involved.

Like Steele, while I gravitate toward the multiple-migration position, I agree with Powell that microevolutionary processes had at least some influence on the morphology of Paleo-Americans and their successors. Small immigrant populations would have experienced the founder effect and, as long as they remained small, would have continued to be subject to genetic drift. The periodic starvation indicated by the Harris lines of leg bones, the tendency for early death among the females, and violence among the males all could have led to further loss of diversity. While some isolated populations might have disappeared entirely, others would have begun to grow, especially in favorable environments such as Mexico and the southeastern United States. Expanding disproportionately, they eventually would have begun to overwhelm their less populous neighbors, a process ultimately leading to relative homogeneity over large regions of the continents.

The founder effect and genetic drift may account in part for why Native Americans differ in appearance from their remote predecessors, but it does not account for why they resemble north Asians. When my students attempt to use the forensic program FORDISC to identify skulls I know to be American Indian, they are as likely to identify their subjects as Japanese, Chinese, or Siberian as they are to match them to some American Indian group.

Joe Powell, in line with his other thinking, posits that the similarities are due to convergence. Assuming that the Asian and American Indian progenitors came from the same parent population, he proposes that they underwent similar selective forces—glacial cold, a warm, dry early postglacial period, and the origin and spread of agriculture. It is possible, he believes, that the microevolutionary pathways of both Asians and American Indians led to similar morphologies on the two continents.

Yes, it is possible, but how *probable* is it?

Highly *improbable,* I think, as does Marta Lahr of Oxford University, an expert in the diversification of modern humans. For one thing, random processes such as mutation, the founder effect, and genetic drift lead toward *divergence,* not *convergence.* In addition, Lahr sees the similarities between the two geographically adjacent populations—Asians and American Indians—as just too great to be accounted for by convergence. Like Powell, she envisions the Asian and American populations as having arisen from a more generalized Asian ancestor, again represented by the late Pleistocene skeletons from Southeast Asia and Upper Cave in China. She believes that representatives of this earlier population were the first immigrants to the Americas. Subsequent to that migration, the more specialized so-called Mongoloid peoples, with their large, flattened faces, rounded crania, and Sinodont teeth, evolved in northeast Asia and colonized the Americas in a second migratory wave. Using the same logic followed by Birdsell and Neumann earlier this century, she detects the modern continuation of characteristics from the earlier population in the most remote corners of the hemisphere—Patagonia, Tierra del Fuego, and the outermost Aleutian Islands. There, in near isolation, the populations were less affected by gene flow from the specialized "Mongoloid" peoples who came to dominate pre-Columbian America.

To evaluate these alternative viewpoints, we can turn to the bones as the only direct evidence of human biological history. Which point of view do the skeletons support? Doug Owsley, who has studied thousands of skeletons from throughout the United States, delivers his answer in direct, confident tones: "The fossil record shows us that people very much like modern Indians appeared in North America by around six thousand B.C."

Walter Neves agrees. "Before seven thousand B.C.," he says, "I see only the Australian-like skulls resembling Luzia and Santana do Riacho, but within a thousand years, they were replaced in most places by the Mongoloids—the Indians."

At least in some areas, this seems to be true. Rather than developing gradually from Paleo-American predecessors, the craniofacial characteristics of skeletons from the United States seem to change abruptly. Many craniofacial analyses that include both Paleo-Americans and "Archaic" skeletons (those from between 7000 and 1 B.C.) find that the Paleo-Americans are distinct from the Archaic peoples but that the latter are often not markedly different from modern Indians. This difference may occur earliest in the Pacific Northwest, where, before 7000 B.C., lived the unusual Kennewick Man and Stick Man, who are farther morphologically from modern Indian peoples than any of the other Paleo-Americans. By 6000 B.C. the few skeletons we have seen, including individuals from Prospect, Oregon, and parts of Idaho, are largely indistinguishable from modern American Indians in the morphology of their faces and skulls.

Elsewhere the transition was slower. Jantz and Owsley see the Polynesian-like morphology of the Paleo-Americans as having lasted in California until later than 3,000 years ago. Working in the southern Great Plains, Gentry Steele observes that even as late as 2,000 years ago the people of the Texas coast had very long, narrow heads and prognathous faces. George Gill's studies in the northern Great Plains show the change occurring at about the same time. In some highland parts of Brazil, according to Neves, the Australian-like Paleo–South Americans lingered until farming peoples moved in around 1000 B.C.

Perhaps the New World was peopled in two, three, or more episodes of colonization, but where did the immigrants come from? The best way of answering this question would, of course, be to compare the human fossils with their contemporaries or predecessors in Asia, which has always been considered to be the most likely source. This would be ideal, but the problem is that there are even fewer well-preserved ancient skeletons from eastern Asia than there are from North America. The situation is considerably better for western Asia and Europe, but east of the longitude of India, no more than a few dozen skeletons have been reported, and most of these are very fragmentary. In eastern Siberia, there have been only three finds: teeth from Okladnikov Cave in the upper Ob Basin and the 25,000-year-old site of Mal'ta, on the Lena River near Lake Baikal, and fragments of two skeletons dated to 16,500 years from Afontova Gora on the upper Yenisey. China has more than two dozen sites where fossils of ancient anatomically modern humans have been found, but only two sites contained well-preserved skulls that appear to be as old as or older than those of the Paleo-Americans; one is Upper Cave at Zhoukoudian and the other Liujiang Cave in the southern province of Kwangxi. A few others have been found in Southeast Asia and on nearby islands, most notably a group of 20,000-year-old skeletons from the Minatogawa site on Okinawa and an 11,400-year-old skeleton from Gua Gunung Cave, Malaysia. Unfortunately, there are no Jomon skeletons that are ancient enough for comparison.

What these Asian fossils, limited as they are, seem to attest is that the modern morphology of north Asians and most American Indians did not exist in eastern Asia at the time of the first Americans. The

"Mongoloid" morphology is, in fact, first recognizable in eastern Siberia and China only in postglacial times, beginning at about the same time as we first detect this morphology in the Americas. This may be due, at least in part, to the poor conditions for bone preservation in the taiga environment of Siberia, but the lack of this specialized morphology in China, where preservation is much better, must indicate that the so-called classic Mongoloid morphology migrated to or developed in that region relatively recently.

The oldest modern humans in Asia show more similarities to the Paleo-Americans, but the same distinction between North and South Americans continues to be seen. When Neves and Pucciarelli compared the South American fossils with late Pleistocene skulls from Europe, Asia, Africa, and Australia, they again found the closest relationship to be with the ancient Australians. When Jantz and Owsley added the Upper Cave 101 fossil to their analysis of northern Paleo-Americans, they found that Spirit Cave and Upper Cave 101 were enough alike to have come from the same population. They were in fact more similar to each other than either was to other Paleo-Americans or modern peoples.

Fossil evidence seems to indicate that the Paleo-Americans came from late Pleistocene Asia, but when we expand our geographic scope westward, into central and even western Europe, this conclusion becomes less certain. Like their Asian and Paleo-American counterparts, fossil skulls from Upper Paleolithic Europe usually differ from those of all modern populations but frequently show the closest morphometric similarities to Australian and Polynesian peoples. Late Pleistocene Europeans also exhibit high crural indices—high ratios of tibia to femur length—like the Paleo-Americans.

Dental evidence also shows ties between ancient Eurasia and America, although the message is a complex one. In his analyses of teeth, Christy Turner identified the Mal'ta skeletons as "Europeoid" due to the presence of the Carabelli cuspid and the lack of incisor shoveling. The Minatogawa skeletons are Sundadont. Both sets of characteristics are also found in the Paleo-Americans—Carabelli's cuspid occurs, for example, in the Minnesota woman and the girl from Horn Shelter. Many Paleo-Americans share the characteristics of Sundadonty with the Minatogawa folk.

The fossils thus do not by themselves give us a definitive answer about where the earliest Americans migrated from, but if we turn for a moment to genetics, we find additional clues. Geneticists have studied nuclear genetics—through blood serum proteins—and the highly variable mitochondrial DNA in living peoples and ancient skeletons in the hope of gaining insights into the source of American peoples. In fact, genetic evidence seems to indicate a combination of Eurasian and Southeast Asian origins for the earliest American immigrants. It also provides support for the fossil evidence that people came to the New World in multiple waves of migration.

In an analysis of the worldwide distribution of the alleles for 110 genes in nuclear DNA, Luigi Luca Cavalli-Sforza of Stanford University found that living American Indians were most similar to peoples of northern Asia, as we would expect from their physical characteristics. However, these two groups linked next not to Southeast Asians, which would seem to be likely from the appearance of the latter, but to Europeans and other "Caucasoids." This would seemingly indicate that all three groups sprang from a common parent population that had previously diverged from the progenitors of other world peoples. Alternatively, it might mean that American Indians share a mixed ancestry that includes the predecessors of both eastern Asians and Europeans.

Mitochondrial DNA obtained from living people shows a more complex pattern of relationships that in the final analysis is not incompatible with the nuclear DNA findings. Most American Indians belong to one of four Asian mtDNA lineages—haplogroups A, B, C, or D—and one Eurasian haplogroup, X. Among the Asian lineages, A, C, and D occur today in Siberia; B is absent there but common in Southeast Asia; and X is found only in Europeans, Middle Easterners, and possibly a few peoples of central Asia, such as Kazakhstan.

These five haplogroups are not found in equal proportions in all regions of the Americas, and the pattern may hint at a complex history of migration. Haplogroups C and D occur alone in Patagonia and Tierra del Fuego, B is predominant with lower frequencies of lineages A, C, and D in northern South America, Central America, and the American Southwest, and A dominates the remainder of North America, becoming almost the exclusive lineage in most Native Alaskan populations. X is rare everywhere, and has so far been found in the New World only in living and ancient North American Indians. The pattern is suggestive of a sequence of migrations, a first one with D and C, a second one dominated by B, and a third consisting only of type A individuals. When haplogroup X came cannot be surmised from the geographic patterns, although there is some indication it may have first arrived on the northwest coast of North America.

Theodore Schurr of the Southwest Foundation for Biomedical Research in San Antonio, Texas, has come to a similar conclusion using mutation patterns within each mitochondrial lineage. He has also identified the sources of the various migrations by seeking the modern Old World populations in which the same mutations occur. He infers that American immigrants came in as many as four waves from different parts of the Eurasian supercontinent. Haplogroups C and D, which are common Siberian haplogroups, were brought by one group—perhaps the first—that originated in the Amur River region between Lake Baikal and the Sea of Japan. Haplogroup B, which is absent in Siberia, may have come in a separate migration from coastal eastern Asia, where the types of haplogroup B that entered the Americas seem to have arisen (which, by the way, would also have taken it through the Amur region). He sees the marked north–south decline in the frequency of haplogroup A in America as evidence of a final expansion of northeast Siberians into the Americas following the arrival of the first three haplogroups. Using the presumed rate of mutation in mitochondrial DNA to estimate the ages of the A, B, C, and D lineages in Siberia and America, Schurr estimates that the American progenitors left their homelands between 24,000 and 35,000 years ago.

Schurr accounts for haplogroup X by a possible fourth migration that brought people to America over the Bering Land Bridge from as far away as western Siberia or even across the Ural Mountains in eastern Europe. Such a migration might also have included other mtDNA types. Haplogroup C, for example, is found as far west as the Caucasus Mountains, where it occurs primarily in forms that are ancestral to the haplogroup C found in America.

Most mtDNA researchers take a different view, seeing the low diversity of mtDNA in America as evidence of a single migratory episode and the pattern of haplogroups in the Americas as merely the product of genetic drift. They seek to identify the source of the single migration, which most believe included only haplogroups A, B, C, and D, by looking for a present-day population that contains all four types. Finding such populations in the region of Mongolia, Lake Baikal, and the Altai Mountains, they have identified central Asia as the source of the first Americans. This approach has two severe limitations: First, it excludes haplogroup X, which does not occur in that part of central Asia. Second, it ignores the role of gene flow—the genetic mixing of peoples—over the past 15,000 to 25,000 years, an unwise strategy given the region's long history of interaction with the Chinese, Russian, and Soviet empires, not to mention the thirteenth-century A.D. conquest by the Mongols of much of Eurasia. Schurr's model also contains this second flaw because it too is based on modern genetics, but when we consider the evidence of mtDNA extracted from the bones of Paleo-Americans, we find some support for his ideas.

To date, mtDNA has successfully been extracted from about a dozen Paleo-Americans from North America. All so far belong to haplogroup B, C, or D. Haplogroup A, the most common haplogroup among living native North Americans, has not yet been found in remains older than 6000 B.C. The earliest haplogroup A yet found was from one of the oldest distinctly American Indian individuals from the Pacific Northwest. The ancient DNA evidence is thus consistent with Schurr's suggestion that haplogroup A represents a late expansion out of Siberia. Its association with distinctly American Indian–like physical characteristics further supports the proposition that the northeast Asian craniofacial morphology of American Indians is attributable to a later wave of immigration.

Ancient DNA also hints that haplogroups other than A, B, C, D, and X might originally have existed in the Americas. Frederika Kaestle, now at Yale University, has been attempting to extract DNA from bone found in a large early Archaic cemetery at Windover, Florida, and, she told me, "They're not A, not B, not C, not D, and not X. We've been able to prove what they're *not*, but we don't know what they *are*." Thus the mtDNA evidence supports the indications of the Paleo-American fossils that some of the original genetic diversity in American populations has been lost.

So what do these various lines of evidence say about who the Paleo-Americans might have been? On the one hand, the fossils appear to be telling us that there may have been several early episodes of American colonization before 7000 B.C. There were the Australian-like people who first arrived in South America and more than one group of vaguely Polynesian/Southeast Asian/European–like early North Americans. Certainly, by 10,000 years ago, North Americans not only were divided into physically distinct groups but, if the variety of burial practices and tool technologies described in previous chapters is any indication, lived by different cultures as well. Were the differences among these peoples the products of separate migrations or of founder effect and genetic drift?

The DNA evidence, with its primary linkages to eastern Asia, may be telling us that Americans are all derived from the peoples who lived west of the Altai Mountains in central Asia, or, as the mtDNA distributions and mutation patterns in living American Indians seem to indicate, there may have been separate migrations from the Amur Basin, coastal Asia, northeastern Siberia, and even western Eurasia. But genetic drift plays such a major role in the persistence of mtDNA haplogroups that the record is difficult to read with confidence. mtDNA from ancient bone does, however, seem to support the idea of earlier and later migrations, with the most recently arriving DNA being associated with north Asian physical characteristics.

Asian fossils are little help, partly because they are so rare and partly because they seem to show little differentiation from an ancestral *Homo sapiens* form. The fossils that have been found are not unlike the earliest Americans in their cranial and dental morphology, but then neither are those of the early Europeans. All three, it seems, are representative of a modern *Homo sapiens* prototype that spread across the globe before becoming differentiated into geographically distinct morphologies. Dental evidence seems to suggest that central Asia was occupied by peoples with dental features common to modern Europeans and Middle Easterners (and Paleo-Americans) at the time, some 25,000 years ago, when some DNA researchers suspect peoples first left there on their way to America. The presence of the Sundadont dental morphology in some ancient Americans, on the other hand, along with haplogroup B, hints at a Southeast Asian origin for at least some immigrants.

Wherever the first people departed from—one place or many—one thing seems clear: they did not resemble modern northeast Asians or American Indians. There is in fact no indication thus far that the so-called Mongoloid cranial and facial characteristics had even evolved by the time the first peoples came to America. As Gentry Steele and Joseph Powell conclude in their paper "Peopling of the Americas, a Historical and Comparative Perspective":

> The founding population of anatomically modern humans that first colonized the New World entered via the Bering Land Bridge prior to the establishment of populations in northern Asia which bore the facial characteristics of northern Asians today. . . . We feel the strong similarities documented between more recent northern Asian populations and those of more recent American Indians indicate a marked degree of gene flow brought about by subsequent colonizations of the Americas by more recent northern Asians.

10

Routes of Passage

WHOEVER THEY WERE, how and when did human beings first enter the New World? A variety of routes has been offered, including boating across the southern Pacific Ocean, but three hypotheses seem credible. One hypothesis, which I have earlier referred to as the conventional view, has people crossing the interior of the Bering Land Bridge from Asia into what is now Alaska about 14,000 years ago. By 13,500 years ago, in what is now the Yukon Territory, they are presumed to have entered a north–south corridor between masses of glacial ice and emerged onto the northern Great Plains, somewhere around Edmonton, Alberta, as the Clovis mammoth hunters. Popular portrayals depict these people as clothed in animal skins, trudging through snow with spears in their hands and the bare essentials of living in bundles strapped to their backs. This is commonly known as the "Clovis First" model.

In the other two models, immigrants do not trek across barren wastelands and between glaciers but boat around them. In the more accepted of these models, the first Americans enter by way of the Bering Land Bridge, but this time they make use of the Pacific coast rather than the interior, working their way along the southern shoreline of Alaska and down the British Columbia coastline into the Pacific Northwest. This is the Pacific Rim model. A few archaeologists who claim that there are close similarities between the Clovis hunters and the Solutrean culture of the European Upper Paleolithic suggest that people boated across the North Atlantic and entered North America first along the East Coast. I'll call this third model the "Solutrean Connection." The Pacific Rim and Solutrean Connection models both posit human expansion into the Americas before the time of Clovis, or before 13,500 years ago. As you will see, each of these proposed models has its advantages and shortcomings, but I find the Pacific Rim arguments the most convincing.

❋

All three models take us back to the most recent glacial period, called in North America the Late Wisconsinan, which lasted from about 75,000 to 11,000 years ago. During the Pleistocene epoch, which has spanned the last 1.8 millon years, the earth has undergone repeated periods of warming and cooling. The cold periods are the glacial epochs, while warm periods, such as the one we now enjoy, are called interglacials or, if occurring as brief respites during a glacial period, interstadials (a stadial is a glacial advance). The most recent interstadial occurred between 34,000 and 25,000 years ago.

Glacial ice blanketed much of the northern hemisphere during the Wisconsinan, developing in vast sheets across eastern Canada and Scandinavia and covering many of the higher mountain ranges of Alaska and Siberia. In the northwestern United States, mountain glaciers coalesced, moving westward into the Pacific Ocean and eastward to meet the ice sheet of eastern Canada. So much water was locked up in ice that sea levels were lowered as much as 400 feet (122 m), exposing millions of square miles of continental shelf. Great coastal plains were exposed around the margins of many continents, extending them sometimes hundreds of miles into what is now ocean and connecting islands to continents. One of the largest of these extensions connected Alaska to Siberia in the so-called Bering Land Bridge, which, along with Alaska and the northeasternmost parts of Siberia, is known to scientists as the glacial-era subcontinent of Beringia.

At 20,000 B.C., when the Wisconsinan was at its coldest, Beringia was a dry, windswept place, supporting across its entire expanse little more than a steppelike tundra of grasses, sedges, and a form of sagebrush. At its worst, in northeasternmost Siberia, it was not unlike parts of Antarctica today, with clouds of ice crystals and dust blowing across lifeless plains. Much of the southern shore of Beringia was a vast lowland crossed by the icy Yukon River. Separated from the Pacific by the greatly reduced Bering Sea and the Aleutian Islands, this land was warmed and moistened only a little by the nearby Pacific Ocean. The ecosystem of Beringia was an eastern extension of a treeless habitat called the Mammoth Steppe, which occupied northern Eurasia as far west as northcentral Europe and as far south as Ukraine, Mongolia, and the northernmost islands of Japan.

In the North Atlantic, exposed continental shelves narrowed the distance between Europe and America to about 1,400 miles (2,250 km). Pack ice extended northward from the British Isles and Newfoundland, filling the North Sea and Labrador Strait. Frigid and ice-filled as they were, the waters at this latitude would have been unusually rich, fertilized by nutrients that melted from the glaciers and welled up from beneath the ice packs. Rock art from coastal Spain, not far from the ice margin, depicts seals and penguins; we can surmise the presence of fish and feeding seabirds as well.

In the center of North America, where the glaciers from the western mountains, called the Cordilleran sheet, met the Laurentide ice sheet from eastern Canada, ice extended a minimum of 1,200 miles (1,930 km) from north to south. Half covered with ice, our continent was much cooler than it is now, with a band of tundra stretching along the glacial front and extending down the Rocky Mountain and Cascade ranges.

This was the picture during the coldest part of the last glaciation, but conditions changed constantly. Warmer episodes reduced the glacial ice cover, raised sea levels, flooded coastlines, and allowed forests to expand into the Mammoth Steppe; cooler episodes locked vast regions in ice.

After 22,000 years ago, the global climate warmed and glacial conditions began to wane, slowly at first, then rapidly between 16,000 and 17,000 years ago. In North America, the Cordilleran ice sheet melted rapidly, exposing enough of the coast that by 15,000 to 17,000 years ago, bears were again living on Prince of Wales Island in southeast Alaska. The great ice sheets in Canada and Scandinavia were slower to melt, however, keeping sea levels low and allowing the land connection between Siberia and Alaska to persist until around 11,500 years ago.

❄

Modern humans—people with not only our physical form but also our cognitive abilities—are now thought to have emerged from a homeland in North Africa or the Middle East sometime between 50,000 and 100,000 years ago. It appears that they expanded in two waves. One went eastward through the subtropics of southern Asia, south of the highlands of Afghanistan, the Himalayas, and the Tibetan plateau. The other emerged north out of the Middle East and spread eastward into the part of Asia that lies north of the highlands and westward into Europe. The southern wave, which appears to have been the earlier one, swept along the southern coast of Asia into the coalesced islands of Indonesia, known as Sundaland. People then crossed from Sundaland into what are now Australia and New Guinea by at least 40,000 to 50,000 years ago. By 35,000 to 40,000 years ago, the northern wave occupied the entire expanse from eastern Spain to southern Siberia and northern China. One wave or the other—it looks like the southern one—moved out onto the Japanese archipelago by 34,000 years ago.

The stone tool technologies that early people used along the southern route are largely what are known as core-and-flake-based. That is, they consist of simple tools produced by striking thin, irregular slabs of stone (flakes) from a larger piece of tool stone (the core). Both core and flake have sharp edges and can be used as tools, the flakes often with little additional shaping. The relative simplicity of these stone tools is probably due to the fact that these peoples used fiber and wood, particularly bamboo, as raw materials for implements and weapons.

The toolmaking traditions that emerged along the northern route are generally known as Upper Paleolithic core-and-blade technologies. This type of technology produces stone tools by preparing a core so that a series of narrow, parallel-sided, ridge-backed flakes can be struck off—sometimes dozens from a single core. The blades are then modified further to create tools for cutting, scraping, and piercing. Bone also played an important part in these northern tool kits in the form of needles, spear foreshafts, harpoon tips, and a wide variety of other items. Because of the importance of bone, one of the common tools in these technologies is the burin, a stone tool with a very narrow, chisel-like edge that is used to shape bone, antler, and ivory. Many of these core-and-blade technologies include implements called bifaces—flat stone pieces shaped by chipping on both surfaces and generally used as knives or spear points—in contrast to unifacial tools, which were chipped on one surface only.

The first peoples to venture northward from the central Asian foothills onto the lowlands of Siberia were members of a culture that seems to have extended as a series of related ethnic groups across the southern Mammoth Steppe, from central Europe at least to the middle Lena River basin. Throughout this vast expanse, people lived in very similar ways: they dwelt in semisubterranean houses; used a tool technology characterized by large blades, bifacially flaked points and knives, and large shafts of mammoth bone or ivory; made characteristic female effigies called "Venus figurines"; and buried their dead amid red ocher and beads made of various materials. The appearance of ocher, shell beads, and a needle among the Upper Cave skeletons at Zhoukoudian indicates that the Mammoth Steppe cultures might have reached as far east as northeastern China.

Increasingly bitter cold drove these Mammoth Steppe people out of central Asia around 24,000 years ago, but their cultures continued, evolving separately, at the eastern and western ends of their former range. Blade and biface industries appeared at this time in parts of Japan, where they replaced the earlier core-and-flake technologies, and remained viable in southern parts of Europe. But Siberia was largely if not entirely depopulated.

This situation persisted until about 20,500 years ago, when warming temperatures again allowed people to venture forth onto the Siberian plains. Emerging from the vicinity of Lake Baikal was a culture labeled the Dyuktai. Apparently descended from the Mammoth Steppe cultures, it included the same large-bladed tools and bifaces as before but added microblades made from distinctive wedge-shaped cores and slotted bone handles into which blades were fitted. The Dyuktai culture expanded northward and eastward as the climate warmed and forests spread down river valleys. Ted Goebel of the University of Nevada, Las Vegas, who has compiled data on the Paleolithic cultures of Siberia, believes this expansion was literally fueled by the northward advance of wood for burning, which had been absent on the open Mammoth Steppe during the depths of glacial cold. The Dyuktai rarely built permanent dwellings but moved frequently from camp to camp. They were accomplished big-game hunters and appear to have concentrated on herd species such as bison, reindeer, red deer, and mountain goat. By 16,500 years ago, the distinctive Dyuktai microblade technology had replaced the blade and biface technologies of Japan, and by about 13,000, it had reached northeastern Siberia and was poised to enter the Americas.

CLOVIS FIRST

This oldest and most widely held view of America's first colonization proposes that Siberian big-game hunters—some say people with a Dyuktai technology—migrated into Beringia toward the end of the last glacial epoch, propelled by the growing populations to the west. They are said to have reached the great Canadian ice sheets, and around 13,500 years ago, after the glaciers had melted far enough to expose an ice-free corridor in central Alberta, a small band worked its way southward. This single group of what some suggest may have included as few as 100 to 150 people found upon its arrival a vast uninhabited continent. With no human competition and an essentially unlimited food supply, they multiplied rapidly and expanded throughout the unglaciated land, occupying all of temperate North

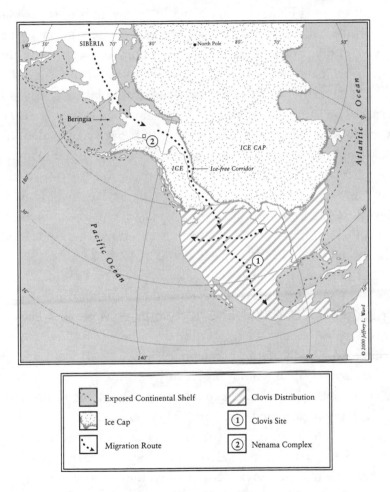

The conventional explanation of how humans entered America, known as the Clovis First model, is that they migrated down an ice-free corridor between the Laurentide (right) and Cordilleran ice sheets. Recent evidence has shown, however, that no habitable corridor existed 13,500 years ago, when this migration was supposed to have taken place.

America within less than 300 years and reaching the southern tip of South America only 200 years later.

The evidence in favor of this model of hemispheric colonization is extensive, supported by the rapid spread and almost ubiquitous distribution in North and Central America of the Clovis stone tool technology. Clovis is very much an Upper Paleolithic blade and biface technology, including large, flat, ovate bifaces, knives and side scrapers made on long blades, scrapers made on the ends of short blades, often with small beaks chipped at one end of the working edge for engraving bone, and cylindrical shafts of bone or ivory about the diameter of a man's index finger. The microblades and wedge-shaped cores characteristic of the Dyuktai are entirely lacking, and burins are rare. The hallmark artifact of this technology is the Clovis Point, a lanceolate to triangular spear point with broad flakes, called flutes, struck from its base. Such spear points have been found in southern Saskatchewan and Alberta, every one of the lower forty-eight United States, and Central America as far south as Panama. In Central America, the lanceolate shape seems to change to a stemmed, fluted form called a fishtail, which has been found down the Andean chain to Tierra del Fuego in sites dating as old as 12,900 years.

What has long made Clovis such an appealing candidate for primacy is the rapidity with which it spread and the thoroughness of its distribution. As David Meltzer of Southern Methodist University points out, it does not seem possible for a people to have expanded its range so rapidly if the hemisphere had already been inhabited upon its arrival. One would expect any existing population to have slowed or even halted the expansion if Clovis migrants had encroached upon occupied territory. This observation seems further supported by the occurrence of large caches of bifaces and spear points, often coated with red ocher, which Meltzer suggests may have been created by Clovis people when they moved into new territory and were uncertain of whether they would encounter new veins of suitable tool stone.

Then there is the fact that many—some would say all—of the

technologies that began to spring up regionally after about 13,000 years ago have an Upper Paleolithic appearance and seem to be descended directly from the Clovis tool kit. One feature of many of the Clovis-derived technologies, the manufacture of tiny needles, has not yet been found in Clovis sites themselves, but I suspect they will eventually turn up.

There is even a suggested connection between early Alaskan peoples and Clovis. The Nenana Complex in the Tanana River basin, north of the Alaska Range, has an Upper Paleolithic technology, including the large blade tools, bifaces, and burins, plus small, triangular knives that, if enlarged and fluted, could have become Clovis spear points. One site even contained cylindrical ivory shafts. Nenana was also in just the right place for entry into temperate America; people just had to follow the Tanana River a few hundred miles eastward, cross into Canada, and enter the ice-free corridor. Most important, Nenana, dating as early as 13,900 years ago, is old enough to have been a progenitor of Clovis.

There are three major problems with the Clovis First scenario. First, the Dyuktai culture was not in northeastern Siberia early enough to have given rise to Clovis. Second, the ice-free corridor was not habitable early enough for Nenana people to have used it before Clovis first appeared in North America. It had barely opened 13,500 years ago; only barren land lay between the ice floes. Third, and most important, Clovis was *not* the first culture in the Americas.

In 1984, Tom Dillehay of the University of Kentucky found two buried campsites along a small stream at a site called Monte Verde in the foothills of southern Chile. In the younger of the two, he found a mere handful of stone and bone tools, including long bipointed spear tips of stone, simple flakes, bola stones, naturally sharp rocks, and a long rod of elephant bone. But the preservative qualities of water and the cold south-temperate environment had saved much more, including tent stakes, pieces of elephant flesh, and the chewed remains of edible plants. There were even human footprints left in hardened mud around the campfires. Radiocarbon dates consistently demonstrated that this upper stratum was 14,500 years old, more than 1,000 years older than the earliest Clovis, 1,500 years older than the Clovis-derived fishtail points of the Andes, and 700 years older than Nenana.

Not only does Monte Verde predate Clovis, but the two technologies have nothing in common. Monte Verde is a simple flake technology that relies as much on found objects—such as rounded stones and natural flakes—as on manufactured ones. Clovis is a highly planned Upper Paleolithic blade and biface assemblage. The two are so dissimilar that it is difficult to conceive of them having been derived, at least recently, from the same parent technology. The deeper stratum at Monte Verde, which Dillehay explored only briefly, is tentatively dated to more than 30,000 years ago.

Dillehay immediately faced a storm of opposition to his discovery from the well-entrenched Clovis First camp, which had held sway in American archaeology for nearly thirty years. The used stones were not artifacts, they said, and either the radiocarbon dates were not associated with the artifacts or there was contamination. They had effectively used these same arguments to debunk nearly every previous pre-Clovis candidate and expected to prevail here as well. After twelve years of rejection, however, Dillehay invited a panel of experts, including some of his most staunch detractors, to examine the site for themselves. They accepted and, after the inspection, validated the antiquity and archaeological significance of Monte Verde. A new era of North American archaeology then began.

The blue-ribbon team's pronouncement was a belated recognition of what many South American archaeologists had known for years. Ruth Gruhn of the University of Alberta, who with her husband, Alan Bryan, has spent a career championing the pre-Clovis sites of America, points out that many South American sites contain evidence of human occupation 13,500 years old or older. Between 14,000 and 15,000 years ago at Taima Taima in Venezuela, for example, people killed a juvenile mastodon with a spear point similar to the ones from Monte Verde. In Colombia, the Peruvian Andes, and Patagonia, sites such as Pachamachay and Los Toldos contain simple flake tool technologies in association with mastodon, horse, and guanaco bones. In highland Brazil, sites such as Lapa do Boquete and Santana do Riacho (the source of the SR1 skull that is so dissimilar from those of modern Brazilian Indians) contain similar simple stone tools but show evidence of an economy of nut and shellfish gathering, fish catching, and small-mammal hunting. By 13,000 years ago, still before the Clovis-derived tool technologies are supposed to have arrived on the southern continent, some South Americans were already living on the Peruvian shore, subsisting on seabirds, fish, and shellfish. Others were occupying the rain forests in the lower Amazon Basin. Clearly, human beings had been living in South America long enough that by the time Clovis spread throughout North America, people were already adapted to every habitat the southern continent had to offer. They must thus have been in residence for a considerable length of time.

If that is the case, though, where are the earliest North Americans? The acceptance of Monte Verde has stimulated a new look at the most promising sites and created a greater willingness to give serious consideration to claims of early finds. An example of the latter is the recent discovery in Idaho of a 13,500-year-old campsite of the Intermountain Stemmed Point Tradition, demonstrating that this tradition may have predated Clovis. In the eastern United States, the most promising sites are Meadowcroft Rockshelter in Pennsylvania, Cactus Hill in Virginia, and Topper in South Carolina, where the human record appears to be much older than those of both Clovis and Monte Verde.

The best documented of these sites is Meadowcroft, which was impeccably excavated by James Adovasio and his students between 1973 and 1995. Beneath a shallow limestone overhang, they found an almost continuous record of human habitation that began perhaps as early as 20,000 years ago and certainly by 15,400 years ago. Below the Clovis strata, which dutifully fell in the 13,000-year age range, they found a series of deeply buried campsite deposits that contained blade tools and small lanceolate spear points similar to Clovis, but without the characteristic basal flutes. In other words, it was not the simple flake technology found in South America but a proper Upper Paleolithic blade and biface technology like the ones found in Siberia before 24,000 years ago and in parts of Japan between 24,000 and 16,500 years ago.

Potential confirmation of Adovasio's finds comes from the site of Cactus Hill, excavated since 1993 by Joseph McAvoy of the Virginia Department of Historical Resources. There, in a stratum below a 13,000-year-old Clovis horizon, he found another layer with blade tools and bifaces clustered around charcoal stains that he interpreted as hearths. Bits of charcoal found in two such hearths—large enough in one case to be identified as white pine—were dated to 18,000 and 20,000 years ago. Finds at the Topper site, although not yet dated, also indicate a blade technology, according to excavator Albert Goodyear of the University of South Carolina.

Thus there is evidence of people in both North and South America before Clovis, but curiously enough, as far back as 15,000 years ago, they were using different stone tool technologies. This may bespeak different origins, as one might interpret the human fossil evidence to mean, or it may simply indicate that people had abandoned or lost the knowledge of blade-making technology en route to the southern continent, either through a cultural analog to genetic drift or because they passed through regions where tool stone was so poor that the blade-making technology, which requires high-quality materials, could not be utilized for a generation or two and was forgotten.

In any case, the archaeological evidence from the Western Hemisphere now shows that human beings were here before Clovis technology developed. This means either that people passed through the ice-free corridor not after the final ice advance but before it, while the ice masses remained apart, or that they did not use the ice-free corridor at all, for the Laurentide and Cordilleran ice masses came together approximately 27,000 years ago and did not open again until around 13,500 years ago, about the time the Clovis progenitors are supposed to have arrived. But if people did not use the ice-free route, how did they enter the Americas?

THE PACIFIC RIM

The idea that people entered America along the Beringian and Alaskan shorelines is not new, but it has long languished in the shadow of the Clovis First model. In 1960, fossil pollen specialist Calvin Heuser found evidence that, contrary to then-conventional belief, glacial ice had not entirely mantled the coast of southeastern Alaska and British Columbia. He speculated that humans might have arrived in America along the Pacific coast. Fifteen years later, archaeologist Knut Fladmark of Simon Fraser University elaborated on the idea, bringing to bear evidence from ocean-bottom studies, paleontology, and pollen. His proposal too was largely ignored until the acceptance of Monte Verde demonstrated that the first Americans could not have come through an ice-free North American corridor. Now the idea has been rapidly gaining adherents, especially among archaeologists who already specialize in human adaptation to marine environments.

When you think about it and compare the coastal environments with those of the Arctic interior, it is not at all unreasonable that the first immigrants to the New World might have hugged the Pacific shore. Marine environments, once thought to have been exploited only after human populations had fully occupied inland habitats, are among the simplest places for omnivorous humans to survive. They offer (in order of increasing difficulty of capture) seaweed, shellfish, bird's eggs and birds, near-shore fish, seals, offshore fish, dolphins, and whales. There are also land mammals, such as otters and bears, that live along shorelines and take advantage of their bounty. Add to this the fact that—contrary to what we might intuitively expect from experience with the terrestrial environment—northern oceans are generally more productive than tropical waters, and it becomes apparent that for people with a maritime way of life, migrating north-

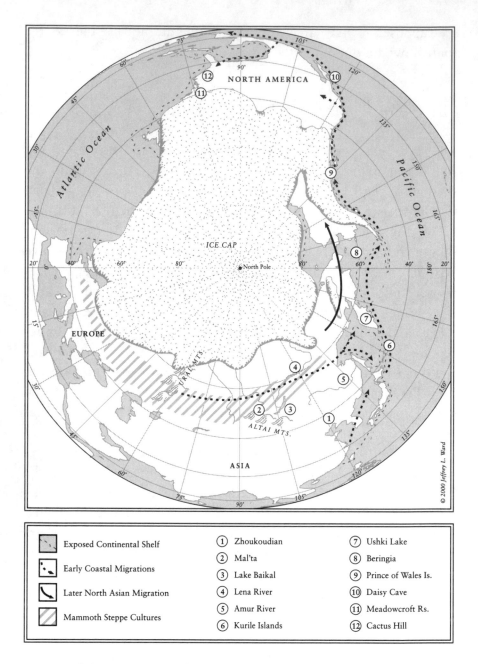

⬚ Exposed Continental Shelf	① Zhoukoudian	⑦ Ushki Lake
⬚ Early Coastal Migrations	② Mal'ta	⑧ Beringia
⬚ Later North Asian Migration	③ Lake Baikal	⑨ Prince of Wales Is.
⬚ Mammoth Steppe Cultures	④ Lena River	⑩ Daisy Cave
	⑤ Amur River	⑪ Meadowcroft Rs.
	⑥ Kurile Islands	⑫ Cactus Hill

It is becoming increasingly evident that most early immigrants entered the Americas along the Pacific Rim, coming from various parts of Asia. Using boats, they would have skirted the ice floes and moved easily from one habitable area to another.

ward into the Arctic need not have meant a reduction in the food supply. Finally, the technology needed to gather food from an Arctic shoreline is not very different from what is needed on a temperate coast: digging sticks (for clams or to pry mussels off rocks), carrying bags, harpoons, fishing lines, hooks, nets, and, if one is to exploit deepwater fish or whales or to move easily from one food source to another, boats. The primary adjustments people need to make as they move to higher latitudes have to do with staying warm in and out of the water and coping with ice.

In proposing a coastal entry for the first Americans, Fladmark used evidence from marine geology to demonstrate that the Alaskan and British Columbian coasts had not been locked in ice, even during the height of the Wisconsinan, and that the Cordilleran glaciers of the western mountains had melted away much faster than the Laurentide sheet of eastern Canada. Ocean-bottom studies show that the most recent glaciers cut broad valleys into the continental shelf but left open large tracts of land between the valleys. Some areas, including (from northwest to south) parts of Kodiak Island, Cook Inlet, Prince William Sound, mainland and island southeast Alaska, the Queen Charlotte Islands, and Vancouver Island, were largely if not entirely ice-free during much of the late Wisconsinan. The vegetation of the ice-free patches was largely tundra-like, and the Queen Charlottes, at least, were inhabited by caribou and bears. Fladmark likens the glacial environment of this region, with its many ice-filled fjords separated by rocky headlands, to the modern-day shore of Greenland. Only the Alaska peninsula, east from Kodiak Island to the eastern edge of the Bering Land Bridge (which lay near the Pribilof Islands), may have been under continuous ice. This reduces the distance between habitable lands to a "mere" 500 miles (800 km). It would have been a long trek on foot, whether a person walked on sea ice or took to the dangerous glacial front, but it would have been a matter of only a few weeks by boat. In Fladmark's words, "People in an umiak moving at two kilometers per hour could go from the eastern Aleutian Islands to the mouth of the Columbia River in one year, and to Chile in only 4.5 years."

The Wisconsinan glaciation in this region reached its height between 23,000 and 19,000 years ago and had begun to melt rapidly by 17,500, leaving the coast entirely ice-free for the last 14,000 years. Paleontologists from the Denver Museum of Natural History have discovered bear dens on Prince of Wales Island, southeast Alaska, in which they found the fossil remains of seals, caribou, and the bears themselves. The bones of brown bears, which have been radiocarbon-dated to as much as 19,000 years old, contain carbon isotope ratios indicating an almost entirely marine diet. This means not only that the coast was free of ice at this early time, reasons project archaeologist and Pacific Rim proponent James Dixon, but also that human beings, who eat essentially the same foods as brown bears, could have survived there as well.

If conditions were suitable for a coastal entry while the glaciers were melting, offers Ruth Gruhn, who is a strong adherent of the Pacific Rim model, they must also have been suitable at earlier times as well—between 28,000 and 23,000 years ago, when the glaciers were advancing at the end of the last interstadial, or toward the beginning of the last interstadial. She favors entry as long as 50,000 years ago by peoples using a simple flake technology of the sort that prevailed in South America during pre-Clovis times. Envisioning what she calls a "linear" pattern of expansion, Gruhn argues that people hugged the coastline, continuing to colonize more southerly shores, until they reached and occupied South America. Adapted to the maritime environment, they had no incentive to colonize the continental interior. We can expand upon her idea and imagine the coastal dwellers moving down the Pacific Rim to Central America, where they discovered the Atlantic coast and proceeded both north and south. This could explain why people were present in Virginia and Pennsylvania as early as 20,000 years ago but did not expand onto the Great Plains until much later.

Evidence now indicates that humans could have moved into North America along the North Pacific coast, but whether they came 15,000 years ago, 20,000 years ago, or earlier, the first Americans had to use boats. No evidence of marine watercraft has yet been found. But this is hardly surprising. Coming from the Arctic, where wood is in short supply and found only as drift, people would have built their boats of skin stretched over a delicate frame. Such craft are unlikely to have preserved well, and we might never find them.

Indirect evidence that early immigrants might have had seaworthy boats has been found on California's Channel Islands in the forms of the 13,000-year-old Arlington Springs woman of Santa Rosa Island and artifacts from Daisy Cave on San Miguel Island that date to almost 13,500 years ago. The Channel Islands were not connected to the mainland at that time, so people would have had to use boats to get there. Although Daisy Cave predates Clovis, it is much younger than Monte Verde, Meadowcroft, and Cactus Hill, leaving open the possibility that people invented marine craft independently after arriving in California. Evidence that America's *first* immigrants could have used boats has had to come from Asia, and it is extensive, if also indirect.

The pattern of human expansion in the Old World leaves little doubt that people have been able to cross open saltwater passages for at least 40,000 to 50,000 years. That is approximately when the people who would become the first inhabitants of Australia and New Guinea crossed from Sundaland over more than one reach of open ocean, one 56 miles (90 km) across even when sea levels were lowered 500 feet (152 m). Modern humans reached Okinawa, which likewise has never been connected to a continent, by 22,000 years ago and moved onto the Japanese archipelago from the Asian mainland by 34,000 years ago. Although Japan may have been connected to Korea earlier, the land connection would have been drowned at 34,000 years ago, the warmest part of the last interstadial. Thus there is no doubt that boats adequate for ocean travel, at least within sight of land, were a part of East Asian technologies early enough to put people in the New World by 20,000 years ago. This is long enough ago for them to have crossed the continent at Central America and left behind the blade tools and small bifaces at Meadowcroft and Cactus Hill and early enough to have reached South America before 15,000 to 16,000 years ago.

If maritime people entered the Americas early, where is the evidence? To date, the Pacific Rim model, which is highly plausible, relies more on possibilities than on archaeological facts. This is largely because whether the colonists came early in the last interstadial, as the Wisconsinan glaciers advanced for a final time, or as the glaciers rapidly retreated at the end of the Pleistocene, the sites they left behind would now be as much as 400 feet under water. Archaeologists are following two strategies to solve this problem. Some, like Dixon and his colleagues on Prince of Wales Island, and Daniel Sandweiss of the University of Maine, working in Peru, are seeking the few places where movements in the earth's crust have raised glacial shorelines above the modern ocean surface. Thus far, they have discovered evidence of coastal habitation as early as 13,000 years ago in Peru and 11,500 years ago in southeast Alaska, but this is still not old enough to provide a convincing argument.

Daryl Fedje of Parks Canada and his colleagues have been seeking submerged sites by creating images of the underwater landscape around the Queen Charlotte Islands to identify likely places for human habitation and then scooping large sea-bottom samples from those spots in search of artifacts. So far they have found nothing older than Clovis, but their work may yet bear fruit.

Despite the absence of an archaeological record supporting it, the Pacific Rim model goes a long way toward explaining evidence in the fossils and DNA for multiple episodes of American colonization. The route was open to any people who had the technology to live on the southern coast of the Bering Land Bridge and the skill to circumnavigate a few hundred miles of ice along the Alaskan peninsula, as long as the Beringian coast itself was habitable. People could have begun coming shortly after their seaworthy ancestors had arrived in coastal East Asia and Japan, or as long ago as 30,000 years ago, and continued immigrating, using boats, even after the land bridge ceased to exist.

Immigration probably came in pulses rather than a continuous flow. Arctic environments, which are certainly what prevailed along the southern margin of Beringia, have a way of periodically annihilating their human inhabitants, opening the way for new colonists when environmental conditions again allow settlement. The prehistory of Greenland and Arctic Canada provides a good example of this process. Three times the region was colonized, first by the Arctic Small Tool Tradition, then by the Dorset Culture, then by the Tule. The latter two must have found the settlements of their predecessors, but there was no one left alive to greet them. Analogously, coastal Beringia, as some sea-core studies suggest, was habitable for only short periods, between which it remained locked in permanent sea ice. It is easy to envision an Asian maritime culture expanding north into Kamchatka and out onto the Beringian coast, occupying the area for a few centuries, and exploring its way to America. When this first group was exterminated or forced to abandon the northernmost coast by the cooling climate, the peoples of Asia and America would have become separated, both culturally and biologically, until Beringia again became habitable and the process could be repeated. Evolutionary processes, including extensive gene flow from other Eurasian groups, would have continued in the parent population for tens or even hundreds of generations between colonization episodes. Each successive wave of immigrants, ultimately sampled from the same large gene pool but subject to strong genetic drift, would have differed genetically, culturally, and probably morphologically from its predecessors.

Whether one is more persuaded by the Pacific Rim model or the Clovis First model (which retains adherents despite its limitations), the problem remains of linking the first American cultures to progenitors in Asia. To date, only one set of sites has been found that might provide the necessary link. Those sites are Ushki Lake I and V on the Kamchatka Peninsula, which lies just southwest of the Beringian coast. The people who dwelt at Ushki Lake around 17,000 years ago used an Upper Paleolithic blade and biface technology not unlike that of the earliest American cultures. But the sites are unique, and archaeologists have thus far been unable to link Ushki to any other cultures of the same age in easternmost Asia. They show no link to the Dyuktai culture, which appeared on Kamchatka only after 13,000 years ago. Several characteristics of the Ushki Lake culture do, however, appear much earlier and farther west in Asia among the middle Upper Paleolithic cultures of the southern Mammoth Steppe. The tool technologies are similar, and, like the Mammoth Steppe peoples, Ushki folk buried their dead with ocher amid hundreds of beads and lived in large semisubterranean houses.

This indirect connection between the earliest American cultures and the peoples of the Mammoth Steppe is attractive, and a connection was suggested by Vance Haynes as early as 1964. Both have core, blade, and biface technologies, cylindrical bone or ivory rods, and fine, eyed needles. Both lack the Dyuktai microblade technology. Many of the Paleo-American skeletons have also been found buried with beads and ocher. A more direct connection between Ushki Lake and the Mammoth Steppe people remains to be made, however. Connecting the two requires that we ignore a separation of 2,000 miles and 6,000 years. Several archaeologists, including John Erlandson of the University of Oregon (excavator of Daisy Cave) and Roger Powers of the University of Alaska, have suggested a connection between Ushki and the blade and biface cultures of northern Japan—which appear to be derived from the Mammoth Steppe cultures—by way of the Kurile Islands. A research team from Harvard University and the University of Washington is now searching for early archaeological sites in the Kuriles, so we may soon have an answer to the question of how the earliest American cultures link to the Upper Paleolithic of Asia. But for now the question lingers.

THE SOLUTREAN CONNECTION

A small group of archaeologists, having become frustrated with their inability to find a direct connection between Asia and the Americas, have begun to look elsewhere. Dennis Stanford of the Smithsonian, stone tool specialist Bruce Bradley of Colorado, and Michael Collins of the University of Texas, Austin, suggest that the earliest Americans, who gave rise to the Clovis Culture in America, are derived not

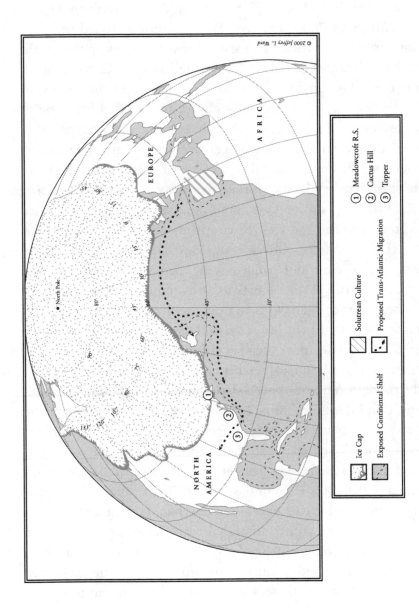

A small group of prominent archaeologists suggests that the people who gave rise to the Clovis phenome-non came across the North Atlantic Ocean from the Iberian peninsula, descendants of the very similar So-lutrean culture.

from *Siberia* but from *Iberia*—the European peninsula that includes Spain and Portugal. The Upper Paleolithic culture they have in mind is the Solutrean, which occupied Iberia and southwestern France from 25,000 to 19,700 years ago. Their premise is based on three observations: Clovis sites are oldest and most abundant in the southeastern United States; nearly all characteristics of Clovis can be found in the Solutrean; and during the last glacial maximum, exposure of the continental shelves brought ice-free parts of Europe to within 1,400 miles (2,250 km) of North America. They suggest that maritime-adapted Solutrean hunter-gatherers moved from northeastern Spain onto the continental shelf west of the British Isles and then, paddling skin-covered boats, worked their way along the permanent pack ice. Camping on ice floes, hunting, and fishing from the ice margin, they reached the ice-free continental shelf east of what is now Newfoundland and moved southward along the broad, now-drowned coastal plain into what is now the eastern United States. Stanford, taking the Eskimo umiak as an example of the kind of simple skin boat that could have been used, estimates that people could have made the trip in as little as two to three weeks—a short enough voyage to have carried their own provisions.

The technological similarities between Clovis and Solutrean are indeed striking. Both are Upper Paleolithic blade technologies, making large, thin bifaces and using lanceolate spear points with ground bases, end scrapers with spurs for bone working, and small numbers of burins. Both loved to make their biggest bifaces out of exotic stone and often cached them together with masses of red ocher. They produced needles (presumed in the case of Clovis) and rods of bone or ivory, with their beveled bases scored to facilitate attachment to a wooden shaft and sometimes decorated with incised lines. They even shared a penchant for scratching designs on flat tablets of soft stone. But what most attracted Bradley's attention was the methods used for making tools, which he sees as virtually identical and unique to the Solutrean and Clovis.

The idea already has staunch opponents. Lawrence Straus of the University of New Mexico, the United States' leading expert in Solutrean culture, finds it ludicrous. The first problem is that Clovis began no earlier than 13,500 years ago, whereas the Solutrean ended by 19,700, replaced by the culture known as Magdalenian. Second, the distance between the two regions is immense in terms of both space and difficulty. The northernmost Solutrean sites are located in France well south of the British Isles. Due to extreme cold, no one was living closer to the glacial ice. Even if they were living out on the continental shelf, Straus argues, floating ice and the stormy seas created by the contact between Arctic waters and the Humboldt Current, just off the northwest corner of Iberia, would have made the voyage too dangerous. Furthermore, in his view, there is no evidence that the Solutrean folk had a maritime adaptation—no evidence of boats, sea-mammal hunting, or deep-sea fishing. In addition, their technology was regionally diverse and much more complex than that of Clovis, with many kinds of tools that are not found in America. The similarities are, in his view, merely convergent, the results of people facing the same kinds of problems with the same limited set of raw materials.

I am inclined to concur, but Stanford and Bradley are preparing a book on their argument and I prefer to await the full exposition of their ideas before forming a final opinion. Among other points they are likely to make in answer to Straus is that it is not Clovis but its American progenitors, represented at such sites as Cactus Hill and Meadowcroft, that we must link to the Solutrean; since nearly all characteristics of Clovis can be found in the Solutrean, the differences between the two may be due merely to cultural drift; and evidence that the Solutrean people were acquainted with—and probably hunted—sea mammals can be found in the depiction of penguins and seals in cave art that now lies in underwater caves nearer the level of the glacial sea. There is also some evidence of the presence of boats. The debate promises to be a lively one.

❖

These three suggested means for Ice Age people to have entered America are all plausible. Science, however, evaluates competing possibilities on the basis of how well they fit the existing evidence and on how few assumptions they require. The best model explains the known evidence and makes the fewest assumptions. If we look at these competing models in light of the evidence from human fossils and modern DNA, all three have value, but the Pacific Rim model, despite the absence of ancient coastal sites, stands out.

Clovis First falls down simply because Clovis was not first but came at least 1,000 years too late to explain the presence of people in South America, not to mention the habitation of such sites as Cactus Hill and Meadowcroft 20,000 years ago. If this were not the case, however, it would fail because it presumes the early entry of but one population and thus does not accommodate the diversity in ancient America of craniofacial morphologies, dental characteristics, or mitochondrial genetics. It certainly has problems explaining the early differences we see between the Australian-like early South Americans and the more Polynesian/Ainu–like early North Americans, not to mention the differences between Paleo-Americans and later American Indians, unless we invoke profound genetic drift and the unlikely hypervariable immigrant group.

The Solutrean Connection model can account directly for why there are similarities between some Paleo-American skulls and some European populations, such as the similarity of Spirit Cave Man to Norse people, why Carabelli cuspids and nonshoveled incisors were common in ancient Americans, and why mitochondrial haplogroup X is found in western Eurasia and America but not in eastern Eurasia. The Solutrean model cannot, however, explain the prevalence of Asian haplogroups, nor the similarity of most Paleo-American skulls to Polynesians/Ainu or Australians, except that early European skulls also somewhat resemble these same groups. It is possible that some ancient Americans came across the Atlantic, but not all or even most of them.

The Pacific Rim model, however, can explain everything we see, especially if helped along by the process of genetic drift. If we assume that the earliest immigrants had a blade and biface technology embedded in a culture that was adapted to cold northern conditions, they can be traced to the Upper Paleolithic cultures of central Eurasia, particularly the peoples of the Mammoth Steppe. These peoples, when divided by glacial cold after 24,000 years ago, were split into eastern and western groups, one of which contributed to the gene pool of later Europeans, the other to the gene pool of the peoples of northern China, the Russian Far East, and Japan. These latter peoples, I presume, would also have had some genetic heritage from Southeast Asia, with which they connected along the Pacific coast. It was the peoples who moved into easternmost Eurasia who, on several occasions, migrated north to Beringia and east along the Pacific Northwest coast into America. This would explain the prevalence among early Americans of dental characteristics that are found primarily in Europe (Carabelli cuspids) and southern Asia (the Sundadont pattern), as well as the DNA evidence. These Mammoth Steppe people may have possessed haplogroups X and C but, through genetic drift following the migration to the Americas, lost C west of the Caucasus Mountains and X in most populations east of there. B would have been contributed by the south Asian ancestry, and D would have evolved locally along the Asian coast. It is also possible that the Mammoth Steppe people possessed all five haplogroups and more. The craniofacial characteristics of Paleo-Americans, Asians, and early Europeans, loosely resembling as they do the Ainu, Polynesian, and Australian peoples, show that neither major contributor to the Paleo-American gene pool had yet differentiated far from the ancestral, generalized *Homo sapiens* form. Retention of tropical proportions in the leg bones is just one more line of evidence for the undifferentiated form of these earliest immigrants. These peoples, in successive waves, perhaps stimulated by brief intervals of climatic warming separated by longer intervals of forbidding cold, migrated to coastal Beringia and thence to the New World.

Only after this first colonization or series of colonizations is it possible to invoke an interior Siberian route of entry. Clovis may have evolved, as the Clovis First model suggests, out of the Nenana adaptation of Alaska, after bearers of the Nenana Culture moved into temperate North America and long after the coastal migrations had taken place. Whether or not that occurred, at least one more immigration event took place after America was already fully populated: bearers of the Dyuktai Culture, who may by then have evolved the specialized "Mongoloid," or north Asian, characteristics during 7,000 years of residence in harshest Siberia, expanded into Alaska sometime after 13,000 years ago. Gene flow, either as discrete colonizations along the coast and through the interior or simply through prolonged intermarriage, led to the dominance of these distinctly north Asian characteristics among modern American Indians.

Thus the peopling of the Americas appears to have been a lengthy process that drew from several populations and cultures over thousands of years. In a very real sense, that process continues today as the Western Hemisphere remains a destination for immigrants from throughout the world.

Epilogue

ON SEPTEMBER 24, 2000, the Interior Department released its determination of Kennewick Man's fate. Interior Secretary Bruce Babbitt announced that he had chosen to support the initial finding by the Walla Walla District Corps of Engineers: Kennewick Man was affiliated with the five tribes who had originally claimed him—the Nez Percé, Umatilla, Wanapum, Yakama, and Colville—and would be turned over to them for reburial.

Although this was the outcome the scientists who had sued for access to the skeleton (and I) had expected all along, it ran counter to nearly every bit of evidence the Interior Department had assembled in the two and a half years since it had taken over the case. A series of reports published on the Internet—about physical anthropology, archaeology, folklore, and language, in addition to the skeletal analysis conducted in 1998 by Powell and Rose—seemed largely to support an argument of nonaffiliation. Kennewick Man did not resemble any modern people, let alone Columbia Basin Indians, in his skull morphology or genetically determined skull and dental characteristics. The region's archaeological record showed no one living in the Tri-Cities area before 9,000 years ago, and seemed to indicate repeated episodes of population decline and subsequent profound cultural change. Linguistic ties could not be made, except conjecturally. Only folklore offered a tenuous link. It contained tales about how the landscape was formed, including metaphorical references to a great flood (and there had been immense floods in the region during the last glacial epoch). It also observed that none of the local tribes had stories of having immigrated from elsewhere. The Interior Department's own staff, in a report entitled "Human Culture in the Southeastern Columbia Plateau, 9500–9000 B.P. [sic] and Cultural Affiliation with Present-day Tribes," dated September 19, 2000, seemed to argue that cultural affiliation could not be established. Significantly, it downplayed the meaning of the flood stories, observing that severe floods had been commonplace in the postglacial history of the Columbia Basin. It also noted that many immigrant peoples, including the ancient Greeks, lacked oral accounts of their arrival, and noted that some of the tribes' origin tales referred to people who occupied the land before the Indians were created.

So why did Babbitt find for the Indian Tribes? He cited only two lines of evidence, rather than, as NAGPRA requires, the "preponderance of evidence," and both are highly suspect: folklore (which Interior calls "oral history") and geography. The folklore claim was based primarily on myths about how the landscape was formed, including the flood story, and the lack of any tales of migrations from elsewhere; the geographic claim was based on an interpretation of the *discussions of,* not (as required by law) a *decision by* the Indian Claims Commission. Although the commission had not made a determination that the land where Kennewick Man had been found had formerly belonged to one tribe, Babbitt felt that their discussions indicated that they *intended* to do so. When asked by reporters about these discrepancies, the Interior Department's lead attorney stated that they were "testing some of the margins of the statute." Babbitt explained that he felt NAGPRA was an Indian law and that, therefore, when there was any doubt, the decision should go in their favor. In other words, it was not incumbent upon the tribes to establish affiliation with a skeleton, but rather up to the government to prove that there was none.

The scientists were appalled by this lack of concern for due process and immediately reopened their suit in Magistrate Jelderks's court. The legal battle will be a long one, pitting the federal government, with its endless source of funds, backed by the Indian tribes with their government-paid lawyers and casino millions, against eight poorly paid academics and their pro bono attorneys. A real David and Goliath scenario. I'm rooting for David.

I am not without sympathy for the Indian position, however. I have worked with tribes for most of my career and advocated for them on a number of occasions on issues related to recognition and religious practice. I have participated in more than a dozen repatriations and have attended several reburial ceremonies. In 1993, the Colville tribe, which appreciated how I treated the dead as people, not specimens, had asked me to relocate and prepare for repatriation the remains of individuals taken from four cemeteries near the confluence of the Okanogan and Columbia Rivers. In completing that task, I was shocked to find that the remains collected by one institution were now scattered among five. Bones were mixed up in the skeleton boxes (in one case there were cadaver bones commingled with an ancient Indian), and in some cases, parts, including skulls, could not be relocated. The archaeology curator from the original institution had even repatriated a skeleton and two skulls—for which I had located the skeletons—to the wrong Indian tribe because she did not know the meaning of the site designations on the boxes. Keeping all of the remains of American Indians that are now in museums would clearly be wrong, and a lack of respectful treatment of the skeletons is only one reason why.

Perhaps an even stronger reason is Indian identity, that is identity with a small "i," not the big "I" that I will address shortly. Imagine how hard it would be for an Indian youth to build a positive self-image when he knows that the graves of his recent ancestors can be dug up as a hobby or excavated by scientists without his agreement or participation. He would feel less human than people of European, African, or Asian ancestry, less than equal in the eyes of the law. And I believe that it truly was a vestige of the pre-twentieth-century view of Indians as less than fully human that was behind the looting of graves. This attitude developed among Euro-American settlers, who displaced Indian peoples in order to ensure the survival of their own families. In coping psychologically with the consequences—seeing men, women, and children destitute, racked by disease, and starving— they had dehumanized those they displaced. To help purge the remnants of this way of thinking, America needed a law like NAGPRA.

But NAGPRA is flawed. Although it states that claims for possession of skeletons must be based on family relationship or cultural affiliation, that is not how it is being applied. Museums, wishing to avoid being called "insensitive," or worse, "racist" by Native American activists, often turn all holdings over to the tribe that owns the loudest voice, not the most supportable claim. The law has been coopted—and in truth was initially demanded—by the Native American Identity movement. That is identity with a big "I." Peoples descended from Pre-Columbian societies as disparate as tiny bands of wandering foragers and farm-fed, theocratic empires seek a unified identity based on outmoded concepts of race. "We have always been one people" is the refrain of the descendants of the conquerors and the conquered of antiquity alike, "and have occupied this land since the beginning of time." I believe it is in the service of this movement, not out of respect for the dead or even true identity with them, that tribes have pursued claims for the earliest Americans, in some cases more vehemently than for more recent remains. Buhla, the Minnesota woman, the Browns Valley man, Spirit Cave Man, and Kennewick Man have all been claimed. Spirit Cave Man and Kennewick Man alone among this group remain unburied (incongruously, the Interior Department determined that Spirit Cave Man was unaffiliated with any modern tribe while affiliating the almost equally old Kennewick Man to Columbia Basin tribes).

As strongly as I believe that it is morally wrong to excavate recent (as in 1,000- to 2,000-year-old) American Indian graves or to keep them in museums without the consent and participation of their cultural next of kin, I believe it is immoral to turn the bones of the most ancient Americans over to modern tribes, who have expressed an intent to bury them without learning what stories they have to tell about themselves and their time. The evidence is mounting that the Americas were peopled in several waves of ancient immigrants. The earliest of these peoples represent only one five-thousandth of the early American skeletons held in collections in the United States and they do not culturally or physically resemble the modern-day peoples of our hemisphere. Spirit Cave Man, for example, was buried wearing moccasins unique to prehistory, wearing a cloak of rabbit skin woven in a previously unknown fashion, and wrapped in a blanket twined in a manner unknown in America after 9,000 years ago. The peoples of the Intermountain West, probably including Kennewick Man's kin, used such tools as bolas and crescents, which, like the unique moccasins and woven fabrics of Spirit Cave, dropped out of use at about the time the people who closely resemble today's Indians arrived. The Paleo-Americans more closely resembled the human prototype that emerged from Africa so recently in the history of the world. NAGPRA should not apply to them; they should be considered the heritage of all the world's peoples.

Kennewick Man lived along the Columbia River 450 generations ago in a culture now forgotten, speaking a language now dead, among a people who may be extinct. If his people are indeed extinct, and if the plaintiff scientists win their case and complete their studies, what should become of Kennewick Man's remains? I fear that I have conflicting perspectives on this question. I teach my students that the forensic anthropologist is the advocate for the dead, and as the individual who gathered this man's remains from the riverbank I feel a personal responsibility and attachment to him. In choosing how best to advocate for him, I am of three minds.

As a humanist, and as a man, I would like to see him at rest, back at peace in the same ground that held him for ninety-five centuries. He is not kept on a museum shelf now, available for use as a teaching specimen, as had been many of the skeletons I repatriated for the Colville, but he has been sorely abused. Nearly whole when I recovered him, he has lost most of both femurs to theft, and parts of a tibia, a few ribs, and several hand and foot bones to overcautious, poorly informed scientific investigations while in the government's custody. Perhaps once we have learned from him all that we can with today's technology, we should return him to the earth, in a ceremony that allows all—the tribes and even the Asatru Folk Assembly—to honor him. If that happens, or if the tribes prevail and rebury him, I hope to be present to pay my respects to one who has had such an impact on my life.

As a scientist, I feel we should retain Kennewick Man under high security as the Neanderthal and Cro-Magnon skeletons of Europe are maintained. Thus kept, he would be accessible in perpetuity to scholars who, armed with methods and technologies not yet imagined, could glean ever more information about these little-known people.

The moralist in me agrees not with the humanist, as one might expect, but with the scientist, but for different reasons. Kennewick Man, Spirit Cave Man, the Wilson-Leonard woman, and the couple from Horn Shelter are all messengers from a long-distant past, who represent a people or peoples who no longer exist. At least some of those peoples represent dead branches on the dense bush of human biological and cultural history. To rebury Kennewick Man and his contemporaries without scientific study by people who are independent of the political process, or to rebury them now after even a full investigation with today's technologies, would in effect silence them forever. It would rob them of their rightful place in the history of the human species. Instead, we should hold such individuals as national treasures— messengers from a long-distant past who can educate and enlighten future generations that through scientific advances may be better able to hear the stories these ultimate American elders have to tell.

One teaching the Paleo-Americans have already brought to us, just by being physically close to the human prototype, is a reminder of how we expanded across the globe as a morphologically uniform species just a few thousand years ago and of how recent and superficial the differences between us really are. We should take that lesson to heart and emphasize not the ethnic and "racial" distinctions that divide us but the characteristics that unite all humankind.

Notes

Chapter 1: The Stone Had Teeth

Page
19 *"I've got some bones for you to look at"*: Much of the dialogue in this book is based on notes from interviews and telephone conversations and is as close to verbatim as possible. Where no such documentation was available, I have made every effort to remain faithful to the content and spirit of each interchange, working from both my own memory and that of others who participated in or witnessed the interaction.

19 *bones always have a story to tell*: A number of excellent books on forensic anthropology and bioarchaeology are available for the layman, including Jeffrey Schwartz, *What the Bones Tell Us* (Tucson: University of Arizona Press, 1993); Konrad Spindler, *The Man in the Ice* (New York: Crown, 1994); Douglas Ubelaker and Henry Scammell, *Bones: A Forensic Detective's Casebook* (New York: M. Evans and Co., 1992); Stanley Rhine, *Bone Voyage: A Journey in Forensic Anthropology* (Albuquerque: University of New Mexico Press, 1998); Mary Manhein, *The Bone Lady: Life as a Forensic Anthropologist* (Baton Rouge: Louisiana State University Press, 1999); and Clark Spencer Larsen, *Skeletons in Our Closet* (Princeton, N.J.: Princeton University Press, 2000).

21 *They had come over from Siberia*: See, e.g., Brian M. Fagan, *The Great Journey* (London and New York: Thames and Hudson, 1987); David J. Meltzer, *Search for the First Americans* (Washington, D.C.: Smithsonian Books, 1993).

Chapter 2: A Question of Time

22 *"a work in progress"*: Despite the fact that the article written following this interview (Dave Schafer, "Skull Likely Early White Settler," *Tri-City Herald*, August 30, 1996) emphasized the possible European identity of the skeleton, it did include my disclaimer in its fourth column.

23 *the second earliest well-documented culture*: See James C. Chatters and David A. Pokotylo, "Prehistory: Introduction," in *Handbook of North American Indians*, vol. 12, *Plateau*, edited by Deward E. Walker (Washington, D.C.: Smithsonian Institution Press, 1998), 73–80.

36 *"Under the authority of the Coroner"*: James Chatters to Richard Charlton, Real Estate Division, Walla Walla District, Corps of Engineers, July 30, 1996.

45 *the major text on radiocarbon dating*: R. E. Taylor, *Radiocarbon Dating* (New York: Academic Press, 1987); see also R. Taylor, A. Long, and R. Kra, eds., *Radiocarbon after Four Decades* (New York: Plenum, 1992).

47 *"with care and sensitivity"*: This statement, which I transcribed at the time of the conversation, is echoed in communications between Tracy and his superiors dated August 5 and August 9, 1996.

47 *the coroner's signed letter of request*: The letter, signed by Deputy Coroner Larry Duncan, read in part:

"We are engaged in the investigation of human skeletal remains recently recovered on the Columbia River in Benton County, Washington. . . . In order to resolve the identification issue, and assure that the remains go to the proper group of descendants for reburial, we are requesting that your laboratory conduct Accelerator Mass Spectrometer radiocarbon dating of the enclosed bone sample.

"We are particularly concerned that the smallest possible amount of material be used to obtain the date. Some of the native tribes in our region object to destructive analysis of the remains of their ancestors, and should the date show this to be Native American, we wish to minimize the offense to the possible descendants. . . .

". . . We hope to be able to use the result to make our determination by August 27th."

48 *analyzing mitochondrial DNA*: Few descriptions of these methods occur in the general literature, but see, e.g., Berndt Herrmann and Suzanne Hummel, "Introduction," in *Ancient DNA*, edited by Herrmann and Hummel (New York: Springer, 1994). An excellent primer on mtDNA can be found in Roger Lewin, *The Origin of Modern Humans* (New York: Scientific American Library, 1993).

51 *One half of it is constantly decaying*: This is the mean half-life computed by Libby and used throughout the world since the inception of the radiocarbon dating method. More recent research has shown that the actual half-life is nearer to 5,730 years, but to keep new radiocarbon dates consistent with earlier computations, all laboratories use the standard half-life.

53 *calendar years, not radiocarbon years*: Where uncorrected radiocarbon dates occur they are described as radiocarbon years or followed by the letters B.P. This may be confusing for some, who are used to seeing radiocarbon years expressed as years ago, as often occurs in the popular press and surprisingly often in professional journals. Calibrated ages are often much older than radio-

carbon ages. The height of the last glacial episode, for example, is given the age 22,000 years ago here, whereas it is usually cited as 18,000 B.P.; the beginning of the postglacial, or Holocene, epoch at 11,500 instead of 10,000 B.P. The program used to do the calibrations is Oxcal 3, and I use the approximate modal (most likely) date only rather than giving a range of possible ages.

Some readers may notice the difference between the age given here for Kennewick Man and that reported in the popular media. The oft-reported age, 9,265–9,535 years, is based on a radiocarbon age that was not yet corrected for the carbon isotope composition of the bone, −14.9 per mil (parts per thousand) relative to standard mean seawater, whereas wood charcoal is usually in the range of −22 per mil. This greater tendency for the bone to contain heavier atoms of carbon means that there will be more carbon 14 than expected and thus the date will appear younger than it actually is. The value 8,410±60 has been corrected for this effect, resulting in a slightly greater calibrated age.

Chapter 3: An Opportunity Lost

59 *usually requested state-of-the-art analyses:* I had recovered four sets of human remains (totaling sixteen individuals) from traditional Colville territory during the 1980s, working with Adeline Fredin and one or more elders in each case. Each time, Fredin had approved radiocarbon dating and stable isotope analyses, which I presented in a series of reports published by Central Washington University. In 1993, she requested that I conduct a large repatriation project, which would include the same kinds of analyses. Thus her claim that analysis of Kennewick Man's remains violated the tribe's religious beliefs seemed to me to ring hollow.

59 *to right a historical wrong:* For an exposition of the NAGPRA issue from the Native American perspective, see David Hurst Thomas, *Skull Wars* (New York: Basic Books, 2000).

70 *"There won't be any more publicity":* This position is repeated in a memorandum entitled "Public Affairs Plan—Involvement with Recently Discovered Ancient Human Remains at [Columbia Park]" (location deleted in released copy), drafted by Duane "Dutch" Meier, public affairs officer for the Walla Walla District Corps of Engineers, August 29, 1996.

74 *the law may not cover very ancient remains:* Report of the NAGPRA Review Committee (Washington, D.C.: National Park Service), August 20, 1996.

Chapter 4: To the Brink of Oblivion

80 *Katie MacMillan and Grover Krantz:* Catherine J. MacMillan, Bone-Apart Agency, to Floyd Johnson, Benton County Coroner, August 31, 1996; Grover S. Krantz, Washington State University, to James C. Chatters, September 2, 1996.

81 *letters I gladly supplied:* These letters read, in part:

"I am writing on behalf of and with the knowledge of the Benton County Coroner. . . .

"We are facing a situation where the Corps of Engineers is attempting to force the Coroner to turn over human remains before he has finished his investigation. . . . The remains consist of a complete skeleton of a man who lived more than 9200 years ago. As such, it is one of a handful of complete remains from more than 8000 years ago that have ever been found in North America. . . . The Smithsonian Institution's Physical Anthropologist, Dr. Douglas Owsley, and Curator of Anthropology, Dr. Dennis Stanford, have stated that the find is of national if not international significance. . . . [T]hey have offered to fly me with the remains to Washington [for] two days to conduct nondestructive studies.

"The remains were found on Corps of Engineers land but, under common law, we understand that the remains are to stay in the coroner's custody until he completes his investigation. He has not done so yet, but we are receiving demands from the Corps . . . that the bones be returned to them. Their intent is to give them to the Umatilla Indian Tribe, who intend to bury them . . . before any study is conducted. . . . Given their stated plans for reburial, this amounts to destruction. . . .

"I am asking your assistance in helping us influence the Corps to let us finish our investigation and preserve this very important scientific discovery for the benefit of all citizens."

87 *"Our oral history goes back ten thousand years":* This oft-reported claim is not based on direct reckoning of time, since the Sahaptian language, spoken by most of the claimants in this case, does not have a concept for "thousand." Most of the oral traditions date to the nineteenth century or perhaps just before white contact. The only story ever brought up as evidence for this 10,000-year tenure is a tale of a great flood on the Columbia River. Since there were glacial floods in the region which have been radiocarbon dated by scientists, Minthorn uses the correspondence to argue for eternal tenure on the land. This claim of being on land since time began is now being echoed by aboriginal groups from throughout the world, regardless of past oral traditions or historical records to the contrary.

90 *his museum's interests:* Interestingly enough, the American Museum's administration did challenge NAGPRA in early 2000. The Grand Ronde tribe, a small group from western Oregon, had filed a claim for the Willamette meteorite, which the museum had bought from an iron and steel company a century earlier. The museum filed suit, stating that natural objects such as the meteorite were not covered under the statute. The case was resolved by a joint custody agreement between the tribe and the museum that permits continued display at the museum. But the lawsuit clearly points out the serious ambiguities of this vague law.

92 *she ran a news story about the work:* Ann Gibbons, "DNA Enters Dust Up Over Bones," *Science* (October 12, 1996): 72.

92 *Reports by the Associated Press:* My actual statement had been that he was not *just* the Umatillas' ancestor but was probably at least an ancestor of all Western Hemisphere peoples (letter from James C. Chatters to Aviva Brandt of the AP, dated September 13, 1996).

94 *"passive genocide":* "Position on the Preservation of Human Remains," submitted October 2, 1996, by Edward Neiburger, chairman, Ethnic Minority Council of America.

96 *partial male skeleton found in Hourglass Cave, Colorado*: Cynthia Mosch and Patty Jo Watson, "The Ancient Explorer of Hourglass Cave," *Evolutionary Anthropology* 5 (1996): 111–115.

100 *The tribes had scheduled the reburial*: In an October 4 letter to Lieutenant Colonel Curtis, the chairman of the Confederated Tribes of the Yakama Nation wrote, "I am informed that tentative reburial dates of 25 October and 30 October have been established. We sincerely hope that the Corps of Engineers–Walla Walla will continue to exert all necessary effort to accommodate these dates."

101 *neither had mentioned deferring to the Umatillas*: Joe Pakootas, chairman of the Colville Business Council, in an October 11 letter to Curtis, stated simply, "This letter is intended to make it absolutely clear that the Confederated Tribes of the Colville Indian Reservation claim all of the human remains discovered at [Kennewick, Washington]." Rex Buck and Robert Tomanawash of the Wanapum band wrote, "I am writing a letter on behalf of the Wanapum Band of Priest Rapids requesting the return of ancestral human remains found at [Kennewick, Washington]. The one remain found the weekend of July 27, 1996 and the five individuals during the weekend of August 24, 1996. We are requesting their return for immediate reburial." (The locations are given in brackets here because the government redacted locations on all documents released on this case, even though everyone knew where the highly publicized find had occurred.)

102 *should be turned over to the Smithsonian*: Letter from John Huerta, general counsel for the Smithsonian Institution, to Lester Edelman, chief counsel for the U.S. Army Corps of Engineers, dated October 15, 1996. I have attempted only to distill the essence of Huerta's argument here. The Act creating the Smithsonian Institution was signed into law on August 10, 1846, and can be found in Title 20 of the United States Code. Cited sections are 50 and 59.

102 *the accidental finding*: This memo, "CENPD [Corps of Engineers North Pacific Division] Comments Regarding the Disposition of Culturally Unidentifiable Human Remains and Associated Funerary Objects," is identified as COE 0663–0666 and was cited extensively in a June 27, 1997, decision by Judge Jelderks. Despite the Corps's evident acknowledgment that scientific study was not prohibited by NAGPRA and that it was in fact necessary in cases such as that of Kennewick Man's, the Corps of Engineers in January 1997 denied all requests for scientific study on the grounds that (a) such study was prohibited without tribal approval and (b) the tribes opposed it. The scientific community was thus left with no recourse but to pursue its lawsuit.

Chapter 5: The Battle for Kennewick Man

104 *attempted to have the scientists' suit*: *Bonnichsen et al. v. US* and *Asatru Folk Assembly v. US*, United States District Court for the District of Oregon 969, Federal Supplement 614, February 19, 1997, and associated documents. The full text of the opinion is reprinted in Richard B. Cunningham, *Archaeology, Relics, and the Law* (Carolina Academic Press, 1999), 637–648.

105 *a blistering fifty-two-page opinion*: *Bonnichsen et al. v. US* and *Asatru Folk*

Assembly v. US, United States District Court for the District of Oregon 969, Federal Supplement 614, February 19, 1997, and associated documents. The full text of the opinion is reprinted in Richard B. Cunningham, *Archaeology, Relics, and the Law* (Carolina Academic Press, 1999), 648–673.

107 *That list did not include:* There is no record that these notes existed prior to December 1996. Alan Schneider had, through legal discovery, requested all Corps documents on the Kennewick Man case and received more than one thousand pages of documents, none of which, he reports, included the purported summary done by the tribe's staff member.

108 *The Nez Percé Tribal Council:* Nez Percé Tribal Executive Committee Resolution NP98-177, dated March 24, 1998, and signed by Samuel N. Penney, chairman. This document states in part: "NOW THEREFORE BE IT RE-SOLVED, that the Nez Perce Tribe opposes any contract that may be contemplated by any federal, state, private corporation, or organizations, to be made with James Chatters, Ph.D., anthropologist; that the Nez Perce Tribe does not feel comfortable with his capabilities, based on the consideration of his known work performance, including his role in the 'Kennewick Man' controversy, which constitutes a conflict of interest and has potential adverse impacts to the interest of the Nez Perce Tribe [upper case and punctuation as in original]."

108 *More bones disappeared:* Declaration by John Leier, May 8, 1998, to the U.S. District Court for the District of Oregon in the case of *Bonnichsen et al. v. US* and *Asatru Folk Assembly v. US* (Civil Nos. 96-1481-JE and 96-1516-JE).

111 *New cracks had developed:* The Interior Department attempted publicly to blame this cracking on my efforts to preserve the skull, but I have preserved many bones before and since using the same polymer I used to treat the Kennewick bones with no ill effects.

113 *The results proved to be inconclusive:* According to attorney Alan Schneider, Joe Powell confided to him that the government had completely rewritten the report he and Rose had prepared, making it necessary for them to work diligently to keep their original findings intact.

116 *McManamon finally released:* www.cv.nps.gov/aad/kennewick.

Chapter 6: A Lifetime of Pain

122 *I studied these records:* For an academic presentation of my observations, see James C. Chatters, "The Recovery and First Analysis of an Early Holocene Human Skeleton from Kennewick, Washington," *American Antiquity* 65 (2000): 291–316.

122 *I pored over anthropological journals:* An excellent introduction to the methods of forensic anthropology or bioarchaeology is Simon Mays, *The Archaeology of Human Bone* (London: Routledge, 1998); for popular presentations of the science, see notes to Chapter 1.

129 *about 66 percent of his protein intake:* There is more than one reason why carbon 13 might vary in relation to carbon 12, so for diet to be accurately assessed, ratios of nitrogen isotopes need to be considered along with those of carbon. Consumers of tropical or hot weather grasses, such as corn (maize) or

some of the short grasses of the Great Plains have high levels of carbon 13 relative to consumers of temperate zone plants, and show carbon 13 levels that are very close to those of marine food eaters. Nitrogen ratios help us to distinguish between marine consumers and tropical grass consumers. Nitrogen 15 increases in relation to nitrogen 14 as one proceeds up the food chain, which means that large marine fish, which are usually higher-order consumers, will have high nitrogen 15 ratios compared with grazing animals. Therefore, salmon eaters should have high nitrogen 15 levels, which is true of the late prehistoric inhabitants of the Columbia Basin. An analysis of nitrogen ratios in Kennewick Man's bone collagen would confirm or disconfirm the conclusion that he ate a lot of salmon. Unfortunately, no such analysis has yet been performed. We can, however, surmise that because Kennewick Man apparently lived along the Columbia River, he probably ate the fish of that river, which have always included anadromous species.

130 *A paleopathologist must interpret:* This field is rarely discussed in popular formats as paleopathology uses a deep, dense jargon. A basic understanding can, however, be gained by perusing Robert W. Mann and Sean P. Murphy, *Regional Atlas of Bone Disease* (Springfield, Ill.: Charles C Thomas, 1990), and Donald J. Ortner and Walter G. J. Putschar, *Identification of Pathological Conditions in Human Skeletal Remains* (Washington, D.C.: Smithsonian Institution Press, 1981), as well as some of the references cited in Chapter 1.

134 *"that's way too much difference":* Several of my colleagues, including Judy Meyers Suchey of California State University, Fullerton, and Phillip Walker of the University of California, Santa Barbara, report seeing such a great asymmetry between right and left arms fairly often, although I have not had that experience. They would attribute the difference simply to a much heavier reliance on the right arm.

139 *Dr. K.'s medical perspective:* For a slightly different analysis, see Joseph F. Powell and Jerome C. Rose, "Report on the Osteological Assessment of the 'Kennewick Man' Skeleton (CENW.97.Kennewick)" (Washington D.C.: National Park Service, U.S. Department of the Interior, 1999). Powell and Rose conducted a brief examination of the skeleton for the Interior Department in February 1999, during which they spent about three days reconstructing the skull, taking measurements, pictures, X rays, and CT scans, and making observations of the skeletal pathologies. They complained that the short working time, poor light, and lack of a good microscope limited their ability to conduct their studies. Their report, which was published on the Internet by the Department of the Interior, contained several differences from my own. They estimated Kennewick Man's height at approximately 5 feet, 9 inches, but did so without the femurs, most of both of which had already been stolen. (Femur measurements are considered to give the most accurate estimates of stature.)

They (largely Rose, according to Joe Powell) also drew some different conclusions about the man's injuries. They did not see the defect of the skull as a fracture, although I have received concurrence with my assessment from Phillip Walker of the University of California, Santa Barbara, who has worked extensively with such injuries in prehistoric skeletons. They did not notice the acute infection in the left temple or the radial head fracture, nor did they comment about the weaker muscle development in the left arm. They did, however, infer a fracture of the right humerus from a slight angle and thickening at about the middle of the shaft. They noted a similar angle in the left arm but interpreted that as muscle development. The thickening was in both cases located at the lower end of the attachment for the deltoideus muscle and is a common occurrence in peoples who lived in the Northwest. It is probably due to hyperdevelopment of the shoulder musculature because of some mechanical stress associated with water, such as swimming, paddling boats, pulling nets, or the like. They saw only three rib fractures, two with false joints, but Doug Owsley (when he conducted his inventory) and I saw more.

The greatest difference in our findings, however, is in the spearpoint wound. Rose interprets the spear as having entered from behind and below, not from the front and above, meaning the man would literally have had to sit upon it with great force. He inferred that the spear had entered and caused no infection, quickly healing so thoroughly that it had left no scar at the entry point. This is not possible. Bone simply does not heal from such a severe trauma without a trace, and the extensive concave area of remodeled bone around the wound clearly shows that there had been an acute infection. Rose's inference was based largely on the opinion of lithic analyst John Fagan, who relied more heavily on a low-resolution three-dimensional CT scan rather than on visual examination to look at the stone point. The chipping patterns that can be seen through the bone window in the ilium clearly show that the base is positioned above and to the outside, a fact confirmed by my CT scans. Finally, Rose suggested that the man's various wounds, such as the ribs that flexed in and out when he breathed, caused him no pain. As a sufferer of many rib fractures, I can confidently say that chronic, or at least recurrent, pain is part of the experience.

Differences of opinion are a part—an important part—of science.

141 *Kennewick Man was nonetheless at risk:* Francis McManamon of the Interior Department confidently told the press that Kennewick Man did not die from the spear wound. The man did not die immediately from the wound, nor did he succumb within a few months or probably a few years from the ensuing infection, but chronic conditions such as this one are known to cause death on some occasions, long after the initial wound seems to have healed.

143 *a method named after the late Russian anatomist:* Gerasimov's method is illustrated in the movie *Gorky Park* (Orion Pictures, 1983), although the results displayed there show a significantly greater likeness to the deceased than one should realistically expect. For an excellent popular presentation of this method and its many applications see John Prag and Richard Neave, *Making Faces* (College Station: Texas A&M Press, 1997).

147 *probably the skin color:* Christopher Stringer and Robin McKie, *African Exodus* (New York: Owl Books, 1996).

Chapter 7: A Place in Time

149 *Intermountain Stemmed Point Tradition:* Roy L. Carlson, "Introduction to Early Human Occupation in British Columbia," in *Early Human Occupation in British Columbia,* edited by R. L. Carlson and L. Dalla Bona (Vancouver: University of British Columbia Press, 1996), 3–10.

152 *After 6,000 years ago:* James C. Chatters, "Population Growth, Climatic Cooling and the Development of Collector Strategies in the Southern Plateau," *Journal of World Prehistory* 9 (1995): 341–400.

152 *these new people probably moved south:* This move was a part of the Salishan expansion, which was first posited by linguist William Elmendorf, who used the degree of language divergence to estimate the time when Salish-speaking people expanded from coastal British Columbia into the interior Pacific Northwest. See Kinkade and others, "Languages," in *Handbook of North American Indians,* vol. 12, *Plateau,* edited by Deward E. Walker (Washington, D.C.: Smithsonian Institution Press, 1998), 49–72.

156 *"the tribes consider this site sacred":* As important as it is that we all respect one another's right to freedom of religion, this action by the Corps was unconstitutional. The courts have found on several occasions that one group's religious beliefs cannot be used by the government to constrain the actions of other citizens on federal property (e.g., *Bandoni v. Higginson,* 1980, 10th Circuit; *Hopi v. Block,* 1981, DC Circuit; *Bear Lodge Multiple Use Association v. Babbitt,* 1996, District of Wyoming). It appears that at that time, the Corps was operating under an Executive Order by President Clinton, which ordered federal agencies to consider the impact of their actions on Indians' free expression of religion.

In this case, the claim of sanctity and prohibition of excavation in undisturbed portions of the site seem specious. In the fall of 1996, the Walla Walla District Corps of Engineers had issued an ARPA permit to the Umatilla tribe to excavate test pits in order to determine the extent of a historic Indian cemetery located only 4 miles away. Further, the Umatillas' own research plan, submitted with their request for a permit to investigate the Kennewick Man site, included digging test pits on the uneroded floodplain.

156 *The Corps took other samples:* Sampling was one area where the Corps team seemed technically outdated, or at best to be using techniques better suited to other purposes. In work of this kind, where one seeks to identify the source of a dislodged fossil, precision is paramount. Stafford and I, who did most of the sampling for the scientific team, first cleaned and described in detail each section, then took soil at 2-cm and 5-cm intervals, from the bottom of the bank to the top, always ending samples at stratigraphic boundaries. Soil was cut from the clean bank directly into clean, prelabeled plastic bags without being handled, to avoid contamination with organic material and other soil. The Corps took its samples in 10-cm blocks, with no apparent attention to the stratigraphic boundaries. They took earth directly into their hands and packed it into fruit jars for transport, labeling the containers only after all had been filled. Then they mailed the jars home. Not surprisingly, many of the jars were broken by the time they reached Vicksburg. The Corps then sent an untrained technician out to replace them, so this sampling was even less precise. It is small wonder that Stein and Huckleberry had a difficult time matching soil from the skeleton with that from the riverbank.

157 *13,100-year-old Glacier Peak ash:* The Corps of Engineers conducted its own radiocarbon dating of soils, but its results contradict the geologic evidence for site age and therefore are not reliable. The Corps obtained dates ranging from nearly 10,000 years ago approximately 1 m below the surface of the river-laid

unit to three dates more than 14,500 years old from below that (Lillian Wakeley and others, U.S. Army Technical Report GL-98-13 (Vicksburg: Waterways Experiment Station, 1998)). While the uppermost date is within the appropriate age range of the skeleton, the lower three would make this lower floodplain older than the Glacier Peak ash-containing terrace on the Yakima River, which is not possible. For this reason, all four dates must be considered suspect on methodological grounds, and I do not discuss them in this text. Radiocarbon dating of soil requires very careful consideration of the soil chemistry and awareness that the various organic components of soil are likely to have different histories. What probably happened here was inclusion of ancient carbon (carried in by the river as part of the sediment) with organic acids that were precipitated in the soil by plants that lived and died on the surface of each stratum. The inclusion of the ancient carbon would give an erroneously old estimate of stratum age.

Chapter 8: Kennewick Man's "Brother"

165 *the only males of that age:* A single skeleton was found in a grave in Marmes Rockshelter, on the Snake River, and a radiocarbon date on shell from the time of the burial was around 7800 B.P. This skeleton has never been reported, and it might never be studied because it is under control of the same Corps of Engineers district as Kennewick Man's. However, most of the human remains in that site are in very poor condition, and none had skulls intact enough for analysis.

165 *mythical beings:* Reference to the Stick People can be found in Click Relander's *Drummers and Dreamers* (Seattle: Pacific Northwest National Parks and Forests Association, 1986), a book about the Wanapum people. Clayton Denman, a retired faculty member at Central Washington University, had worked as an archaeologist on the Columbia River during his graduate student days at the University of California, Berkeley. Whenever human bones were found, he recalls, the project director would call in Frank Buck, leader of the Wanapum Band, and ask if they were the remains of his people. Sometimes Buck would claim the dead as tribal members and take them for reburial. Other times, however, he would say, "Those aren't Indians, those are Stick People. They were here before the Indians; they belong in a Museum." And that is where they went until claimed by the next Wanapum generation as revered ancestors.

170 *a short note to this effect:* James Chatters, "Encounter with an Ancestor," *Anthropology News* 38 (1997): 3 (www.ameranthassn.org, January 1997).

172 *Races were then seen as distinct groupings:* See Stephen Jay Gould, *The Mismeasure of Man* (New York: W. W. Norton, 1996). There has been some resurgence of this attitude in books by Richard Herrnstein, Charles Murray, Arthur Jensen, and J. Philippe Rushton. Alarm over the social implications of the works by these authors may in part explain the overreaction to the use of "Caucasoid" in the Kennewick case.

172 *we all know that races don't exist:* A lively discussion about the topic of race in anthropology can be found in *Anthropology News* from September 1997 through June 1998 (see www.ameranthassn.org). Of particular interest is the interchange among Alan Goodman, Jonathan Marks, me, and three of the

plaintiffs in the Kennewick Man case—George Gill, Richard Jantz, and Douglas Owsley.

177 *modern Nubians and ancient Lower Egyptians:* C. L. Brace, D. P. Tracer, L. A. Yaroch, J. Robb, K. Brandt, and A. R. Nelson, "Clines and Clusters Versus 'Race': A Test in Ancient Egypt and the Case of Death on the Nile," *Yearbook of Physical Anthropology* 36 (1993): 1–31.

181 *Sinodont, or "Chinese-toothed":* For a popular account of this work, see Christy Turner, "Teeth and the Prehistory of Asia," *Scientific American,* February 1989, 88–96.

182 *The Ainu are the vestiges:* For an excellent recent discussion of the Ainu, see William Fitzhugh and Chisato Dubreuil, *Ainu: Spirit of a Northern People* (Seattle: University of Washington Press, 2000).

184 *Relative newcomers:* Geoffrey Irwin, *The Prehistoric Exploration and Colonization of the Pacific* (Cambridge, England: Cambridge University Press, 1992); Patrick Kirch, *The Lapita Peoples: Ancestors of the Oceanic World* (London: Basil Blackwell, 1996); for an excellent popular summary, see Jared Diamond, *Guns, Germs, and Steel: The Fates of Human Societies* (New York: W. W. Norton, 1997).

Chapter 9: Who Were the Paleo-Americans?

188 *The team found more of Marmes Man:* A fascinating popular account of this discovery is Ruth Kirk, *The Oldest Man in America* (New York: Harcourt Brace Jovanovich, 1970).

189 *he later came to see ritual cleaning:* Grover Krantz, "Oldest Human Remains from the Marmes Site," *Northwest Anthropological Research Notes* 13 (1979): 159–173.

190 *Hrdlička had gone to great pains:* Aleš Hrdlička, "The Origin and Antiquity of the American Indian," *Annual Report of the Board of Regents of the Smithsonian Institution* (1923), 481–493; "Early Man in America: What Have the Bones to Say?" in *Early Man as Depicted by Leading Authorities at the International Symposium at the Academy of Natural Sciences, Philadelphia, March 1937,* edited by G. MacCurdy (Philadelphia: Lippincott, 1937), 93–104.

190 *very few ancient human bits:* See H. M. Wormington, *Ancient Man in North America,* 4th ed. (Denver: Denver Museum of Natural History, 1957).

192 *the Spirit Cave mummy:* The better-preserved and -documented Paleo-American skeletons are described in the following sources:

Spirit Cave, Wizards Beach, and Grimes Burial Shelter: Donald Tuohy and Amy Dansie, eds., *Nevada Historical Society Quarterly* 40, no. 1 (1997) (entire issue).

Horn Shelter: Albert Redder and John Fox, "Excavation and Positioning of the Horn Shelter Burial and Grave Goods," *Central Texas Archaeologist,* 11 (1998): 1–12; Dianne Young, "An Osteological Analysis of the Paleoindian Double Burial from Horn Shelter, Number 2," *Central Texas Archaeologist,* 1 (1998): 13–105.

Buhl: Thomas Green et al., "The Buhl Burial: A Paleoindian Woman from Southern Idaho," *American Antiquity* 63 (1998): 437–456.

Notes

The Minnesota woman: Albert Jenks, *Pleistocene Man in Minnesota* (Minneapolis: University of Minnesota Press, 1936).

Browns Valley: Albert Jenks, "Minnesota's Browns Valley Man and Associated Burial Artifacts," *Memoirs of the American Anthropological Association* 49 (1937).

Gordon Creek: David Breternitz et al., "An Early Burial from Gordon Creek, Colorado," *American Antiquity* 36 (1971): 170–182.

Hourglass Cave: Cynthia Mosch and Patty Jo Watson, "The Ancient Explorer of Hourglass Cave," *Evolutionary Anthropology* 5 (1996): 111–115.

Gore Creek: Jerome Cybulski et al., "An Early Human Skeleton from South Central British Columbia: Dating and Bioarchaeological Inference," *Canadian Journal of Archaeology* 5 (1981): 49–59.

J. C. Putnam: T. D. Stewart, "Report on the J. C. Putnam Skeleton from Texas," *Bulletin of the Texas Archaeological and Paleontological Society* 16 (1945): 31–38.

On Your Knees Cave (aka Tongass Caves): E. James Dixon, *Bones, Boats, and Bison: Archaeology and the First Colonization of Western North America* (Albuquerque: University of New Mexico Press, 2000).

Wilson-Leonard: "Human Biological Remains," in *Wilson-Leonard: An 11,000-Year Archaeological Record of Hunter-Gatherers in Central Texas,* edited by M. Collins (Austin: Texas Department of Transportation): 1441–1458.

197 *perhaps his daughter or very young wife:* Opinions about the child's sex differ. Dianne Young (see reference above) interpreted the remains as those of a male, but Doug Owsley (personal communication), who reanalyzed the bones in the fall of 1998 as part of a study of Paleo-American and archaic skeletons from the Great Plains, identified it as a female. I use the female designation here in deference to Owsley's greater experience and the association of the child with a needle, specimens of which were also associated with the Buhl female and possibly with Marmes I.

199 *have been discovered by chance:* This statistic is a reason for concern. Finds usually are not made during controlled archaeological excavations but are inadvertent. Under federal law, skeletons found in the course of archaeological excavations may be studied for a time before they are reburied by modern Indian groups, but the part of the law that addresses inadvertent discoveries contains no mention of study. This means that if all future finds are made on federal land or in states that have copied NAGPRA in their own statutes, we are unlikely to learn much more about the first peoples of America. One positive outcome of the Kennewick Man case has been the federal government's acknowledgment that for NAGPRA to be applied correctly, extensive studies are needed even in cases of inadvertent discovery.

203 *buried her:* One of the ironies of this story is that the Shoshones and other Numic-speaking peoples were traditionally very informal about disposal of the dead. Most ethnographies indicate that corpses were typically left in rock crevices or other places of exposure with little or no ceremony.

208 *the teenage male:* Douglas Owsley and Richard Jantz, "Biography in the Bones," *Discovering Archaeology,* February 2000, 56–58.

215 *As they recently wrote:* D. Gentry Steele and Joseph Powell, "Peopling of the

Americas: A Historical and Comparative Perspective," in *Who Were the First Americans?*, edited by Robson Bonnichsen (Corvallis: Center for the Study of the First Americans, Oregon State University, 1999), 97–126.

216 *In counterpoint to Hrdlička:* See, e.g., Kenneth McGowan and Joseph A. Hester, *Early Man in the New World* (Garden City, N.Y.: Anchor Books, 1962).

218 *linguist Alan Greenberg and geneticist Steven Zegura:* See Joseph Greenberg, *Language in the Americas* (Stanford, Calif.: Stanford University Press, 1987); Joseph Greenberg, Christy Turner, and Steven Zegura, "The Settlement of the Americas: A Comparison of the Linguistic, Dental and Genetic Evidence," *Current Anthropology* 27 (1986): 477–497; see also Christy Turner reference in Chapter 8. For an opposing viewpoint, see Johanna Nichols, "Linguistic Diversity and the First Settlement of the *New* World," *Language* 66 (1990): 475–521.

219 *Steele and Powell reexamined:* D. Gentry Steele and Joseph Powell, "Paleobiology of the First Americans," *Evolutionary Anthropology* 2 (1993): 138–146; "Paleobiological Evidence for the Peopling of the Americas: A Morphometric View," in *Method and Theory for Investigating the Peopling of the Americas,* edited by R. Bonnichsen and D. G. Steele (Corvallis: Center for the Study of the First Americans, Oregon State University, 1994), 141–163.

223 *the oldest individuals formed:* "Databases for Paleo-American Skeletal Biology Research," in *Who Were the First Americans?*, edited by Robson Bonnichsen (Corvallis: Center for the Study of the First Americans, Oregon State University, 1999), 79–96.

224 *Walter Neves and his colleagues:* See, e.g., W. A. Neves and H. M. Pucciarelli, "Morphological Affinities of the First Americans: An Exploratory Analysis Based on Early South American Human Remains," *Journal of Human Evolution,* 21 (1991): 261–273.

225 *a similar analysis:* Walter Neves and Max Blum, "The Buhl Burial: A Comment on Green et al.," *American Antiquity* 65 (2000): 191–193.

225 *pooled a large number:* Joseph Powell and Walter Neves, "New Craniofacial and Dental Perspectives on Native American Origins," in *Yearbook of Physical Anthropology* 42 (1999), 153–188.

230 *just too great:* Marta Lahr, "History in the Bones," *Evolutionary Anthropology* 6 (1997): 2–6.

232 *In eastern Siberia:* Anatoliy Derev'anko, *The Paleolithic of Siberia* (Springfield: University of Illinois Press, 1998).

232 *one is Upper Cave:* For a nontechnical description of the Upper Cave and Liujiang finds, see *Atlas of Primitive Man in China* (New York: Van Nostrand Reinhold, 1980); for a technical review, see Johann Kamminga and R. V. S. Wright, "The Upper Cave at Zhoukoudian and the Origins of Mongoloids," *Journal of Human Evolution* 17 (1988): 739–767. Kamminga and Wright contend that on the basis of associated animal fossils, the Zhoukoudian fossils are less than 11,000 years old, but a recent radiocarbon date on remaining skeletal parts indicates an age closer to 27,000 years for at least some of the remains. Kamminga and Wright are also convinced that the Liujiang individual is probably younger than 10,000 years old and represents a recent, fairly typical Southeast Asian male. These authors also summarize other discoveries from Southeast Asia and Indonesia.

233 *"Mongoloid" morphology:* A school of thought known as "multilineal evolution" believes that modern humans evolved as a group in all regions of Africa and Eurasia simultaneously because they had kept in continuous genetic contact since their original spread as *Homo erectus* about a million years ago. Adherents of this school, including C. Loring Brace and many Russian and Chinese scholars, see evidence of Mongoloid morphology as early as the *Homo erectus* from Zhoukoudian (Peking Man) as well as in the Upper Cave skulls. V. Alekseev (see Derev'anko reference above), who is a member of this school, thus interprets the Mal'ta and Afontova Gora fragments as "Mongoloid" on the basis of the nasal bones and the minimal shoveling of the incisors.

233 *fossil skulls from Upper Paleolithic Europe:* William Howells, "Who's Who in Skulls," *Papers of the Peabody Museum of Archaeology and Ethnology,* vol. 82 (1995); Johann Kamminga and R. V. S. Wright, "The Upper Cave"; Walter Neves and Hector Pucciarelli, "The Zhoukoudian Upper Cave Skull 101 as Seen from the Americas," *Human Evolution* 34 (1998): 219–222.

234 *the worldwide distribution:* The most thorough recent popularized presentations of global patterns of human genetics are Luigi Luca Cavalli-Sforza, Paolo Menozzi, and Alberto Piazza, *The History and Geography of Human Genes* (Princeton, N.J.: Princeton University Press, 1994), and Luigi Luca Cavalli-Sforza and Francesco Cavalli-Sforza, *The Great Human Diasporas: The History of Diversity and Evolution* (Reading, Mass.: Addison-Wesley, 1995). See also Michael Crawford, *The Origins of Native Americans: Evidence from Anthropological Genetics* (Cambridge, England: Cambridge University Press, 1998).

234 *Most American Indians belong:* A thorough recent discussion of the mtDNA record and its implications for the peopling of the Western Hemisphere is Theodore Schurr, "Mitochondrial DNA and the Peopling of the New World," *American Scientist* 88 (2000): 246–253; see also Theodore Schurr, "The Story in the Genes," *Discovering Archaeology* 2, no. 1 (2000): 59–60.

234 *X is found only:* M. D. Brown et al., "Haplogroup X: An Ancient Link Between Europe/Western Asia and North America?" *American Journal of Human Genetics* 63 (1998):1852–1881.

236 *Most mtDNA researchers:* See, e.g., Andrew Merriwether et al., "Distribution of the Four Founding Lineage Haplotypes in Native Americans Suggests a Single Wave of Migration for the New World," *American Journal of Physical Anthropology* 98 (1995): 411–430; C. J. Kolman et al., "Mitochondrial DNA Analysis of Mongolian Populations and Implications for the Origins of New World Founders," *Genetics,* 142 (1996): 1321–1334.

237 *But genetic drift plays:* mtDNA is more strongly subject to drift than most nuclear DNA because it is inherited only from the mother. A family that has all sons brings to end the mtDNA of the mother's line. Additionally, population size plays a major role in the loss of diversity. The ancient populations of Asia and America were small and, we presume, highly subject to genetic drift of even their nuclear DNA. This is especially true of Siberia, the climate of which has never been especially hospitable to its human occupants. Extinction of whole families, whole bands, and whole peoples is likely to have occurred repeatedly in the history of both regions. Types A and B may be rare or absent in

many groups in eastern Siberian not because they never existed there but because they were lost through genetic drift. The presence of haplogroup X in America may not mean that some of the earliest colonists were western Eurasians. It is possible that haplogroup X was once widespread in Eurasia and was simply lost through drift in the vast region of Siberia that now separates the populations who carry it. For the same reason, haplogroups A, B, C, D, and X may not be the only ones ever to have existed in the Americas; some of the founding lineages may be extinct.

Chapter 10: Routes of Passage

239 *how and when:* Numerous books and hundreds of scholarly articles address this topic. Some readily available examples are: Jared Diamond, *The Third Chimpanzee* (New York: HarperCollins, 1992); Brian Fagan, *The Great Journey: The Peopling of Ancient America* (London and New York: Thames and Hudson, 1987); David J. Meltzer, *Search for the First Americans* (Washington, D.C.: Smithsonian Books, 1993). More academic coverage can be found in Robson Bonnichsen and D. Gentry Steele, eds., *Method and Theory for Understanding the Peopling of the Americas* (Corvallis: Center for the Study of the First Americans, Oregon State University, 1994); Robson Bonnichsen and Karen Turnmire, eds., *Ice Age Peoples of North America* (Corvallis: Center for the Study of the First Americans, Oregon State University, 1999); Alan Bryan, ed., *Early Man in America from a Circum-Pacific Perspective* (Edmonton: University of Alberta Press, 1978); Ronald Carlisle, ed., *Americans Before Columbus: Ice Age Origins* (Pittsburgh, University of Pittsburgh Press, 1988); Tom D. Dillehay and David J. Meltzer, eds., *The First Americans: Search and Research* (Boca Raton, Fla.: CRS Press, 1991); plus the works by Crawford, Dixon, Greenberg, Nichols, Schurr, and Turner cited above and by Dillehay, Haynes, and West cited below.

240 *called in North America:* This global glaciation is known by various names: the late Wurm in Europe, the Sartan in Siberia, and the Fraser in the Pacific Northwest of North America. For the sake of simplicity, I use the North American term Wisconsinan here. For a discussion of ice ages and their causes, see J. Imbrie and K. Imbrie, *Ice Ages: Solving the Mystery* (Cambridge, Mass.: Harvard University Press, 1986).

241 *Beringia was a dry, windswept place:* See papers in Frederick West, ed., *American Beginnings: The Prehistory and Paleoecology of Beringia* (Chicago: University of Chicago Press, 1996).

241 *a treeless habitat:* R. D. Guthrie, *Frozen Fauna of the Mammoth Steppe: The Story of Blue Babe* (Chicago: University of Chicago Press, 1990).

241 *fertilized by nutrients:* Formed by electrical discharges in the atmosphere, particularly by the electromagnetic charges that build up near the poles and are manifested as auroras, nitrates become concentrated in glacial ice and move with it to the melting edge. Glaciers melting along both margins of the North Atlantic and North Pacific would thus have fertilized the seawater, leading to substantial production of phytoplankton, which form the base of the marine food chain. See Mort Turner, Edward Zeller, Gisela Dreshhoff, and Joanne

Turner, "Impact of Ice Margin Environments on Glacial Margin Environment," in *Ice Age Peoples of North America,* edited by Robson Bonnichsen and Karen Turnmire (Corvallis: Center for the Study of the First Americans, Oregon State University, 1999).

242 *North Africa or the Middle East:* For popular or highly readable academic accounts of world prehistory and the expansion of *Homo sapiens,* see Richard Klein, *The Human Career* (Chicago: University of Chicago Press, 1989); "The Archaeology of Modern Humans," *Evolutionary Anthropology* 1 (1992): 5–14; Roger Lewin, *The Origin of Modern Humans* (New York: Scientific American Library, 1993); and Christopher Stringer and Robin McKie, *African Exodus* (New York: Owl Books, 1996). That the emergence might have been as recent as 50,000 years ago is based on recent findings and does not yet appear at this level, an emergence of around 100,000 years is ordinarily suggested, although only Lewin seems to see expansion into central Eurasia as having been earlier than 40,000 years ago.

243 *a series of related ethnic groups:* Readable academic discussions of the Mammoth Steppe peoples and later Paleolithic of Siberia include Richard Klein, *Ice Age Hunters of the Ukraine* (Chicago: University of Chicago Press, 1973); Olga Soffer and N. D. Praslov, eds., *From Kostenki to Clovis: Paleolithic Paleo-Indian Adaptations* (New York: Plenum, 1993); Anatoliy Derev'anko, *The Paleolithic of Siberia* (Chicago: University of Chicago Press, 1998); Theodore Goebel, "Pleistocene Human Colonization of Siberia and Peopling of the Americas: An Ecological Approach," *Evolutionary Anthropology* (1999).

244 *oldest and most widely held:* Publications on the Clovis phenomenon and its rapid spread are multitudinous; see the books by David Meltzer and Brian Fagan cited above, plus C. V. Haynes, "The Earliest Americans," *Science* 166 (1969): 709–715; Paul Martin, "The Discovery of America," *Science* 179 (1973): 969–974; Robson Bonnichsen and Karen Turnmire, *Clovis: Origins and Adaptations* (Corvallis: Center for the Study of the First Americans, Oregon State University, 1991). Watch for additional publications from the 1999 Clovis Conference from the Center for the Study of the First Americans, Corvallis (in production).

247 *Tom Dillehay:* A thorough presentation of finds at this controversial site is Thomas Dillehay, *Monte Verde: A Late Pleistocene Site in Chile* (Washington, D.C.: Smithsonian Institution Press, 1997). The December 1999 issue of *Discovering Archaeology* contained a blistering critique of the report by Stuart Feidel of Alexandria, Virginia, who took issue with every minor editing error to again cast doubt upon the site's veracity. The critique seems to have little merit, however, and except for giving heart to a few other staunch Clovis First advocates, it has not robbed Dillehay of his hard-won victory.

248 *belated recognition:* For an encyclopedic discussion of the earliest prehistory of South America, see Thomas Dillehay, *The Settlement of the Americas* (New York: Basic Books, 2000).

251 *people entered America:* For a popular but also thorough academic treatment of this issue, see E. James Dixon, *Bones, Boats, and Bison* (Albuquerque: University of New Mexico Press, 1998).

256 *11,500 years ago in southeast Alaska:* The discovery in On Your Knees Cave (aka Tongass Caves), Prince of Wales Island, of a young man whose bone

chemistry indicates an almost purely marine diet has been touted as evidence
that the early immigrants to America came along the coast. The skeleton,
however, radiocarbon-dates to only about 10,300 years old, thousands of
years after the glaciers had melted and centuries after the Bering Land Bridge
had become entirely submerged. Evidence of even earlier maritime adaptations
has long been known from such sites as Namu on the British Columbia coast,
which is still younger than Clovis and provides no insights into the real antiquity of coastal habitation.

258–59 *derived not from* Siberia *but from* Iberia: Stanford and Bradley are writing
a book on their Solutrean Connection theory for the University of California
Press, Berkeley, due out in 2001 or 2002. For academic overviews of Solutrean
archaeology, see Clive Gamble, *The Paleolithic Settlement of Europe* (Cambridge, England: Cambridge University Press, 1986), and Lawrence Straus,
"The Last Glacial Maximum in Cantabria: The Solutrean," in *The World at
18,000 BP,* (vol. 1, edited by Olga Soffer and Clive Gamble (London: Unwin
Hyman, 1990). For Straus's objections in detail, see Lawrence Straus, "Solutrean Settlement of North America? A Review of Reality," *American Antiquity* 65 (2000): 219–226.

Index

Page numbers in *italics* refer to illustrations.